Arete

ARETE

GREEK SPORTS FROM ANCIENT SOURCES

Third Edition, with a New Foreword by Paul Christesen

STEPHEN G. MILLER

University of California Press

BERKELEY   LOS ANGELES   LONDON

University of California Press, one of the most distinguished university presses in the United States, enriches lives around the world by advancing scholarship in the humanities, social sciences, and natural sciences. Its activities are supported by the UC Press Foundation and by philanthropic contributions from individuals and institutions. For more information, visit www.ucpress.edu.

University of California Press
Berkeley and Los Angeles, California

University of California Press, Ltd.
London, England

ISBN 978-0-520-27433-4

Library of Congress Cataloging-in-Publication Data

  Arete : Greek sports from ancient sources / Stephen G. Miller, [editor].—3rd and Expanded ed.
    p. cm.
  Includes bibliographical references and index.
  ISBN 978-0-520-24154-1
  1. Sports—Greece—History—Sources. 2. Sports in literature.
I. Miller, Stephen G.
GV21.A73 2004
796'.0938—dc21   2003019000

18   17   16   15   14   13   12
12   11   10   9   8   7   6   5   4   3   2   1

Contents

Abbreviations

BCH	*Bulletin de correspondance hellénique*
BSA	*Annual of the British School at Athens*
CID	*Corpus des Inscriptions de Delphes*
CR	*Classical Review*
ID	*Inscriptions de Délos*
IG	*Inscriptiones Graecae*
IvO	*Inschriften von Olympia*
PLond	*London Papyri*
POxy	*Oxyrhynchus Papyri*
PZenon	C.C. Edgar, *Catalogue général des antiquités égyptiennes du museé du Caire*, nos. 59001–59139; *Zenon Papryi I* (Cairo 1925)
SEG	*Supplementum Epigraphicum Graecum*
SIG³	*Sylloge Inscriptionum Graecarum*

Foreword to the Third Edition

The book that you hold in your hands has as its title a single Ancient Greek word, *arete*, but *thesauros*, another word from the same language, might better describe its contents. A *thesauros* is a treasure, or the container for a treasure, and Stephen Miller's *Arete* contains a particular kind of treasure, in the form of a carefully selected collection of primary source evidence for the history of sports in ancient Greece. The wide range of material found in *Arete*, taken from literary works, papyri, and inscriptions, reflects Professor Miller's unmatched scholarly expertise and decades of experience in teaching courses on Greek sports at the University of California, Berkeley. As will become apparent, all this source material is nicely organized, carefully explained, and translated into highly readable English. For anyone new to the subject, especially those who cannot easily make their way through the relevant texts in the original languages, *Arete* represents an invaluable resource that admirably serves its intended purpose of facilitating the study of Greek sports.

The publication of the first edition of *Arete* in 1979 reflected and was part of a major shift in the study of sports history, and the republication of the third edition is a fitting occasion to take stock of the enduring significance of *Arete*, and, more generally, of Professor Miller's work on the history of Greek sports.

The present volume appears at a time when new books and articles on Greek sports are produced regularly and in considerable quantity. It may, therefore, come as something of a surprise that until very recently there was little scholarly interest in the history of sports, either ancient or modern.

Scholarly disinterest in sports is in and of itself a remarkable phenomenon. Sports were a fundamentally important element of life in ancient Greece. To give but one example, the various communities on the Greek mainland had a difficult time assembling an army to oppose a massive Persian invasion force in the late summer of 480 B.C., in part because so many men wished to attend the Olympic Games. (The interested reader can find the story in Herodotus' *History*, 7.206.) The ubiquity and importance of sports in the modern day is apparent from the fact that the 2010 FIFA World Cup was broadcast in every country and every region of the planet, including Antarctica, and reached an audience of over three billion people.

Yet until the 1960s scholars managed to ignore sports almost entirely. There was, of course, always a trickle of scholarship on sports. The cultural critic Joseph Strutt published the first edition of *The Sports and Pastimes of the People of England* in 1801. The creation of the modern Olympics in 1896 almost inevitably stirred a continuing interest in their ancient counterpart. In the early twentieth century E. Norman Gardiner produced three separate books on Greek sports, including *Athletics of the Ancient World*, which remained influential and in print for decades thereafter. Frederic Paxson's 1917 article "The Rise of Sport," which traced the growing importance of sports in the America of Paxson's own time to the closing of the frontier and concomitant need for a social safety valve, is typically seen as the first serious scholarship on American sports. Gardiner and Paxson had their successors, but scholarly books and articles on sports were few and far between.

The willingness of scholars to turn a blind eye to a social phenomenon of such importance was in large measure the product of a long-standing tendency on the part of academics to privilege the intellectual to the virtual exclusion of the physical. As Harry Edwards has observed: "The slow emergence of the study of sport as a subdiscipline in the social sciences is attributable to the Western educational tradition of emphasizing intellectual development as opposed to physical expression. Such a tradition demands the avoidance of any academic association with sport which, despite its complexities and significance, nonetheless maintains physical expression as its most dominant and obvious characteristic."[1]

All of this changed rather suddenly in the 1960s and the early 1970s, when sociologists and historians began to evince a sustained interest in sports as played in a range of different times and places. Heightened interest in sports history was the product of a number of factors, including a shift in focus toward social (as opposed to military or political) history. Changing academic attitudes toward the study of sports were reflected in the foundation of the North American Society for Sport History in 1972, and of the

---

1. Harry Edwards, *The Sociology of Sport* (Homewood, IL: Dorsey, 1973) 6–7.

Journal of Sport History in 1974. The journal *Stadion*, established in 1975, published a considerable number of articles on ancient Greek sports. The existence of professional organizations and journals dedicated to sports history signaled its recognition as a valid subdiscipline.

Scholarship on sports thus became significantly more common than it had been before, but, as might be expected of an emergent field, much of the resulting work was initially, in terms of the analyses undertaken and the methodologies used, not terribly sophisticated. Many publications offered relatively straightforward descriptive narratives, which can in retrospect seem almost simplistic, but which represented important and necessary first steps toward dealing with a large and largely unexplored body of evidence. Scholars writing about ancient Greece, like Gardiner before them, showed a particular interest in the basic mechanics of Greek sports and focused on questions such as how Greeks threw the discus and whether the jumping contest that formed part of the Greek pentathlon was a long jump or triple jump. The evidence on which they drew to answer such questions consisted largely of passages from ancient Greek authors, supplemented by relevant vase paintings. Good examples of such work can be found in H. A. Harris's *Greek Athletes and Athletics* (1964) and *Sport in Greece and Rome* (1972).

It is against this background that we need to understand Stephen Miller's scholarship on Greek sports, the roots of which lay in the excavations that he undertook at Nemea starting in 1973. Nemea, like Olympia, Delphi, and Isthmia, was a religious sanctuary and the site of a major set of athletic contests that attracted competitors from all over the Greek world. Although it had received a certain amount of attention before he arrived, Miller's excavations represented the first thoroughgoing investigation of Nemea. The overriding importance of athletic activity at Nemea meant that Miller necessarily began to delve into the history of Greek sports, as part of the process of making sense of what he and his team were finding at the site.

Over the course of the decades that followed, Miller produced a series of groundbreaking treatments of Greek sports that differed in three major ways from what had come before. First, he brought to bear a broader range of evidence and deeper expertise than many of his predecessors. Beginning in the late nineteenth century, there was a substantial and continually growing body of archaeological and epigraphic evidence for Greek sports. This was the result both of excavations at places such as ancient Olympia, where German archaeologists set to work in 1875, and also of finds of inscriptions, such as the catalogs of victories that were carved onto the bases of honorific statues of athletes. However, sports historians such as Harris did not evince a high level of familiarity with or interest in this material. Miller, drawing in part on first-hand and fine-grained knowledge developed in the course of his excavations at Nemea, made exemplary use of an array of literary, artistic, archaeological, and epigraphic sources to expand our understanding of Greek sports. For example, starting with the remains of the stadium at Nemea, he proposed a new (and now standard) understanding of how turns and lanes were variously arranged in footraces of different lengths.[2]

Second, Miller brought to his work on Greek sports a consistently high level of analytical sophistication, supplemented by a strong sense of the practical exigencies faced by athletes and organizers of athletic contests. For example, Miller resolved a long-standing question about the timing of the ancient Olympics by showing that the games were arranged to coincide with the second full moon after the summer solstice.[3] In formulating the relevant arguments, he made subtle use of all of the relevant evidence, and the insight that the system employed by the authorities at Olympia had to be one that was easily comprehensible to Greeks scattered all over the Mediterranean in hundreds of autonomous communities, each with its own calendar.

Third, Miller took crucial first steps toward asking and answering more complex questions that involved the role of sports in Greek society as a whole; in other words, he helped initiate a move from writing about the history of sports to writing a social history of sports in ancient Greece. Even after sports history became a recognized subdiscipline, the results were frequently not integrated into the wider picture of what was known about ancient Greek society. Hence, in the introduction to the second edition of Arete, Miller lamented the "artificial division by which the study of athletics has been divorced from the remainder of the ancient world." He helped remedy that regrettable situation by delving into some of the effects of sports on Greek society. For example, he argued that the leveling effects of athletic nudity contributed meaningfully to democratization at Athens.[4]

In addition to his contributions to the scholarly literature, Miller has played a leading role in making ancient Greek sports accessible and interesting to wider audiences. As a sought-after public speaker, he has regularly and generously shared his expertise about Greek sports with audiences of all

2. Stephen G. Miller, "Turns and Lanes in the Ancient Stadium," *American Journal of Archaeology* 84 (1980): 159–66.
3. Stephen G. Miller, "The Date of Olympic Festivals," *Mitteilungen des Deutschen Archäologischen Instituts Athenische Abteilung* 90 (1975): 215–31.
4. Stephen G. Miller, "Naked Democracy," in *Polis and Politics: Studies in Anciet Greek History*, edited by P. Flensted-Jensen, T. H. Neilsen, and L. Rubinstein (Copenhagen: Museum Tusculanum Press, 2000), 277–96.

kinds, ranging from Greek schoolchildren to the viewers of broadcasts of the modern Olympic games. As the director of the excavations at Nemea, he helped found the Society for the Revival of the Nemean Games, which has since 1994 organized athletic contests closely modeled on those of the ancient Nemean Games, held in the ancient stadium at Nemea.[5] These contests, open to people of all nationalities, ages, and abilities, have attracted thousands of participants from all over the world.

And as a faculty member at the University of California at Berkeley, he taught for over three decades a course on ancient athletics to large and appreciative groups of students. Miller's approach to teaching about Greek sports was based on his respect for the intellect and curiosity of his students, and his belief that students should be exposed to as much of the primary evidence as possible and asked to think for themselves about what it might mean. As Miller put it in his introduction to the second edition of *Arete,* "questions produce more knowledge and understanding than do ready-made answers."

With that in mind, Miller compiled a collection of source material for ancient Greek sports taken from literary texts, papyri, and inscriptions and gave it the title *Arete.* The reader will find Professor Miller's thoughts on the meaning of this crucial and complex term in the pages that follow. *Arete* is not intended as a textbook, but rather as a supplement to a text that provides a more traditional narrative of the history of Greek sports. In the introduction to the original version of *Arete,* Miller suggested using it alongside Gardiner's *Athletics of the Ancient World.* The fact that Gardiner's work was, when *Arete* first appeared, nearly fifty years old shows just how little sports history was written for much of the twentieth century.

The present version of *Arete* is the result of continuing changes made by Miller in response to an ever-expanding body of relevant evidence and his own evolving views of the history of Greek sports. In recent years the number of textbooks on ancient Greek sports has increased exponentially, but none is better than Miller's own richly illustrated *Ancient Greek Athletics,* which, not coincidentally, can be used very effectively together with *Arete.*

Speaking as someone who has had the opportunity to teach courses on Greek sports to undergraduates on multiple occasions, I can say from first-hand experience and without hesitation that the current version of *Arete* remains an indispensable resource for anyone interested in ancient Greek sports. Its republication is a vivid demonstration of the continuing fascina-

5. See nemeangames.org.

tion that Greek sports exercise upon the modern imagination, and a testament to the enduring importance of Professor Miller's work. It is, therefore, with considerable pleasure and anticipation that I urge you to turn the page and to begin exploring the *thesauros* that is Stephen Miller's *Arete*.

Paul Christesen

Introduction

The Greek word *arete* comes down to us inextricably connected to the athletics of ancient Greece and laden with a plethora of meanings. A definition of *arete* would include virtue, skill, prowess, pride, excellence, valor, and nobility, but these words, whether taken individually or collectively, do not fulfill the meaning of *arete*. *Arete* existed, to some degree, in every ancient Greek and was, at the same time, a goal to be sought and reached for by every Greek. It cannot be translated by a direct one-to-one equivalent into the idiom of modern American English, and even though the context of a particular use of the word may refine its meaning in that context, the word *arete* still carries with it a notion of ephemeral excellence and of transient triumph that makes its translation an exceedingly risky business. In addition, the word *arete* has imbued ancient athletics with an aura of the quest of man for perfection, a quest which—at least in the eyes of moderns—was isolated from more practical matters such as politics and economics. *Arete*—incompletely understood—has thereby dimmed our picture of the realities of antiquity and has robbed us of many of the real lessons to be learned from ancient athletics.

At the same time *arete* has come to represent—again to modern scholars—an artificial division by which the study of athletics has been divorced from the remainder of the ancient world. Scholars who would be quick to insist that all evidence for our knowledge of the political, literary, philosophical, and cultural institutions of Greece must be examined with great care accept an *arete*-colored image of the Greek athlete without question. And the facts that education in antiquity was set in the gymnasium, that the Akademy of Plato was first and foremost a place of exercise for the body, that the literature of fifth-century Athens abounds with direct references to and metaphors derived from athletics, and that football players do have brains are all too frequently neglected. If this little book avoids offering simple answers and attempts rather to set out factual bases for asking questions, it is because of the belief (which has been strengthened over the years) that questions produce more knowledge and understanding than do ready-made answers. If this book refuses to provide a set definition of *arete*, but challenges the reader to see how the word is used in each case and then to arrive at his or her own definition, the refusal is due to the notion that those who are interested in athletics are not and never have been *ipso facto* unable to think for themselves. If this book introduces many sources that seem to have little to do with athletics, it is with the realization that, in antiquity, *arete* was not limited to athletes.

Nonetheless, the athletics of Greek antiquity are the focus of this book. This subject has proven to be a continuing source of interest to undergraduate students, and it is toward them that this book is directed. Most of these students have no prior experience of the Classical world but are bright and eager. They are usually willing to confront the problems of a paucity of evidence, or of conflicting evidence from antiquity, and they understand, or come to understand, the importance of primary evidence, but they lack the ancient-language skills needed to deal with that evidence. Although I hope that the general reader will be stimulated by *Arete*, the first purpose of this book is to provide students with translations of the ancient written evidence about athletics. It is not, by itself, the complete tool for the study of athletics because so much evidence also exists in visual form. It should be used with a compendium of vase paintings, sculpture, and athletic gear that have survived to us—for example, my *Ancient Greek Athletics* (New Haven 2004).

The validity of this approach seems to have been recognized in other parts of the world, for somewhat similar presentations have appeared in other modern languages. *Arete* itself has been translated into modern Greek. A detailed and comprehensive collection of sources has been assembled and translated into German under the direction of Ingomar Weiler in the series *Quellendokumentation zur Gymnastik und Agonistik im Altertum* of which five volumes have appeared, each dedicated to a particular event:

1. M. Lavrencic, G. Doblhofer, and P. Mauritsch, *Diskos* (Vienna and Cologne 1991)

2. G. Doblhofer, P. Mauritsch, and M. Lavrencic, *Weitsprung* (Vienna, Cologne, and Weimar 1992)

3. G. Doblhofer, P. Mauritsch, and M. Lavrencic, *Speerwurf* (Vienna, Cologne, and Weimar 1993)

4. G. Doblhofer and P. Mauritsch, *Boxen* (Vienna, Cologne, and Weimar 1995)

5. G. Doblhofer and P. Mauritsch, *Pankration* (Vienna, Cologne, and Weimar 1996)

Finally, an elegant illustrated volume of sources translated into French has been produced recently by the International Olympic Committee: P. Badinou, *Olympiaka: Anthologie des sources grecques* (Bienne, Switzerland, undated).

This version of *Arete* has been considerably expanded beyond the second edition, due in part to the work of the aforementioned scholars, and in part to my own expanding experience and still growing appreciation of the role of athletics in music, the arts, literature, education, and ancient society in general. It seems to me ever clearer that we can better understand those aspects of ancient civilization by a better understanding of athletics.

The thematic organization of the book arises from its didactic goal and has been designed to augment and complement successive classroom lectures and discussions upon topics both specific, such as the individual competitive events, and general, such as the role of politics in athletics (and vice versa). There is considerable overlap between many of those topics and between the sources of evidence for them; the ancients failed to organize their lives and literature around my lectures, and I have provided cross-references to point out some of the links between topics. The arrangement of topics has been made with certain themes in mind, and these are shown in the table of contents. I have found that they serve reasonably well as the outline for a course on ancient athletics, but one does need sometimes to remember an earlier reading in the context of a topic discussed at a later point in the book. For example, a passage from the orator Antiphon (see no. **64**) is presented as evidence bearing on the question of accuracy as a criterion of victory in the javelin throw. However, that same passage is also useful in illustrating some of the activities carried out in the *palaistra* and *gymnasion*—a topic introduced much later in Chapter X. Again, Galen's *On Exercise with the Small Ball* is presented in the chapter concerned with ball playing (see no. **177**). But some of his comments (as, for example, that it is better to give a job to pigs than to those who compete in wrestling) are of interest in the discussion of professionalism four chapters later. There is one pitfall unavoidable in such an arrangement: evidence of very different dates is thus brought together even though practices may have changed dramatically between the times of different documents. On the positive side, such juxtaposition prompts important questions: as a student once asked, "Did the rules stay the same from Xenophon to Philostratos?"

Once again translations are my own and will be recognized to be as idiosyncratic as the choice of the original passages themselves. I have tried to present readable, perhaps even enjoyable, translations with something of the flavor of the original but without doing violence to the meaning of the original. I have taken liberties, especially in poetry, for the sake of clarity. Thus, for example, in the Homeric poems some metaphors have disappeared completely, others have been put into a more contemporary idiom, and proper names have replaced pronouns and substantive patronymics. I have taken no liberties with technical terms. These are simply transliterated, italicized, and defined in the glossary at the back of the book.

I have continued the attempt, in the case of incompletely preserved texts, to indicate what is actually preserved on the papyrus or the stone and what has been restored by modern editors.

Introductions to entries are intended sometimes to provide the dramatic background for action described in the course, sometimes to indicate particular problems to which the source is relevant, and sometimes to give pertinent information about the author or the document. In every case the goal has been to aid the student in understanding the importance of the source of ancient athletics.

A continuing problem concerns the translations of sums of money into dollars. It would be easier for me simply to transliterate the sums and to give a general indication for the value of the drachma or the talent or the denarius at various periods of time. But I have yet to find a student to be satisfied with such an explanation when the question is raised: "How much is that worth today?"

As in the second edition of *Arete* the values presented here are based on the value of olive oil. Since the Panathenaic amphoras given as prizes in the games in Athens typically hold about forty liters, and since we know that the average value of the oil in them was about eighteen drachmas,[1] a liter of oil must have been worth about 0.45 drachmas. At the time of the second edition of *Arete*, a liter of olive oil cost $9.88 in Berkeley. On April 6, 2002,

---

1. This is the highest average usual price as cited by D. C. Young, *The Olympic Myth of Greek Amateur Athletics* (Chicago 1984) 116, n. 13, but Young also cites extraordinary examples of prices as high as 55 drachmas per amphora. I cannot, therefore, be entirely comfortable with the figures I have derived even though I believe in the validity of the basic method. Of course, values changed from time to time in antiquity, and inflation in our own society guarantees that whatever figures are used today will be out-of-date for tomorrow's students.

the price had changed, but was more complicated, for olive oil had been "discovered" in California meanwhile, and the price for a liter now ranged from $6.99 to $16.49. I therefore decided to continue, as in 1989, to use the $9.88 price, which yields a value of $22.00 for the drachma. This rate of exchange yields, in turn, a price of some $26,400 for a horse (no. **66**), fines of $44,000 for athletes who transgressed rules of the games at Epidauros (no. **104**), and a first prize in the men's *stadion* in the Panathenaic Games worth $39,600 (no. **114**). It will be obvious that these figures, by today's standards, are probably too low. At least they will be consistently too low, and the reader is entitled to reckon a significantly higher rate of exchange.

My indebtedness for help with earlier editions can be found in the acknowledgements to them. The debt continues, but my creditors have grown, and the people who have added to this version include E. Baughan, J. Bouyia, M. Chambers, F. Cope, W. Decker, S. Fay, F. Frost, K. Georgiades, M. Golden, D. Kyle, E. Miller, B. Rieger, T. Scanlon, U. Sinn, E. Spathari, P. Valavanis, and I. Weiler.

Once again, and as always, my greatest indebtedness is to the thousands of students over the years who have read through the ancient echoes of *arete* and frequently have achieved their own. If future generations emulate them, this *Arete* will have been a success.

Stephen G. Miller
Berkeley, California
November 2003

I
The Earliest Days of Greek Athletics

In the two passages from Homer which are presented here a picture emerges of what we may call Homeric athletics. The question is, however, whether that picture is one of his own day or a valid, if somewhat blurred, reflection of the athletic practices of the Mycenaean era. Comparison with archaeological discoveries from that era finds relatively little in common with the Homeric picture, while comparison with the development of the Olympic program (Appendix) suggests that the Homeric picture would have been valid only as of the early 7th century B.C. If so, the informality of the Homeric games might have been the case as well for the early days of the Olympics.

1   Homer, *Iliad* 23.256–24.6   *ca.* 750 B.C.

Patroklos, the childhood and lifelong friend of Achilles, has fought in Achilles' place and been killed by Hektor outside the walls of Troy. The corpse of Patroklos has been cremated and the crowd at the funeral begins to disperse:

But Achilles held the people there and sat them in a broad assembly, and brought prizes for games out of his ships, cauldrons and tripods and horses and mules and high-headed powerful cattle and beautifully girdled women and gray iron. First he set forth the glorious prizes for equine feet: a woman faultless in her work to be led away and a tripod with ears holding twenty-two measures for the first prize. Then for the second he set forth a six-year-old unbroken mare carrying an unborn mule foal. Then for the third prize he set forth a beautiful unfired cauldron holding four measures, still new and shiny. For the fourth he set forth two gold talents, and for the fifth a two-handled unfired bowl. Then he stood up and spoke out to the Argives:

"These prizes are placed in competition awaiting the horsemen. If we Achaians were not competing for the sake of some other hero, I myself would take the first prizes away to my tent. You know by how much my horses surpass all others in their *arete*, for they are immortal, a gift of Poseidon to my father Peleus who handed them in turn to me. But I and my solid-hoofed horses stay aside; such is the fame of the charioteer whom they have lost, the gentle one, who so many times rubbed soft oil into their manes after he had washed them with shining water. Therefore they both stand here grieving him with manes trailing on the ground, both hearts grieving as one. But the rest of you take your places in the field, whoever has confidence in his horses and compact chariot."

So spoke the son of Peleus, and the swift riders gathered. By far the first to rise was Eumelos, son of Admetos, who surpassed all in horsemanship. After him rose Diomedes, strong son of Tydeus, and yoked the Trojan horses which he had taken by force from Aeneas. Next rose fair-haired Menelaos, son of Atreus, and yoked his swift horses. Fourth to prepare his flowing-maned horses was Antilochos, glorious son of high-hearted king Nestor. He stood nearby and gave well-intentioned advice to his son:

"Antilochos, Zeus and Poseidon have loved you, though you are young, and have taught you all aspects of good horsemanship. Therefore, I have no need to instruct you, for you know well how to double the *terma*. But I think that your horses are the slowest, and that your work will be harder. The horses of these men are faster, but they do not know better than you how to plan. Remember then, my dear boy, always to have your plan in mind so that the prizes will not elude you. The woodcutter is far better with skill than with brute force; it is with skill that the pilot holds his swift ship on course though buffeted by winds on the wine-colored sea. Thus too by skill one charioteer passes another. But whoever puts his trust in his horses and chariot and recklessly turns wide coming and going, his horses drift out of the course and he cannot hold them. But the man who takes advantage is he who, though driving the slower horses, always watches the *terma* and turns it tightly, nor forgets how much oxhide rein to give and take, but holds his horses well and studies the man in front. I shall give you a marker, and you cannot miss it. There is a dry stump about six feet high above the ground, either oak or pine, but not rotted by rain water, with two white stones against it on either side, and there the course is smooth around it; it may be the marker of some man long dead and buried, or the *nyssa* set up by earlier men, but now Achilles has made it the *terma*. Having approached this, you must drive your horses and chariot near it, and you in your well-woven chariot box lean toward the left; then call out to your right horse and goad him on, and give him full rein. Your left horse must be driven up close to the *nyssa* so that the hub of the wheel seems to touch, but do not let it graze the stone lest you harm your horses and break your chariot. That would be a thing of joy for the others and a source of shame for you. My dear boy, keep your wits about you and be careful, for if at the *nyssa* you drive hard and slip ahead, there is no one who by sprinting can catch you, let alone pass you."

So spoke Nestor, son of Neleus, and sat back down in his place, having told his son the way to win.

The fifth to prepare his flowing-maned horses was Meriones.

Then they mounted their chariots and tossed in their lots. Achilles shook them, and the first to fall out was that of Antilochos, son of Nestor, and after him strong Eumelos drew the next place, and next was Menelaos, son of Atreus. Meriones drew the next lane to drive, and last of all the best of them all, Diomedes, drew the lane to drive his horses. Standing in line, Achilles showed them the *terma*, far away on the level plain. Next to the goal he set godlike Phoinix, squire of his father, to remember the running and certify it.

Then all held their whips high above their horses, and together flicked with their reins, and bellowed out for speed. Quickly they spread out over the plain and left the ships behind. The swirling dust clung beneath the chests of the horses like clouds of a whirlwind; their manes streamed out in the wind's current; the chariots plunged down to the ground and, again, shot up like meteors. The drivers rocked in their chariots, and the heart of each beat high with the hope of victory; they shouted to their horses, and they flew over the plain in a cloud of dust.

But when the fleet horses turned back toward the shore, then the *arete* of each began to show, and at once the field of horses was stretched out. Quickly the swift-footed horses of Eumelos went in front, and after them the stallions of Diomedes, not far behind and seemingly always about to climb into the chariot of Eumelos with their breath hot on his back and broad shoulders. And Diomedes might have passed, or at least drawn even had not Apollo been angry with him, and dashed the whip from his hands. The tears of rage started from his eyes which watched the mares of Eumelos running even better while his own horses slackened without the goad. But Apollo's cheating of Diomedes did not escape Athena; quickly she swept to him and returned his whip, and inspired his horses with strength. Then she descended in wrath upon Eumelos and broke the yoke of his horses. They ran off the road, the pole dragging on the ground, and he was catapulted out of the chariot over the wheel, ripping his elbows and mouth and skin, and smashing his forehead so that the tears flowed but his voice would not. Then Diomedes rushed past him, and led the field by far, for Athena had inspired strength in his horses and glory in him.

After him came fair-haired Menelaos, but Antilochos cried out to his father's horses:

"Step it up, you two! Pull as fast as you can! I'm not telling you to catch those horses of Diomedes—Athena has now inspired strength in them and glory in him—but beat the horses of Menelaos! Don't be left behind! Faster! For shame to let his mares beat you stallions! Why are you falling behind, my brave boys? Do you know what's going to happen? You'll get no more care from Nestor; he'll cut you up for dog food, if we carry off the lesser prize because you didn't try. Get going! As fast as you can! I know what I'll do, I'll slip past him where the road gets narrow. He won't get away from me!"

So he spoke, and they were terrified by their master's shouts and ran harder for a little while, and then Antilochos saw the narrow spot in the road. There was a gully where the winter rain had run from the road creating a large pothole, and into this he forced Menelaos who shrank from a collision, but Antilochos turned his horses off the road and drove along for a bit on the shoulder. Menelaos was frightened and called out to Antilochos:

"Antilochos, that is reckless driving! Hold your horses! The road is too narrow here, but it will soon be wide enough for passing. Don't crash up your chariot and wreck the both of us!"

So he spoke, but Antilochos drove all the harder and lashed his horses for greater speed, as if he had not heard him. They ran even for about the length of a boy's diskos throw, but then the mares of Menelaos fell back, for he let up lest the horses crash, the chariots overturn, and they in their struggle for victory end up in the dust. But fair-haired Menelaos called out in anger:

"Antilochos, you are the most wretched of men! Damn you! We Achaians were wrong to say you had good sense! But you won't get the prize without swearing that you played fair!"

So he spoke, and then shouted out to his horses:

"Don't slacken up, don't stop, even though your hearts are heavy! Their feet and knees will tire before yours! Their youth is gone."

So he spoke, and they were terrified by their master's shouts and ran harder and soon caught up with the others.

Meanwhile, the Argives sitting in their assembly were watching for the horses which flew through the dust of the plain. Idomeneus, lord of the Cretans, was first to make out the horses, for he sat apart from the others, and higher up where he had a panoramic view. He heard and recognized the shouting of Diomedes, and made out his conspicuous horse, leading the others, all red except for a white mark like a full moon on his forehead. Idomeneus stood up and called to the Argives:

"Friends, am I the only one who sees the horses, or do you see them too? It seems to me that other horses are leading, another charioteer ahead. The mares of Eumelos must have come to grief on the plain, for I saw them running in front around the *terma*, but now they are nowhere to be seen and I have looked over the whole Trojan plain. Perhaps the reins slipped away from the charioteer and he could not hold them around the *terma*, and did not make the turn. I think that he must have been thrown out there and his chariot wrecked, and his mares bolted away wildly. But do get up and see for yourselves, for I cannot make it out clearly. I think that strong Diomedes is in the lead."

And swift Ajax, son of Oileus, spoke shamefully to him:

"Idomeneus, can't you hold your wind? The horses are still far out on the plain. You are not the youngest of us, and your eyes are no better than ours, but you must always blow on and on. There is no need for your wind since there are others here better than you. Those are the same mares in front as before, and the same Eumelos who holds the reins behind them."

Then the lord of the Cretans angrily answered him to his face:

"Ajax, although you are the best in abuse and stupidity, you are the worst of the Argives with that donkey's brain of yours. Now put your money where your mouth is and bet me a tripod-cauldron. We'll have Agamemnon, son of Atreus, hold the bet so that you will pay up when you find out which horses are in front."

So he spoke, and swift Ajax jumped up again in anger to retort, and the quarrel would have gone on had Achilles not risen and said to them:

"Ajax and Idomeneus, be quiet. This is not becoming, and if others were acting like you, you yourselves would be angry with them. Sit down with the others and watch for the horses. They are into the stretch and will be here soon, and then you can see for yourselves which are first and which are second."

While he spoke, Diomedes had come driving hard upon them lashing his horses. They still ran with feet high and light, and dust still splashed at the charioteer, and the chariot plated in tin and gold still rolled hard behind the flying feet of the horses. So quickly they flew that the wheels scarcely left a trace in the soft dust. Diomedes stopped them in the middle of the crowd with the sweat dripping densely to the ground from their necks and chests. He vaulted from his shining chariot to the ground, leaned his whip against the yoke, and did not delay to take his prize, the woman and the tripod with ears which he gave to his comrades to take away, and unyoked his horses.

Next in was Antilochos who had passed Menelaos by trick rather than by speed. But even so Menelaos held his swift horses near behind and would have won clearly had the course been longer. Then came Meriones, noble squire of Idomeneus, a full spear cast behind Menelaos. His horses were beautiful but slow, and he the least talented at chariot racing. Last and behind all the others came Eumelos, dragging his lovely chariot and driving his horses before him. Seeing him, Achilles took pity and stood up among the Argives and spoke out:

"The best man has come in last, but let's give him a prize as he deserves: the second prize. The first should go to Diomedes."

So he spoke, and all agreed, and he would have given the horse to Eumelos had not Antilochos stood up to argue:

"Achilles, I shall be very angry with you if you do as you suggest. You mean to take my prize away from me, thinking that, even though he is a wretched driver he is a good man. Well, he ought to have prayed to the gods, and then he would not have been last. If he is so dear to you and such a good friend, then there is plenty of gold in your tent, and bronze and sheep, and women and horses. From those give him a prize, even better than mine, and the Achaians will applaud you, but I will not give up the mare, and if any-one wants her he will have to fight me to get her."

So he spoke, but Achilles was delighted with his good friend and smiled and answered him:

"Antilochos, if you would have me bring out something special to give to Eumelos, then I will do so for your sake. I will give him a bronze corselet with a tin overlay. It will be worth something to him."

He spoke and told Automedon, his beloved companion, to bring it out of his tent. This was done, and he placed it in Eumelos' hands, and he accepted it joyfully. But then Menelaos, with heart full of bitterness and anger against Antilochos, stood up, and the herald put the staff in his hands and called for silence among the Argives, and he proceeded to speak:

"Antilochos, you used to play fair, but what have you done now? You have besmirched my *arete*, you fouled my horses by throwing your own in front of them, even though yours are far inferior. Come now, Argives, leaders and rulers of men, judge between us, with no prejudice, so that no man can say: 'Menelaos used lies and force against Antilochos and went off with the mare Antilochos had won, for Menelaos' horses were inferior, but he has greater power and prestige.' Or rather I will judge myself, and no man will question the decision, for it will be fair. Come here, Zeus-nurtured Antilochos, and do what is right. Stand in front of your horses and chariot, take in your hand the whip with which you drove them before, take hold of your horses and swear by Poseidon the Earthholder and Earthshaker that you did not foul up my chariot with a dirty trick."

Then Antilochos, once more the sportsman, answered him:

"Enough now. I am much younger than you, lord Menelaos, and you are my elder and better. You know how greedy transgressions sprout up in a young man, for his mind races on, but his judgement is lightweight. Please be patient with me. I will give you the mare which I won. If you demand something of my own besides, I would give it to you, Zeus-nurtured, rather than have fallen for all time from your favor and be wrong in the eyes of heaven."

He spoke, and led up the mare and gave her to Menelaos whose anger softened. He said:

"Antilochos, although I was angry I will now give way to you, since you were not flighty or lightheaded before now. Your youth got the better of your brain. You will not play tricks on your betters another time. Another man might not have won me over, but you have suffered much and worked hard for my sake, as have your noble father and your brother. Therefore, I shall be swayed by your supplication, and I will even give you the mare, although she is mine, so that all may see and know that my heart is never arrogant and stubborn."

He spoke, and gave the mare to a comrade of Antilochos to lead away, and took for himself the glittering cauldron. Fourth, in the order he had driven, Meriones took the two talents of gold. But the fifth prize, the two-handled bowl, was left over. Achilles carried it through the assembly, gave it to Nestor, and stood by him and said:

"Let this now be yours, venerable sir, to keep in memory of the burial of Patroklos, since never again will you see him among the Argives. I simply want to give you this prize, since never again will you fight with your fists, nor wrestle, nor compete in the javelin, nor the footraces, for already the difficulties of old age are upon you."

So speaking, he placed it in Nestor's hands. And he received it joyfully and answered:

"You're right, my boy, everything you said is true. My joints aren't what they used to be, nor my feet, and my hands no longer shoot out lightly from my shoulders. If only I were young and strong again as I was back then when the Epeans were burying Amarynkeas in Bouprasion and his sons set up prizes in honor of the king. There wasn't a man like me then, not a one. I beat Klytomedeas, son of Enops, in the boxing. In the wrestling, only Ankaios of Pleuron stood up to me, and I beat him too. Iphiklos was fast, but I beat him in the races, and I beat both Phyleas and Polydoros in the javelin. I only lost in the horse race because the Aktorians—they were Siamese twins, you know—outmanned me in pursuit of the biggest prizes. One of them took the reins and did the driving while the other used the whip and talked to the horses. That's what I was like back then, but now the young-sters have to do such things. I have to bow to old age, but then I bowed to no man. Now you go along and honor your fallen comrade with these games. I accept this gladly; it does my heart good that you remember me as your faithful friend, and that you do not forget the honor which is my due among our people. May the gods grant you proper joy for this."

So he spoke, and Achilles, having listened to all these praises of Nestor, returned to the assembly of the Achaians. Next he set out the prizes for the painful boxing. He led out and tethered in the field a mule, six years old, hardworking, and unbroken, and for the loser he set out a two-handled gob-let. He then stood up and spoke to the Argives:

"I invite two men, the best among you, to box for these prizes. All you Achaians bear witness that he to whom Apollo gives endurance will take away to his tent this hardworking mule. The one who is beaten will take the two-handled goblet."

He spoke, and immediately a huge and powerful man, Epeios son of Panopeus, well skilled in boxing, rose up, seized the mule, and said:

"Let the one who wants the two-handled goblet come near, for I say that none of you will beat me at boxing and take the mule; I am the greatest. Isn't it enough that I am deficient on the battlefield? A man can't be number one in everything. But I know what's going to happen here to any opponent of mine. I'll tear him limb-from-limb and smash his bones together. Let his friends huddle nearby to carry him out after my fists have beaten him to a pulp."

So he spoke, and they all kept their mouths shut. At last one Euryalos stood up. Diomedes was his second, and encouraged him, and wanted the victory for him. First he pulled the boxing belt around his waist, and then gave him the *himantes* carefully cut from the hide of an ox. The two men, belted up, stepped into the middle of the assembly, squared off, and put up their hands. Then they fell upon each other with their heavy hands mixing it up. There was a gnashing of teeth, and sweat poured off their limbs. Then Epeios rushed in and hit him on the jaw as he peered through his guard, and his knees buckled. As in the water rippled by the north wind a fish jumps in the seaweed of the shallows and disappears again into the dark water, so Euryalos left the ground from the blow. But great-hearted Epeios held him upright in his hands. Euryalos' friends gathered around him and led him through the assembly with his feet dragging as he spat up thick blood and rolled his head over on one side. They led him completely dazed, and they had to return for the two-handled goblet.

Now Achilles set out the prizes for the third contest, the painful wrestling. For the winner there was a huge tripod to be set over the fire. The Achaians among themselves valued it at twelve oxen. He placed a woman, skilled in the work of her hands, for the loser, and they rated her at four oxen. Then Achilles stood up and spoke out:

"Rise up, two who would try for this prize."

So he spoke, and up rose huge Ajax, son of Telamon, and to oppose him the crafty Odysseus who knew every trick. The two men, belted up, stepped into the middle of the assembly, and grabbed each other with their heavy arms looking like rafters which a renowned architect has fitted in the roof of a high house. Their backs creaked under the force of violent, stubborn, tugging hands. Wet sweat poured down, and raw places all along their ribs and shoulders broke out bright red with blood, and they continued to struggle for victory and the wrought tripod. Odysseus could not bring down Ajax nor throw him, nor could Ajax throw Odysseus who was too strong. Gradually the Achaians began to be restless, and huge Ajax said:

"Son of Laertes, either lift me, or I will lift you. The outcome is known to Zeus."

So speaking he lifted but Odysseus did not forget his tricks. Odysseus caught him with a stroke behind the knee, and threw him over backward, so that he fell on the chest of Ajax as the crowd applauded. Next, Odysseus tried to lift Ajax, but could not raise him clear of the ground, so he hooked his knee again but they fell together and both were soiled with dust. Then they would have wrestled a third time, but Achilles stood up and called to them to stop:

"Wrestle no more now! Don't wear yourselves out and get hurt! You are both winners. Go off and divide the prizes and let the rest of the Achaians compete."

So he spoke, and they listened to him and obeyed, and wiped off the dust and put on their clothes.

Now Achilles set out prizes for the footrace: a silver mixing bowl, a work of art, which held only six measures but surpassed all others in its loveliness. This Achilles made the prize for the fastest runner in memory of his comrade. For second place he set out a large and fatted ox, and for the last place he set out half a talent of gold. Then Achilles stood up and spoke out:

"Rise up, you who would try for this prize."

So he spoke, and there stood up swift Ajax, son of Oileus, and crafty Odysseus, and Antilochos the son of Nestor, the best runner of the young men. They lined up, and Achilles showed them the *terma*. They sprinted from the *nyssa*, and soon Ajax was in front, but Odysseus was running so close behind that his feet were hitting Ajax' tracks before the dust could settle back into them, and his breath was hitting the back of Ajax' neck. All the Achaians were cheering his effort to win, shouting for him to turn it on. But when they were in the stretch, Odysseus said a silent prayer to the gray-eyed Athena:

"Hear me, Goddess, be kind to me and come with extra strength for my feet."

So he prayed, and Pallas Athena heard him, and lightened his limbs, feet and arms, too. As they were making their final sprint for the prize, Ajax slipped and fell (Athena tripped him) where dung was scattered on the ground from bellowing oxen, and he got the stuff in his mouth and up his nose. So Odysseus took away the mixing bowl, because he finished first, and the ox went to Ajax. He stood with his hands on the horns of the ox, spitting out dung, and said to the Argives:

"Oh, shit! That goddess tripped me, that goddess who has always stood by Odysseus and cared for him like a mother."

They all roared in laughter at him, and then came Antilochos to take the prize for last place, and grinned as he spoke to the Argives:

"Friends, you all know well the truth of what I say, that still the gods continue to favor the older men. Look here, Ajax is older than I, if only by a little, but Odysseus is out of another age and truly one of the ancients. But his old age is, as they say, a lusty one. I don't think any Achaian could match his speed, except Achilles."

So he spoke and glorified the swift-footed son of Peleus. And Achilles answered him:

"Antilochos, your kind words for me shall not have been said in vain, for I shall add another half talent of gold to your prize."

So speaking he placed it in his hands, and Antilochos received it joyfully. Then Achilles brought into the assembly and set out the spear and shield and helmet of Sarpedon which Patroklos had stripped from his body. Then he stood up and spoke out:

"I invite two men, the best among you, to contend for these prizes. Let them put on their armour and take up their bronze spears and stand up to each other in the trial of close combat. The fighter who is the first of the two to get in a stroke at the other's body, to get through armour and draw blood, to that man I will give this magnificent silver-studded sword. Both men will carry off the armour of Sarpedon and have it in common, and I will treat them both to a good dinner in my tent."

So he spoke, and huge Ajax son of Telamon rose up, and the son of Tydeus, strong Diomedes. When they had donned their armour, they came together in the middle, furious for combat, with fierce faces, and all the Achaians were astonished. They closed and made three charges at one another. Then Ajax stabbed at Diomedes' shield, but did not get through to the skin, for the corselet held. Then Diomedes reached over the great shield and tried to hit his neck with the tip of his spear again and again. When the Achaians saw this they feared for Ajax and called for them to stop and divide the prizes evenly. But Achilles gave to Diomedes the sword with its sheath and belt.

Next Achilles set out a lump of pig iron, which Eëtion the mighty used to hurl. But when Achilles killed him, he brought this away in his ships with the rest of the booty. Then Achilles stood up and spoke out:

"Rise up, you who would try for this prize. Whoever wins will have a supply of iron for five years, and neither his shepherd nor his ploughman will have to go to the city for iron, but will have it already at home."

So he spoke, and up stood Polypoites and Leonteus and Ajax son of Telamon, and Epeios. They stood in a line, and Epeios took the weight, and whirling let it fly, but the Achaians all laughed. Second to throw was Leonteus, and third huge Ajax hurled it from his heavy hand, and surpassed the marks of all the others. But when Polypoites took the weight, he over-threw the entire field by as far as an ox-herd can cast his stick, and they applauded him. The comrades of Polypoites took the prize from the king to the hollow ships.

Once again Achilles set out gloomy iron, this time for the archers. He set out ten double-bladed axes, and ten with single blades. Far away in the sands he planted the mast of a ship, and to it tethered a tremulous wild pigeon by a thin string attached to her foot, and challenged the archers to shoot at her:

"He who hits the wild pigeon will take home all the double axes. He who hits the string, having missed the bird, will be the loser and take the single axes."

So he spoke and up stood Teukros and Meriones, squire of Idomeneus. They shook their lots in a bronze helmet, and Teukros' jumped out first. He let fly a strong shot, but did not promise a sacrifice to Apollo, and so missed the bird, for Apollo begrudged him that, but did snap the string with his arrow, and the pigeon soared swiftly up toward the sky, while the string dangled toward the ground. The Achaians thundered approval. Meriones in a fury of haste caught the bow from Teukros' hand, and readied his arrow, and promised Apollo a grand sacrifice of first-born lambs. High up under the clouds he saw the wild pigeon and as she circled he struck her in the body under the wing. The shaft passed clean through and out of her and dropped back to stick in the ground next to his foot, but the bird dropped onto the top of the mast. Her head drooped and the beating wings went slack and the spirit of life fled from her and she dropped down from the mast, and the people were astonished. Then Meriones gathered up all ten double axes, and Teukros carried the single axes back to his ship.

Next Achilles carried into the assembly and set out a long spear and an untarnished cauldron with flowery designs on it, worth an ox. And the spear-throwers stood up. The son of Atreus, king Agamemnon rose, and so did Meriones, squire of Idomeneus. But Achilles said to them:

"King Agamemnon, since we all know that you surpass all others and are the best by far of spear-throwers, take the cauldron, but let us give the spear to Meriones, if you agree."

So he spoke, and Agamemnon, the lord of men, did not disagree.

Now the games broke up, and the people scattered, each to his own ship. The rest of them thought of their dinners and of sweet sleep, but Achilles alone still wept as he remembered his beloved companion. All-conquering sleep would not come to him, and he tossed from side to side in longing for Patroklos.

2   Homer, *Odyssey* 8.97–253   *ca.* 725 B.C.

Odysseus, in the tenth year of wandering in his attempt to return home to Ithaka after the fall of Troy, has been washed up on the shore of a strange land. He is treated hospitably by the native Phaeacians, who inquire nothing of him, and after a meal the bard, Demodokos, entertains them with songs of the Trojan War which evoke memories and tears from Odysseus. His host, the gracious Alkinoös, notes this, and speaks:

"Leaders and councillors of the Phaeacians, we have had enough now of feasting and of lyre-singing which properly accompanies an abundant table.

Let us instead go out and divert ourselves with various athletic contests so that when our guest goes home he will tell his friends how we surpass others in boxing and wrestling and jumping and foot-racing."

So he spoke and went out, and a crowd of thousands followed him, and many sturdy youths stood up as contestants.

The first contest was in running. They sprinted from the *nyssa*, and flew in a cloud of dust across the plain. Klytoneus won by a long way; he left the others behind by the width of a field which a team of mules can plough in a day. Next they tried the painful wrestling, and Euryalos was the best of all. Amphialos jumped the furthest, and Elatreus won easily with the *diskos*. In the boxing the winner was Laodamas son of Alkinoös. When all had enjoyed the contests, Laodamas said to the young men:

"Hey gang! Let's go ask the stranger if he knows any sport and can show us something. He's well built, and from the look of his thighs and calves, as well as his arms and neck, he must be strong. He's not so old either, although he does look worn-out by hardships. There's nothing like the sea for knocking the stuffing out of the strongest man."

Euryalos answered him and said:

"Okay, Laodamas, you've made your point. Now let's see you do something about it."

Hearing this, Laodamas went into the middle of the crowd and addressed Odysseus:

"Won't you too, sir, try your hand at some contest, that is, if you know any, but you have the look of an athlete to me. There is no greater fame for a man than that which he wins with his footwork or the skill of his hands. Have a try now and put away your cares. Your journey home is near at hand, and we have already prepared for you a ship and crew."

Crafty Odysseus replied to him:

"Laodamas, why do you young chaps mock me with such an invitation? My heart is more set on grief than games, for I have toiled long and suffered much. I am here in your gathering only as a suppliant to get my passage home from your king and your people."

Then Euryalos interrupted and sneered at him:

"As I see it, stranger, you're no good at sports like a real man. You remind me of a master peddling sailors, one who trades from port to port with thoughts for nothing but cargoes and loads and especially profits. You're no athlete."

Crafty Odysseus glared at him and thundered:

"You're no gentleman, sir! You behave like a clod! It is so true that the Gods do not give total grace, a complete endowment of both beauty and wit, to all men alike. There will be one man who is less than average in build, and yet the Gods will so crown his words with a flower of beauty that all who hear him are moved. When he holds forth in public it is with assurance, yet with so sweet a modesty that it makes him shine out above the general run of men. Another man will be as handsome as the Gods, yet will lack that strand of charm twined into his words. Take yourself, for example: a masterpiece in body which not even a god could improve, but empty in the head. Your sneering made my heart beat faster. I am no ninny at sports, as you would have it. Indeed I think I was among the best in my time, but now I exist in pain and misery, having risked and endured much in the wars of men and the wilds of the sea. Yet despite the ravages of these evil things I will try your tests of strength. Your sneer has galled me and your words have stung me."

He spoke and sprang to his feet still clothed and seized a *diskos* which was bigger and heavier than those the Phaeacians had been hurling among themselves. Whirling, he hurled it from his mighty hand, and the stone whistled through the air. Those Phaeacians of the long oars, those master mariners, hit the dirt beneath the hurtling stone which soared so freely from the hero's hand that it overpassed the marks of every other. And Athena, now disguised as a Phaeacian, set the *terma* and called out:

"Even a blind man, sir, could judge your throw by feeling for it; it is not mixed in with the others, but far out in front. You may take heart from this contest, for no Phaeacian will come close, much less beat you."

So she spoke, and Odysseus was cheered to have found a friend in that crowd, and with lighter heart he said to the Phaeacians:

"Now then, young sports, match this throw, and as soon as you do, I'll throw another even longer. For the rest, let anyone whose spirit or temper prompts him step out and take me on in boxing or wrestling or foot-racing, or whatever. You have worked me up to such a pitch that I shall not flinch from anything, nor refuse a bout to any single Phaeacian, except my host Laodamas. Only a dimwitted fool would compete with his benefactor. To challenge one's host, while being kindly treated in a foreign land, would be to cut off one's nose to spite one's face. But I refuse no other man, nor dodge the polished bow, and I can send my spear further than others can shoot their arrows. I fear only that in the footraces some of the Phaeacians may beat me, for I have been shamefully mauled by constant waves on a bare ship. The joints of my knees are therefore feeble."

So he spoke, and all were hushed in silence. Then Alkinoös answered and said:

"Sir, what you have said to us is not unwelcome, for it is natural that you should want to show your *arete* since you were angered by that man standing up in the gathering and sneering at you as if at your *arete*, although no man in his right senses would do so. But come now, listen and remember the abilities which Zeus has given us so that you can relate them to some other hero when you dine in your own house with your wife and children. I confess that we are not polished fighters with our fists, nor wrestlers, but we can run swiftly and are experts on shipboard. We love eating and harp-playing and dancing and changes of clothes and hot baths and our beds. But come, let us have the best dancers of the Phaeacians dance before us so that when our guest goes home he will tell his friends how we surpass others in seamanship and running and dancing and singing."

II
Nudity and Equipment

The custom of competing in the nude is perhaps the most striking aspect of Greek athletics, and the Romans certainly mistrusted it (no. **5**). Aside from equipment required for specific events (e.g. the *halteres* in the *halma*), which we will consider in the appropriate place, the gear common to every athlete can be discerned in the written sources (nos. **6–10**) as well as in ancient vase painting: the *aryballos* (or *lekythos*) for oil, the *stlengis,* and the sponge. Although various types of dust *(konis)* were certainly used as well during the Roman period (no. **11**), such practice is not so well attested in Classical Greek times.

3 Pausanias 1.44.1   *ca.* A.D. 170

Pausanias was an avid tourist who visited Greece in the middle of the second century after Christ and who ultimately wrote a "guide book" to Greece based upon his observations and research. His descriptions of statues at Olympia make him the single most important ancient source for the names and careers of various athletes. He also frequently reveals details of athletic practices which were incidental to the monuments which he was describing. One such case is in his description of the cemetery at Megara:

Near the tomb of Koroibos is buried Orsippos who won the *stadion* at Olympia [720 B.C.]. While the other athletes in the competition wore *perizomata* in accordance with the ancient practice, he ran naked. . . . I think that the *perizoma* slipped off deliberately at Olympia, for he recognized that a nude man can run more easily than one who is girt.

4 Dionysios of Halikarnassos,
Roman Antiquities 7.72.2–3   *ca.* 20 B.C.

Dionysios is discussing a traditional procession in early Rome as well as the Roman refusal to adopt all the practices of the Greeks, whom they had conquered.

After (the young men of Rome) came charioteers driving *tethrippa* and *synorides* and unyoked horses. After them came the competitors in both the light and the heavy events, entirely naked, except they were covered around their unmentionables. This custom has continued down to my time in Rome, just as it was in the beginning among the Greeks. In Greece it was ended by the Lakedaimonians. The first to strip his body and run nude was Akanthos the Lakedaimonian at the 15th Olympiad [720 B.C.]. Before then all the Greeks were ashamed to appear at the games with their bodies entirely naked, as Homer, who is the most credible and earliest of witnesses, shows when he has the heroes girding up.

5 Thucydides 1.6.5–6   *ca.* 420 B.C.

The Athenian historian Thucydides was an eyewitness to many of the events of the struggle between Sparta and Athens, and his account of the Peloponnesian War is usually very reliable. Here he speaks of the more general history of the Greeks and appears to contradict the evidence both of Pausanias (above, no. 3) and of archaeology. It is unfortunate that we cannot know what Thucydides had in mind by the phrase "not many years since."

The Lakedaimonians were the first to take off their clothes and, having stripped in the open, to anoint themselves with oil during their exercises. In early times, even in the Olympic Games, the athletes competed with *diazomata* around their genitals, and it is not many years since that custom has stopped. Even still today those barbarians, especially in Asia, who have contests in boxing and wrestling, compete wearing *diazomata*. Indeed, one could show that the Greeks of old practiced many customs like those of today's barbarians.

6 Aelian, *Varia Historia* 14.7   *ca.* A.D. 220

Aelian (A.D. 170–235), although a native of Praeneste near Rome and a teacher of rhetoric at the latter city, wrote in Greek a collection of moralizing anecdotes from earlier times.

This is a Lakedaimonian law. It goes thusly: None of the Lakedaimonians is to be seen with a more effeminate complexion of body or with more weight than the *gymnasia* will give it. One is a confession of laziness, the other of effeminacy. It was also written in the law that every ten days the *epheboi* would present themselves publicly naked to the *Ephors*. If they appeared well-built and strong, and coming from the *gymnasia* as if sculpted and chiselled, they were praised. But if their limbs had any flabbiness or softness, any slight pudginess or fatty bloating from idleness, they were flogged and punished on the spot.

7 Lucian, *Anacharsis* 24   *ca.* A.D. 170

*Lucian moved to Athens in his fortieth year (A.D. 160) and there wrote dozens of literary pieces that reflect the society of his day, albeit sometimes in a "historical" fiction. For more on this essay, see below, nos. **35, 113, 127**.*

We strip their bodies when they are no longer soft and completely formless, first because we think they should become accustomed to the air, regardless of the season, so that heat will not bother them or cold cripple them. Then we rub their bodies with olive oil and work it in so that they will have better tone. It would be extraordinary if, since we think that lifeless leather softened by oil is more durable and has greater longevity, we did not believe that the body—still alive—would be improved by oil.

8 Pliny, *Natural History* 15.4.19   *ca.* A.D. 75

The elder Pliny produced an encyclopedia of information on hundreds of subjects. Indeed, his curiosity led him to sail into the eruption of Vesuvius in A.D. 79. In this book he discusses the olive.

Olive oil by nature makes the body warm and protects against cold, and also cools the head when heated. The Greeks, progenitors of every vice, have perverted it to luxury by its public use in the *gymnasia*. Their magistrates have been known to sell the scrapings of oil *[gloios]* for as much as $450,000.

9 Theophrastos, *Characters* 16 ca. 319 B.C.

In his characterization of the superstitious man, Theophrastos includes the following trait:

When he passes oiled stones at a crossroad, he pours oil from his *lekythos* on them and leaves only after falling on his knees and prostrating himself.

10 James 5.14 ca. A.D. 50

The brother of Jesus who was called the Christos (the Anointed One) directs members of the early church.

Is one of you sick? Let the elders of the church be convened to pray over him having anointed him with oil in the name of the Lord.

11 Pausanias 10.24.6 ca. A.D. 170

Pausanias, at Delphi, has left the Temple of Apollo and has visited the tomb of Neoptolemos, son of Achilles.

As you continue above the tomb there is a stone that is not very big. The Delphians pour oil over it every day. . . . It is thought that this stone was given to Chronos [to eat] instead of his child [Zeus], and that he regurgitated it.

12 Plutarch, *Moralia* 274D–E ca. A.D. 100

Plutarch, a native of Boeotia, was a learned and prolific author of biographies of important Greek and Roman historical figures, and of essays on a vast array of Greek and Roman subjects. His interest in the antiquities of his world was augmented by his priesthood at Delphi during the last 30 years of his life (A.D. 90–120). In his series of essays on Roman customs, Plutarch noted that custom had in earlier times prevented Roman boys from stripping in front of their fathers and sons-in-law from stripping in front of their fathers-in-law and even from bathing with them, and further notes:

Many regulations are revealed to everyone by the (Roman) priest; one of these is the prohibition on anointing oneself in the open air. The Romans viewed oil rub-downs with extreme suspicion, and they think that there is no greater cause of the slavery and effeminacy of the Greeks than their *gymnasia* and *palaistrai,* which breed much useless idleness and indolence and paederasty in their cities and the erosion of the bodies of young men by sleep and strolls and rhythmical movements and exact diets because of which they have omitted weapons and are said to be dexterous and beautiful *palaistra*-rats rather than good soldiers and knights.

13 Phrynichos (ed. I. deBorries, Leipzig 1911) p. 85   *ca.* A.D. 180

Phrynichos compiled a lexicon of Attic words which survives in fragments, including the following:

"Kynodesmai" [dog-leashes]: These are the things with which the Athenians tied up their private parts when they stripped, because they called the penis a dog.

14 Philostratos, *On Gymnastics* 18   *ca.* A.D. 230

Although many handbooks on physical training were available in antiquity, only one has survived. Although later in date than the period in which we are most interested, Philostratos' manual still contains much information of interest, and it often reflects earlier practices. We will examine many passages from this manual that relate to the different competitive events.

The *gymnastes* carries a *stlengis* at Olympia, perhaps for the following reason. It is necessary that the athlete in the *palaistra* at Olympia be dusted and sunburned; in order that these circumstances not ruin his condition, the *stlengis* reminds the athlete of oil and that he should apply it so liberally that it can be scraped off easily.

15 Plato, *Hippias Minor* 368b–c   *ca.* 390 B.C.?

In this dialogue, which may not be by Plato, Sokrates talks with Hippias of Elis, a famous sophist and the man credited with the first critical edition of the list of Olympic victors in about 420 B.C. But our interest here is not in the talents of Hippias, but in what is clearly the standard gear of the ancient Greek.

By all means, Hippias, you are the wisest of men in the most arts, for I once heard you bragging at the tables of the money-changers in the *agora* here in Athens as you recounted your wide and enviable wisdom. You said that you once went to Olympia with everything on your body the work of your own hands. First there was the finger-ring which you had made yourself, showing that you were skilled in carving signet rings, and another seal-stone was also your work, as were your *stlengis* and your *lekythos*. And you said that you yourself had made the shoes, and had woven the cloak and the T-shirt, that you were wearing.

16 Plutarch, *Moralia* 239B   *ca.* A.D. 100

In this essay Plutarch lists the customs of the Spartans which make them so different from the other Greeks. Among these is the following:

They use reeds rather than iron for their *stlengides*.

17 Diodorus Siculus 13.82.8   *ca.* 40 B.C.

Diodorus wrote a history of the world from earliest times to the Gallic Wars of Caesar. Although his historic sensibilities were not strong, his chronological framework was valid and he preserves the traditions of earlier historians.

On the whole the citizens of Akragas [in the period around 412 B.C.] conducted their affairs voluptuously right from childhood, wearing soft clothes and gold to the point of excess and beyond, and even using *stlengides* and oil flasks of silver and even gold.

18 Hippokrates, *On Regimen in Acute Diseases* 55.20   400 B.C.?

Many writings concerning ancient medicine have survived under the famous name of Hippokrates, but it seems that none were actually written by him. Nonetheless, this passage reveals something about the use of the stlengis *and the* spongos.

A bath will be good for many of the ill . . . if done properly . . . a large quantity of lukewarm water is to be prepared and poured over him quickly. Then *spongoi* are to be used instead of *stlengides* and the body to be rubbed down with oil before it becomes completely dry. But the head is to be dried as completely as possible with the *spongos*.

19 Philostratos, *On Gymnastics* 56   *ca.* A.D. 230

The dust of clay is good for disinfecting and for giving balance to excessive sweaters; dust from terracotta is good for opening closed pores for perspiration; dust from asphalt is good for heating the chilled; black and yellow earth dusts are both good for softening and for maintaining, but yellow dust also adds glisten and is a delight to see on a nice body which is in good shape. The dust should be sprinkled with a fluid motion of the wrist and with fingers spread apart and the dust more like a cloud than a thunderburst so that it covers the athlete like soft down.

III

The Events at a Competition

A. RUNNING

20   Philostratos, *On Gymnastics* 32–33   *ca.* A.D. 230

The best candidate for the *dolichos* should have a powerful neck and shoulders like the candidate for the *pentathlon,* but he should have light, slender legs like the runners in the *stadion.* The latter stir their legs into the sprint by using their hands as if they were wings. The runners in the *dolichos* do this near the end of the race, but the rest of the time they move almost as if they were walking, holding up their hands in front of them, and because of this they need stronger shoulders.

No one any longer makes any distinction between the physiques of the contestants for the *hoplitodromos,* the *stadion,* and the *diaulos* since Leonidas of Rhodes won all three races in four successive Olympiads (164–152 B.C.). Still, we should distinguish between those entering just one of these races and those who enter all of them. The entrant in the *hoplitodromos* should have a long waist, a well-developed shoulder, and a knee tilted upward in order that, with these parts supporting it, the shield may be carried easily. Of the runners in the *stadion,* which is the least strenuous of the sports, those of symmetrical build are very good, but better than these are those who are not too tall but yet a bit too tall for their proportion. Excessive height, however, lacks firmness, like a plant which has shot up too high.

They should be solidly built, for the fundamental thing in running well is to stand well. Their proportions should be as follows: the legs should balance with the shoulders, the chest should be smaller than normal and should contain sound inner organs, the knee must be limber, the shank straight, the hand above average size, the muscles should be only medium, for oversize muscles are fetters to speed. Candidates for the *diaulos* should be stronger than those for the *stadion*, but lighter than those in the *hoplitodromos*. Those who compete in all three races should be put together from the best and should possess a combination of all the qualifications which are needed in each single race. Do not think that this is impossible, for there have been such runners even in our own day.

21 Lucian, *On Slander* 12   *ca.* A.D. 170

Immediately the *hysplex* has fallen the good runner thinks only of what is in front of him and, stretching his mind toward the *terma* and putting his hope of victory in his feet, does not plot against the fellow next to him or even consider his competitors; but the bad runner and worthless competitor has no hope in speed but only in tricks and he thinks only of how he might hold up or trip the runner, believing that this is his only possibility of winning.

22 *ID* 1409 Ba II 43–45   166–135 B.C.

A long inventory of items stored in the Oikos of Andros on the island of Delos includes the following entries which give some idea of the elements of the starting mechanism for the races:

3 *hysplex* elbows; 4 *hysplex* posts; 2 rods; 2 eagles.

Another inventory (ID 1400.9) adds to the list:

2 pipes from the *hyspleges*.

Cf. nos. **69, 82.**

23 Lucian, *Timon* 20   *ca.* A.D. 170

Wealth is explaining to Hermes that he is slow to come, but quick to leave.

Indeed, at the moment when the *hysplex* has fallen, I am already proclaimed the victor, having traversed the *stadion* so fast that the spectators did not even see me.

24 *Anthologia Graeca 11.86*

Did Perikles run or sit for the *stadion?* No one knows. A demon of slow. The whack of the *hysplex* falling was in our ears, and another was being crowned, and Perikles had not moved a toe.

25 Plutarch, *Moralia* 224F   *ca.* A.D. 100

In his collection of pithy sayings attributed to Spartans, Plutarch includes the following from Leo, son of Eurykratidas, king of Sparta in the early 7th century.

Seeing the runners at Olympia engrossed at the *aphesis* with how to gain an advantage, he said, "Look at how much more the runners care about advantage than about justice."

26 Pausanias 6.10.4   *ca.* A.D. 170

Damaretos of Heraia, his son, and his grandson each won twice at Olympia. The victories of Damaretos took place at the 65th Olympiad [520 B.C.] when the *hoplitodromos* was held for the first time, and at the following Olympiad. His statue holds not only the shield that competitors still carry in my time, but also a helmet on his head and greaves on his legs. Over the years these were removed from the competition both by the Eleans and by the Greeks in general.

27 *IG* IV^2.1.618   *ca.* 320 B.C.?

The distance from Olympia to Epidauros is about 225 kilometers. Drymos' victory was presumably in the dolichos. *His statue base at Epidauros provides us with the following information:*

I am Drymos the son of Theodoros who announced his Olympic victory here in Epidauros on the same day, running to the glorious grove of the god, an example of manliness. My fatherland is horsy Argos.

28 Herodotus 6.105–106   *ca.* 430 B.C.

Herodotus, who was born a little before the Persian Wars, frequently relied upon the accounts of eyewitnesses in his history. Here he describes a part of the preparations of the Athenians to meet the Persians on the plain of

Marathon in 490 B.C. In particular, we are concerned with the courier sent to Sparta to appeal for help. It should be noted that we do not know his name for certain: he is called Philippides in some manuscripts, Pheidippides in others. It should also be noted that Herodotus appears not to have known of Philippides running back to Athens to announce the victory at Marathon.

Before leaving for Marathon and while they were still in Athens, the generals sent a messenger to Sparta, one Philippides, an Athenian who was also a *hemerodromos* who was used to doing this sort of thing. According to him, as he reported to the Athenians later, Pan appeared to him on Mt. Parthenion above Tegea. Pan called out his name and ordered Philippides to ask the Athenians why they paid no honors to him, even though he was well-intentioned toward them, and had been helpful to them many times in the past, and would be so again in the future. The Athenians believed that this story was true and, when their affairs were settled once more, they established a shrine of Pan at the foot of the Acropolis, and they have appeased him from the time of his message with annual sacrifices and a torch-race. This Philippides, who had been sent by the generals then when he said that Pan appeared to him, arrived in Sparta on the day after he left Athens.

29   Plutarch, *Moralia* 347C   *ca.* A.D. 100

The story of the last-gasp announcement of victory at Marathon, apparently not known to Herodotus, is cited by Plutarch from other, earlier authors.

As Herakleides of Pontos [mid-4th century B.C.] states, Thersippos of Erchia announced the battle of Marathon. But most say that it was Eukles, who, running with his armor hot from the battle and falling in the doors of the *prytaneis*, could only say "Be happy! We have won!" and immediately expired.

30   Lucian, *A Slip of the Tongue in Greeting* 3   *ca.* A.D. 170

Lucian is discussing the uses and meanings of the word chairein, *literally "to rejoice" (but closer to our "be happy" or "cheers"), which was used, and still is today in Greece, in the singular* chaire *and the plural or formal* chairete, *as a form of greeting. Lucian here also recognizes its use for farewells and final greetings, and we here have the earliest reference, perhaps 660 years after the event, to a run by Philippides to Athens to announce the victory at Marathon.*

It is said that the *hemerodromos* Philippides first used the word in this context when, announcing the victory after Marathon, he said to the magistrates back in Athens "Be happy! We have won!" and having said that he died, so that his announcement and that "Be happy!" died together.

31 Pliny, *Natural History* 7.20.84 ca. A.D. 75

The elder Pliny here presents a catalogue of famous long-distance runs, but appears not to know of Philippides running back from Marathon. Neither did Plutarch (no. 29).

It was a great feat for Philippides to have run 1140 *stadia* [= ca. 220 km.] from Athens to Lakedaimonia in two days, until the Spartan runner Anystis and Philonides the runner of Alexander the Great ran the 1305 *stadia* [= ca. 248 km.] from Sikyon to Elis in one day. We are not ignorant of the fact that some can tolerate 160,000 *passus* [= ca. 243 km.] in the circus, and that recently in the consulship of Fonteius and Vipstanus [A.D. 59] an eight-year-old boy ran 75,000 *passus* [= ca. 114 km.] from noon to nightfall. The degree to which this feat is to be marvelled at will be appreciated if one remembers that the longest recorded journey by carriage of a single night and day was that of Tiberius Nero who was hastening to his brother Drusus who was ill in Germany [9 B.C.]; it was 200,000 *passus* [= ca. 304 km.].

B. WRESTLING

32 Philostratos, *On Gymnastics* 35 ca. A.D. 230

Let us turn to the wrestlers. The proper wrestler should be rather taller than one who is precisely proportioned, but formed like those who are precisely proportioned with a neck which is neither long nor set down into the shoulder. The latter is, to be sure, suitable, but it looks more deformed than athletic, just as among the statues of Herakles, the more pleasing and god-like are those which are noble and without short necks. The neck should, then, be upright like that of a horse which is beautiful and knows it, and the throat should come down to the collarbone on either side. The shoulders should be drawn together and the tops of the shoulders should stand up straight; this contributes size to the wrestler and a noble appearance and strength and a greater wrestling ability. Such shoulders are good guards when the neck is bent and twisted by wrestling, for they give the head a firm base which extends all the way from the arms. A well-marked arm is good for wrestling. What I call a well-marked arm is the following: broad veins begin from the neck, one on each side of the throat, and travel across the shoulders to descend into the hands, and are prominent on the upper arms and forearms. Those who have these veins close to the surface and more visible than usual derive no strength from them, and the veins themselves look ugly like varicose veins. Those who have veins which are deep and slightly swelling appear to have a delicate and distinct spirit in their arms. Such veins make the arms of an aging man grow younger, while in a young man they reveal potential and promise in wrestling.

The better chest is prominent and protruding, for the organs are situated in it as if in a stout and well-shaped room, and the organs are excellent, strong, healthy, and showing spirit at the appropriate time. But the moderately protruding chest is also beautiful, if it has been hardened with ridges all around, for it is strong and vigorous and, even though it is not the best for wrestling, it is better than the other kind of chest. I hold that hollow sunken chests ought not to be seen, much less be exercised, for they suffer from stomach cramps, poor organs, and short wind. The lower abdomen should be drawn in—this is a useless burden to the wrestler—and it should rest upon thighs which are not hollow, but well rounded. Such thighs press together and are adequate for everything in wrestling, and pressed together they give pain rather than receive it.

The straight back is beautiful, but the slightly curved is more athletic since it is better adapted to the bent and forward-leaning posture of wrestling. The back should not be distinguished by a hollow backbone, for this will be lacking in marrow and the vertebrae can be twisted and compressed by wrestling, and can even slip inward; but this is my opinion rather than established fact. The hip joint, since it serves as the pivot for the parts of the body both above and below it, must be supple, well turned, and easy to rotate. This is affected by the length of the hip and by its extraordinary fleshiness. The part of the leg under the hip should not be either too smooth or too fleshy, for the former is a sign of weakness, the latter of a lack of exercise. Rather, it should protrude markedly and in a way suitable for a wrestler.

Sides which are flexible and which also lift up the chest are adequate for both offensive and defensive wrestling. Men with such sides who are beneath their opponents are difficult to subdue, and they are no easy burden when on top of their opponents. Narrow buttocks are weak, fat ones slow, but well-formed buttocks are an asset for everything. A solid thigh turned outwards combines strength with beauty, and it gives good support which is even better if the lower legs are not bowed, for the thigh then rests upon a straight knee. Ankles which are not straight but slant inward overthrow the whole body just as crooked bases tip columns over.

33 *Anthologia Graeca* 11.316

Once Milo was the only wrestler who came to the games [*ca.* 520 B.C.] and the *athlothetes* summoned him to be crowned immediately. But he slipped and fell on his back as he came up, and the crowd shouted that he should not be crowned since he fell down all by himself. Milo stood up in their midst and shouted back: "That was not the third fall, I fell once. Let someone throw me the other times."

34 Pausanias 6.4.3   *ca.* A.D. 170

Were the tactics of Leontiskos legal? See no. 101.

Next to the statue of Sostratos [no. **46**] is one of a wrestler in the men's category, Leontiskos from Messene on the Sicilian straits. He was crowned once at Delphi and twice at Olympia. It is said that his wrestling style was similar to that used by Sostratos in the *pankration;* that is, he did not know how to throw his opponents and thus beat them by bending their fingers.

35 Lucian, *Anacharsis* 1–8 and 28–29   *ca.* A.D. 170

This essay is set in Athens and purports to be a conversation between Solon, the Athenian lawgiver, and the Skythian Anacharsis who had come to Greece from his home on the Black Sea in quest of wisdom. Lucian appears to want us to understand Solon as the representative of civilization and Anacharsis as the representative of naive barbarism, and he seems to have picked athletics for the topic of their "conversation" as that aspect of Greek civilization which would be the strangest to the foreigner. It is not completely clear who "wins" the debate, nor exactly where Lucian's own sympathies lie; perhaps the ambiguity is deliberate. The athletic details which we learn from Lucian are sometimes vague or even anachronistic for the supposed date (ca. 590 B.C.) of the confrontation between Solon and Anacharsis, but Lucian does give us a general impression which is correct, a vivid image of the role of athletics in everyday Greek civic life. See also nos. 7 above, and 113 and 127 below.

ANACHARSIS: Solon, what are your young men doing? Some of them are all wrapped up together but trying to trip each other; others are strangling and tackling one another, and grovelling in the mud, wallowing around like pigs. But in the beginning, as I saw for myself, as soon as they took off their clothes they oiled themselves and took turns rubbing each other down quite peacefully. But I don't understand what has happened to them, for now they push and tug at one another and butt their foreheads together like rams. Now look there! That man picked up the other man by the legs and threw him to the ground, and then fell on top of him and will not let him up, but keeps pushing him into the mud. Now he has got his legs wrapped around the other man's midsection and he is grabbing his throat with his forearm and strangling him, and the other one is slapping the first on the shoulder in order to signal, I guess, that he has had enough and doesn't want, poor fellow, to be choked completely. Not even on account of the expensive oil do they avoid getting dirty. Instead they rub off the ointment, and pile on the mud mixed with buckets of sweat and make themselves ridiculous, at least to me, as they slip from each other's hands like eels.

In the open part of the courtyard others are doing exactly the same thing, though not in the mud. Rather, they have put down a thick layer of sand in a trench and they sprinkle one another voluntarily, piling the dust on like roosters, so that (I guess) it will be difficult to escape from the holds since the sand removes the slipperiness and gives a better grip on a dry surface.

Others, upright and covered with dust, are hitting and kicking each other. This one looks like he is going to spit out his teeth, poor fellow, with his mouth so full of blood and sand. As you see, he got a belt on the jaw. And the official—I take him to be one of the officials from his purple cloak—does not separate them and stop the fight; rather, he incites them and cheers the man who landed the punch.

Over there others are all in a lather, bobbing up and down as if they were running, but never moving from their places. Now they are jumping up and kicking the air.

Please tell me what good is being accomplished by all this. Frankly, it looks to me more like insanity than anything else, and you are not going to convince me easily that men who act like that don't belong in the loony bin.

SOLON: Of course they look that way to you, Anacharsis, because what they are doing is strange to you and very different from the customs of your native Skythia. There is probably much in your education and exercises which would seem strange to us Greeks if one of us happened to look in upon it as you are doing now. But take heart, my good man, it is not insanity, nor even for the sake of wanton violence that they beat one another and wallow in the mud and throw dust over each other. What they are doing has some usefulness and is not without pleasure, and it strengthens their bodies to a great extent. As a matter of fact, if you stay for a time in Greece, as I hope you will, before long you will belong to the muddy or the dusty club. You will find out that what they are doing is very pleasant as well as useful.

ANACHARSIS: Thank you very much, Solon, but you Greeks can keep such pleasures for yourselves. If anyone tries to treat me to such pleasures he will find out why we carry daggers in our belts! But tell me anyway, what do you call these things? Are there words to describe what they are doing?

SOLON: We call the place a *gymnasion*, Anacharsis, and it is sacred to Apollo Lykeios. You see his statue over there, the one in the pose of leaning against a *stele* with a bow in his left hand. His right hand, bent back over his head as if from the fatigue of long exertion, shows that the god is resting. What is going on is called athletics in general. The specific name for what is happening in the mud as well as in the dust is wrestling. Those who are standing upright and punching one another are practicing what we call the *pankration,* and we have other types of athletics too—the *pygme,* the *diskos,* jumping, etc. For all of these we hold contests and the winner in each is the one who is the best, and he gets prizes.

(28–29)

SOLON: The mud and the *konis,* which seemed so ridiculous to you in the beginning, are put down for the following reasons. First, so that they may fall safely on a soft surface rather than a hard one. Next, they are necessarily slipperier when they are coated with sweat and mud. Although you compared this to eels, it is neither useless nor ridiculous; it makes a considerable contribution to strength when they are slippery and one tries to hold on while the other tries to slip away. And don't think that it is easy to pick up a man who is sweaty and muddy and has on oil as well. As I said earlier, all this is useful in war in the event that one has to pick up a wounded comrade and carry him out of the fight, or grab an enemy and bring him back to one's own lines. For such reasons we train them to the limits and set the most difficult tasks so that they can do the lesser ones with greater ease.

We believe that the *konis* is useful for the opposite purpose, to prevent a man from slipping away once caught. Once they have been trained with the mud to hold on to what would get away because of its oiliness, they are taught to escape from the opponent's hands when they are caught in a firm grip. In addition, the *konis* is thought to stop profuse sweating, to prolong strength, and to prevent harm to their bodies from the wind blowing on them when their pores are open. Finally, the *konis* rubs off the filth and makes the man cleaner. I would like to take one of those white-skinned fellows who live in the shade and put him next to any athlete you might pick out of the Lykeion after I had washed off the mud and *konis,* and then find out which you would rather resemble. I know that you would choose immediately, without even waiting to see what each could do, to be firm and hard rather than soft and like a marshmallow with thin blood withdrawing to the interior of the body.

36   *POxy* III.466 ii   second century A.D.

A fragmentary papyrus from Oxyrhynchus, perhaps part of a manual of physical education, presents a series of wrestling instructions. Each section concludes with the verb plexon: *to weave, intertwine, tangle. I translate it as "mix it up," with the understanding that, the instruction having been given, it is time to put it to the test by actually wrestling.*

Get alongside him. Take his head in your right arm. Mix it up!
Get around him. Grab him from below. Step through. Mix it up!
Get under his right arm. Get around the arm you are under and hook your left leg on his flank. Throw him over your left leg. Step through. Mix it up!
Turn around. Grab both [???]. Mix it up!
Put a foot forward. Grab him around the body. Push forward and bend him back. Face forward and push back against him . . .

C. BOXING (see also no. **35**)

37   Philostratos, *On Gymnastics* 9–10 and 34   *ca.* A.D. 230

Boxing was a discovery of the Lakedaimonians, and Polydeukes was the best at it and for this reason the poets sang of him in this event [see below, no. **39**]. The ancient Lakedaimonians boxed for the following reason: they had no helmets, nor did they think it proper to their native land to fight in helmets. They felt that a shield, properly used, could serve in the place of a helmet. Therefore they practiced boxing in order to know how to ward off blows to the face, and they hardened their faces in order to be able to endure the blows which landed. After a time, however, they quit boxing and the *pankration* as well, because these contests are decided by one opponent acknowledging defeat and this might give an excuse for her detractors to accuse Sparta of a lack of spirit.

The ancient boxing equipment was the following: the four fingers were bound up so that they extended beyond the strap sufficiently to allow the boxer to clench his fist. The strap continued to the forearm as a support for the wrist. Now the equipment has changed. They tan the hide of a fat ox and work it into the boxing *himas* which is sharp and protrudes from the hand, and the thumb is not bound up with the fingers in order to prevent additional wounds, and thus the whole hand does not fight. For this reason they also prohibit pigskin *himantes* in the stadium because they believe them to cause painful and slow-healing wounds.

(34)

The boxer should have a long hand and strong forearms and upper arms, broad shoulders and a long neck. Thick wrists strike harder blows, thinner ones are flexible and strike more easily. He should have solid hips for support, since the thrust of striking out will unbalance him if his body is not set upon firm hips. I regard fat calves as worthless in every sport, and especially boxing. They are too slow for both offensive and defensive footwork. He should have a straight calf of proper proportion to his thigh, and his thighs should be set well apart from each other. The shape of the boxer is better for offense if his thighs do not come together. The best boxer has a small belly, for he is nimble and has good wind. On the other hand, a big belly will give some advantage to a boxer, for it will get in the way of the opponent who is striking for the face.

38   Pausanias 8.40.4–5   *ca.* A.D. 170

There is a similar story [to the one about the death of Arrhichion, no. **44**] which I know about the Argives in the case of Kreugas, a boxer from Epidamnos. The Argives gave the crown of victory at the Nemean Games to Kreugas although he was dead, because his opponent, Damoxenos of Syracuse, broke the agreement which had been reached between them. While they were boxing evening came on and they agreed in front of witnesses that each would allow the other in turn to land a punch. Now at that time boxers did not yet wear the sharp *himas* on the wrist of each hand, but boxed with the soft *himantes* which were bound in the hollow of the hand so that the fingers were left bare. These soft *himantes* were thin oxhide thongs plaited together in some ancient way. Now Kreugas aimed his punch at Damoxenos' head. Then Damoxenos told Kreugas to lift his arm and, when Kreugas had done so, Damoxenos struck him under the ribs with his fingers straight out. The combination of his sharp fingernails and the force of his blow drove his hand into Kreugas' guts. He grabbed Kreugas' intestines and tore them out and Kreugas died on the spot. The Argives expelled Damoxenos on the ground that he had broken his agreement by giving his opponent several blows [i.e. one for each of his fingers] instead of the agreed-upon one blow. They gave the victory to the dead Kreugas and erected a statue of him in Argos.

39 Theokritos, *Idylls* 22.27–135   *ca.* 275 B.C.

The Hellenistic poet Theokritos here gives us his version of an episode in the myth of Jason's quest for the Golden Fleece in his ship Argo.

Now the Argo had escaped the Clashing Rocks and the baneful mouth of snowy Pontus [the Bosphorus] and had come to the land of the Bebrykians, bearing the dear sons of the gods. There the heroes converged from both sides of the ship, descended the gangplank, and left Jason's ship. They stepped off onto a deeply sanded shore of a headland protected from the wind and busied themselves with spreading their bedrolls and gathering firewood. But Castor and Polydeukes went off by themselves straying apart from their comrades and marvelling at the many varieties of trees growing wild on the mountain. Beneath a smooth cliff they found an everflowing spring, filled to the brim with pure water; the pebbles below flashed like crystal or silver from the depths. Lofty pines grew nearby, poplars, plane-trees, tapering cypresses, and there were also fragrant flowers, work for fuzzy bees. A gigantic man was sitting there and sunning himself, an awesome sight. His ears were crushed from the rigors of boxing, his mighty chest and his broad back bulged with flesh of iron; he was like a colossal statue of hammered metal. The muscles on his firm arms just below the shoulder stood out like rounded stones which a winter's torrent rolls and polishes in great swirling eddies. Over his back there was slung a lion's skin fastened at his neck by the paws. And Polydeukes spoke to him thus:

POLYDEUKES: Good day, stranger, whoever you are. What people are they who own this land?

AMYKOS: Good day? How can the day be good when it brings to me men I never saw before?

POLYDEUKES: Do not be afraid. We are not evil men, nor were our fathers before us.

AMYKOS: I'm not afraid, and I'm not likely to learn to be afraid from the likes of you.

POLYDEUKES: Are you completely uncultured, always perverse and sneering?

AMYKOS: I am what you see, and I'm not trespassing on your land.

POLYDEUKES: Oh, well, come along with us and you will return home again with gifts of friendship.

AMYKOS: I don't want any gifts, and I've none for you.

POLYDEUKES: Well, may we at least have a drink of this water?

AMYKOS: You'll find out when you're a lot thirstier than now.

POLYDEUKES: If you want money just say how much.

AMYKOS: I want you to put up your dukes and fight me like a man.

POLYDEUKES: In boxing? Or may we kick each other's legs, too, and . . .

AMYKOS: Shut up, put 'em up, and do your damndest.

POLYDEUKES: Wait! Is there a prize for which we will fight?

AMYKOS: If you win, you beat me, and if I win, I beat you.

POLYDEUKES: Gamecocks fight on such terms.

AMYKOS: I don't give a damn if we look like gamecocks or lions. You wanted a prize, and that's it.

So spoke Amykos and he picked up and blew upon a hollow shell at whose blast the Bebrykians, whose hair is never cut, swiftly gathered beneath the shady plane trees. And Castor, that mighty fighter, went and called the heroes from the Argo.

When the two combatants had strengthened their hands with oxhide straps and had wound the long *himantes* around their arms, they met in the middle of the gathering and breathed out mutual slaughter. At this point there was jostling between them in their eagerness to see who would get the sunlight at his back. By quick skill Polydeukes slipped by the huge man and the sun's ray struck Amykos full in the face. Then Amykos, enraged, rushed forward aiming his fist straight at the mark, but Polydeukes sidestepped and struck him on the point of his chin. Then, even more aroused, the giant battled wildly and hunching over he rushed heavily upon Polydeukes. The Bebrykians roared applause, while the heroes on the other side shouted words of encouragement to Polydeukes, for they feared that the giant fighter would press him into a corner and finish him. But Polydeukes, shifting his ground this way and that, striking now with his right, now with his left, cut Amykos up and checked his attack in spite of his huge size. The giant came to a standstill drunk with blows, and spat out red blood while all the heroes cheered when they saw the gashes around his mouth and jaws, and as his face swelled his eyes became narrower and narrower. Then Polydeukes continued to bewilder him by making feints from all directions, but when he saw that Amykos was utterly helpless, he drove his fist against his brow smack above the nose and laid bare his forehead to the bone, and Amykos went down hard, stretched out on the layers of leaves.

But he got up again, and the fight became truly bitter; they dealt each other deadly blows from the hard *himantes*. But the giant kept throwing his punches at his opponent's chest and just below his neck while Polydeukes kept on battering Amykos' face all over. The giant's flesh shrank as he sweated and from a huge man he was fast becoming a small one whereas Polydeukes displayed ever stouter limbs and a healthier color.

Then Amykos, hoping desperately for a knockout punch, seized Polydeukes' left hand in his own left hand, and leaned sideways in his forward lunge, and reached down to his right side to bring up a huge haymaker. Had he landed the blow, he would have knocked out the Spartan prince, but Polydeukes ducked out of the way and at the same time he hit Amykos beneath the left temple with a crisp right hand delivered straight from the shoulder; and blood spurted forth from Amykos' gaping temple. Immediately, with his now free left hand, he planted a punch on the giant's mouth, and the teeth rattled loose. With blows that thudded ever sharper and sharper, he battered the man's face until his cheeks were crushed in. Then finally Amykos went down flat on the ground and, dazed, he raised his hand and gave up the fight since he was close to death. But Polydeukes, though he had won, did nothing brutal to Amykos, but did make him swear never again to insult strangers.

40 Plato, *Laws* 830a–c   *ca.* 350 B.C.

In describing his ideal political constitution, Plato insists that practice in military exercises is necessary in peacetime. As a part of his argument, he uses the following analogy:

If we were in charge of boxers or pankratiasts or competitors in similar athletics, would we send them straight into the contest without any prior training or practice? If we were boxers, for example, we would be spending the days before the bout in learning how to fight, and training and practicing all the methods which we intended to use on the day of the real fight, and imitating the real thing as far as possible. Thus, we would wear the *sphairai* instead of the *himantes,* in order to get the best possible practice in punching and counterpunching. If we happened to be short of sparring partners, do you think that the laughter of fools would stop us from hanging up a lifeless effigy and practicing on it? Even if we were in a desert and had neither live nor lifeless sparring partner, would we not resort to a very literal shadowboxing, practicing on ourselves as it were?

41 Plutarch, *Moralia* 825E   *ca.* A.D. 100

In this treatise the would-be statesman is advised to be mild and conciliatory in his private disagreements, avoiding anger and passion and, hence, harshness and bitterness.

Just as we put *episphairai* on the hands of those boxing in the *palaistrai* so that the contest will not come to anything irreparable since the blows will be soft and painless.

42 Plutarch, *Moralia* 38B ca. A.D. 100

In the midst of a discussion about the sense of hearing comes the following statement:

Xenokrates [*ca.* 330 B.C.] urged that *amphotidai* be fastened on children rather than on athletes because athletes may have their ears disfigured by blows, but children have their characters disfigured by words.

43 Philostratos, *On Gymnastics* 57 ca. A.D. 230

A *korykos* should be suspended for boxers, but even more for those who are students of the *pankration*. The *korykos* for the boxers should be lightweight because the hands of the boxer are trained only for sparring, but the *korykos* for the pankratiasts should be heavier and bigger, so that they can practice keeping their balance withstanding the onslaught of the *korykos*, and so that they can exercise their shoulders and fingers against some resistance. And his head should smash into it and the athlete should use it to assume all the upright positions of the *pankration*.

D. *PANKRATION* (see also nos. **22, 23, 29**)

44 Pausanias 8.40.1 ca. A.D. 170

In the *agora* of Phigaleia there is a statue of Arrhachion the pankratiast which is of the archaic style, especially in its form; the feet are not separated and the hands hang down along the side to the hips. The statue is made of stone, and they say that there was an epigram written on the stone. This has vanished over the years, but Arrhachion won two Olympic victories before the festival of the 54th Olympiad [564 B.C.]. At this latter festival, he won a third time, partly due to the fairness of the *Hellanodikai*, and partly because of his own *arete*. As he was fighting with the last remaining of his opponents for the olive, his opponent, whoever he was, got a grip first and held Arrhachion with his legs squeezed around Arrhachion's midsection and his hands squeezing around his neck at the same time. Meanwhile, Arrhachion dislocated a toe on his opponent's foot but was strangled and expired. At the same instant, however, Arrhachion's opponent gave up because of the pain in his toe. The Eleans proclaimed Arrhachion the victor and crowned his corpse.

45   Philostratos, *Pictures in a Gallery* 2.6   ca. A.D. 240

*This Philostratos is probably the son-in-law of the author with the same
name who wrote the treatise on gymnastics (above, nos. **12, 20, 24,** and **29**).
He was a sophist and rhetorician who chose a description of a series of
paintings as a device to exhibit his knowledge and, occasionally, to present
a moral. We are to imagine him in a gallery describing the paintings to a
young student companion.*

Now you have come to the Olympic Games and to the best of the contests at
Olympia. This is the *pankration* for men. Arrhachion is being crowned
although he dies at the moment of his victory, and the *Hellanodikes* is
crowning him. The natural contours of the land form the stadium in a simple,
but ample, glen, and the Alpheios River flows by—it is a light stream, you
know, and that is why it alone of all rivers flows on top of the sea—and
around it grow olive trees with gray-green leaves curling like parsley.

This part of the painting over behind the stadium we will examine
presently, and many other details too, but let us now inquire into Arrhachion's deed before it is over. He seems to have overpowered not only his opponent, but the Greeks in the audience as well. They are jumping up from their
seats and shouting, some waving their hands, some leaping from the ground,
and others are slapping one another on the back. His astonishing feat has left
the spectators beside themselves. Who is so stolid as not to shriek aloud at
this athlete? This present accomplishment surpasses his already great record
of two previous victories at Olympia, for this one has cost his life and he
departs for the land of the blessed with the dust still on him. But do not think
that this is accidental, for he planned his victory very cleverly.

And what about the wrestling? The pankratiasts, my boy, practice a dangerous brand of wrestling. They have to endure black eyes which are not safe
for the wrestler, and learn holds by which one who has fallen can still win,
and they must be skillful in various ways of strangulation. They bend ankles
and twist arms and throw punches and jump on their opponents. All such
practices are permitted in the *pankration* except for biting and gouging.
Indeed, the Lakedaimonians permit even this, I suppose because they are
training for battle, but the Elean Games prohibit biting and gouging although
they do allow strangling. For this reason Arrhachion's opponent, having
already a grip around his waist, thought to kill him and put an arm around
his neck and choked off his breath. At the same time he slipped his legs
through Arrhachion's groin and wound his feet inside Arrhachion's knees,
and pulled back until the sleep of death began to creep over Arrhachion's
senses. But Arrhachion was not done yet, for as his opponent began to relax
the pressure of his legs, Arrhachion kicked away his own right foot and fell

heavily to the left holding his opponent at the groin with his left knee still holding his opponent's foot firmly. So violent was the fall that the opponent's left ankle was wrenched from the socket. For Arrhachion's soul, though it leaves his body feeble, still gives him strength for his purpose.

The one who is strangling Arrhachion is painted to look like a corpse as he signals with his hand that he is giving up. But Arrhachion is painted as are all victors. His blood is in full flower, and sweat still glistens, and he smiles like a living man who sees his victory.

46 Pausanias 6.4.2   *ca.* A.D. 170

There [at Olympia] is a statue of a Sikyonian man, a pankratiast, named Sostratos. His nickname was Akrochersites [Fingerman], because he would grab his opponent by the fingers and bend them and not let go until his opponent surrendered. He won twelve victories at Isthmia and Nemea combined, three at Olympia, and two at Delphi. The 104th Olympiad [364 B.C.] at which Sostratos won his first victory is not accredited by the Eleans, because the games were not held by them, but by the Pisatans and the Arkadians.

E. PENTATHLON

47 Philostratos, *On Gymnastics* 31 and 35   *ca.* A.D. 230

The pentathlete should be heavy rather than light, and light rather than heavy. He should be tall, well built, with good carriage, and with musculature which is neither superfluous nor inadequate. His legs should be long rather than strictly proportionate, and his hips should be flexible and limber for the backward bending of throwing the *akon* and the *diskos* and for the *halma*. He will jump with less pain and less likelihood of breaking something in his body if he can land softly by letting his hips down gradually. It is necessary that his hands and fingers be long. He will hurl the *diskos* considerably better if there is a large grip for the rim of the *diskos* provided in the hollow of a long-fingered hand, and he will have less trouble in throwing the *akon* if his fingers are not so short that they barely reach the *ankyle*.

(35)

The *halter* is a discovery of the pentathletes which was invented for use in the *halma* from which it gets its name. The rules regard jumping as the most difficult of the competitions, and they allow the jumper to be given advantages in rhythm by the use of the flute, and in weight by the use of the *halter*. This is a sure guide for the hands, and leads to a clear and firm landing on the ground. The rules show the value of this point, for they do not allow the jump to be measured unless the footprints are perfect. The long *halteres* provide exercise for the shoulders and the hands; the spherical *halteres* for the fingers as well. They should be used in all exercises, both the light and the heavy, except for the relaxing exercises.

48 Aristotle, *Rhetoric* 1361b   *ca.* 330 B.C.

Each age has its own beauty. In youth, it lies in the possession of a body capable of enduring all kinds of contests, whether of the racecourse or of bodily strength, while the young man is himself a pleasant delight to behold. It is for this reason that pentathletes are the most beautiful; they are naturally adapted both for exertion of the body and swiftness of foot. In the prime of life, beauty lies in being naturally adapted for the toils of war, in being both a pleasure to look at and yet awe-inspiring. In old age, beauty lies in being naturally adapted to confront unavoidable tasks and not causing annoyance to the beholder by being devoid of the disagreeable aspects of old age.

Strength consists of the power of moving another man as one wants, and for this it is necessary to pull or push, to lift, squeeze, or crush. A strong man is defined as being strong by virtue of his ability to do some or all of these things.

Excellence of size is defined as being superior to most men in height, weight, and girth, but in such proportion so that the movements of the body are not slowed down by excess.

Athletic excellence in a body is defined in terms of the above: strength and size, as well as in terms of speed, for to be swift is to be strong. One who can move his legs rapidly and in long strides makes a good runner. One who can grab and grapple makes a good wrestler. One who can thrust away his opponent by a blow of the fist makes a good boxer. One who excels in both boxing and wrestling makes a good pankratiast. But he who excels in everything is fit for the *pentathlon*.

49 [Plato], *The Lovers* 135c–137d   [400 B.C.]

Although this dialogue has come down to us together with other writings by Plato, we can be certain that he did not author this piece. We do not know the date of its composition either, but its dramatic date is obviously during Sokrates' lifetime. An attempt is being made to define philosophy, and the analogy drawn between philosopher and pentathlete is interesting and perhaps revealing about an attitude toward the pentathlete. As usual, Sokrates plays devil's advocate.

I next asked him if it was not impossible for any one person to learn equally well two crafts, not to say many, or even two of the principal crafts. He replied:

"Do not think, Sokrates, that I would maintain that the philosopher must have the same depth of knowledge about each of the crafts as the professional working in them. I mean only such knowledge of them as may reasonably be expected of a free and educated man; that is, he should be able to follow the explanations of the craftsman more readily than the others around him. He should be able to contribute an opinion of his own which will make him seem to be the most clever and accomplished of the group which might be present at any verbal or practical display of a craft."

Then, since I was still quite unsettled about his meaning, I asked him:

"Do I understand correctly the sort of man whom you mean by the philosopher? You seem to mean someone like the pentathletes in the competition with the runners or the wrestlers; the former yield, you know, to the latter in their specialities, and are their inferiors, but are superior to the run-of-the-mill athletes and beat them. It is something of this sort which you seem to suggest is the effect produced by philosophy upon those who make it their pursuit; they yield to those who are first-rate in their understanding of the crafts, but surpass the others by taking second place. In this way, the man who studies philosophy finishes second in everything. That is the sort of man whom you appear to be indicating."

"It seems to me that you are quite right, Sokrates," he said, "in your concept of the philosopher's position, and in your comparison of him to the pentathlete. It is precisely his nature not to be bogged down with any business, or to work things out exactly and in detail, for to do so would mean that his excessive attention to one thing would make him deficient in the rest like a craftsman. Rather, he should have moderate contact with everything."

After this answer, I was eager to know clearly what he meant, so I asked him whether he thought of good men as useful or useless.

"I would say useful, Sokrates," he replied.

"Then if useful men are good, are useless men wicked?"

He agreed that they were.

"Again, do you think that philosophers are useful men or not?"

He opined that they were not only useful, but the most useful men of all.

"Come now, let us see, if what you say is true, how these second-best men are useful to us; clearly the philosopher is second-best to any particular workman in the crafts?"

He agreed.

"Well now," I went on, "if you, or one of your close friends, were to fall sick, would you fetch the second-best man into the house in order to get well again, or would you summon a doctor?"

"For my part, I would have both," he replied.

"Please do not say 'both,'" I said, "but which of the two you would prefer and would summon first."

"Of course," he replied, "anyone would prefer the doctor and summon him first."

"And again, if you were in a ship that was in rough weather, to which would you rather entrust yourself and your things, the pilot or the philosopher?"

"I would chose the pilot."

"And so it will go in everything else? So long as there is a craftsman, the philosopher will not be useful?"

"Apparently," he replied.

"So now we find that the philosopher is a useless person, assuming that we will always have craftsmen, and we have agreed that useful men are good and useless men are bad?"

He had to agree with this.

"Then what follows? Shall I ask you, or will it be too ill-mannered?"

"Ask whatever you please."

"I would like," I said, "merely to recall our agreement upon what has been stated. We agreed that philosophy is honorable, and that philosophers are good; we also agreed that useful men are good, and useless men wicked. But then again we agreed that philosophers, so long as we have craftsmen, are useless. Have we not agreed to all of this?"

"Yes, of course," he replied.

"Then we are also agreed, according to your definition of philosophy as having the kind of knowledge which you describe about the crafts, that philosophers are useless and wicked. But I suspect that philosophers are not really wicked, my friend, and that philosophy is not just dabbling in the crafts or spending one's life in meddlesome snooping and prying and in an accumulation of learning, but something else."

50 Pausanias 3.11.6   *ca.* A.D. 170

One of the most difficult questions concerning ancient athletic practices is the method by which the victor in the pentathlon *was determined. The following story, which also appears in Herodotus (9.33) and the date of which is to be placed at around 500 B.C., gives some tantalizing information. Note that the Iamids were the family of prophets at Elis; cf. no. 79.*

Tisamenos, an Elean of the Iamid family, received an oracle that he would win five very remarkable contests. He therefore practiced for the *pentathlon* at the Olympic Games, but was defeated even though he did win two contests, for he beat Hieronymos of Andros in the *dromos* and the *halma*. But when Hieronymos beat him in the *pale* and Tisamenos lost the victory, he came to understand that the oracle meant that the god had given to him the fate to win five military victories by means of his own prophesying.

51 Xenophon, *Hellenica* 7.4.29   364 B.C.

The Arkadians have ousted the Eleans from Olympia and are celebrating the Olympic Games (cf. nos. 46 and 241) when, much to their surprise, the Eleans march against them and into the Altis. The Games have reached the following stage when the Eleans appear, and we therefore learn something of the order of the competitions in the pentathlon:

They had already finished the horse-race, and the stadium events of the *pentathlon*. The competitors who had reached the wrestling were no longer in the stadium, but were wrestling in the region between the stadium and the altar.

52 *SEG* 15.501   first century B.C.?

The following inscription from the island of Rhodes is sadly fragmentary, but the text which does survive provides clues about the order of the events in the pentathlon. *The parts which are enclosed in brackets are not preserved on the stone.*

> [. . . . . .] they are to be in charge of [. . . . .]
> [. in] turn until each five times [has thrown the *diskos*. . . . . . .]
> [first] shall jump the one who threw the *diskos* farthest [. . . . . .]
> [. . . .] they have ? the *skamma* nor the [. . . . .]
> [. . . . .] of the surface of the stadium [. . . . .]
> let it be two feet. Similarly [. . . . .]
> of the *kanon* and the [. . . . .]
> ? and the one at the *te*[*rma*. . . . .]
> of those who are [. . . . .]
> of the wrestler [. . . . .]

53   Artemidoros, *Interpretation of Dreams* 1.57   ca. A.D. 180

A native of Lydia in Asia Minor and a near contemporary of Pausanias and Lucian, Artemidoros collected hundreds of dreams and the meanings that had been assigned to them. The dream given here may reflect the order of the competitions in the pentathlon.

It seems to me that if someone dreams of competing in the *pentathlon* it signifies, first of all, a movement from place to place because of the *dromos*, and then some kind of extraordinary fines or expenses or unfamiliar outlays because of the *diskos*, which is made of bronze [like typical ancient coins] and flung from the hands. Often it signifies cares or anxieties as well, because of the jumping with *halteres*. For we say that those beset by unforeseen cares have been jumped. It furthermore signifies fights and disagreements with people because the swish and speed of the *akon* are like wound-up tense words. Finally, it signifies for the wealthy land disputes, and for the poor illness because of the *pale*.

54   *Anthologia Graeca* 11.84   ca. A.D. 60

The following epigram was written by Lucillius who specialized in satirical jokes. It, like the dream interpretation of Artemidoros, appears to indicate the same sequence of competitions in the pentathlon *although the* pale *is first here.*

None of the competitors fell more quickly than I, and none ran the *stadion* more slowly. I never came near the others with the *diskos*, my legs never got strong enough to jump, and a club-footed cripple could hurl the *akon* better than I. I am the first in the *pentathlon* to be proclaimed vanquished in all five.

55   Philostratos, *Pictures in a Gallery* 1.24   ca. A.D. 240

Read the hyacinth, for it is inscribed and says that the hyacinth sprang from the ground in honor of a lovely lad, and that it laments him in early spring, I suppose because it was born from him when he died. Do not be delayed by the flower in the meadow, for it grows from him as well, no different from the earthborn blossom. The painting says that the lad's hair is "hyacinthine" and that his blood, coming to life in the earth, colors the flower. It flows from his head where struck by the *diskos*. The mistake told of Apollo is terrible and scarcely creditable, but we are not here as critics of the myths and are not ready to refuse them creditability. Rather, we are simply viewers of the paintings, and thus let us examine the painting and first of all the *balbis* for the *diskos*.

A *balbis* has been separated off; it is small and adequate only for a single standing man, and even then it holds back only the rear and the right leg (the back is facing forward) with the weight on the left leg reduced, for it is necessary that this leg is straightened and advanced together with the right arm. The attitude of the man holding the *diskos* must be that he turn his head to the right and bend over so far that he can see his side, and to throw he must draw himself up and put his whole right side into the throw.

This is how Apollo has thrown the *diskos*, for he could not have thrown it otherwise. The *diskos* has struck the youth who lies on top of it. He is a Lakonian youth with a straight calf which is no stranger to running; his arms are already developed and the fine lines of his bones show forth. Apollo is still standing on the *balbis* with his face averted and looking down at the ground. You might say that he is frozen there by the great consternation which has befallen him.

No gentleman is Zephyros who, because he was angry with Apollo, made the *diskos* strike the youth, and the scene makes the wind laugh as he jeers at Apollo from his hideaway. I think that you can see him with wings at his temples, with his delicate appearance, and with a garland about his head with every kind of flower in it. Presently he will be weaving the hyacinth in with them.

56 Pausanias 6.19.4   *ca.* A.D. 170

In the Treasury [of the Sikyonians at Olympia] are kept three *diskoi*, the number used for the competition of the *pentathlon*.

57 Aristotle, *On the Progression of Animals* 705a   *ca.* 330 B.C.

The animal moves by pushing off against that which lies beneath it, so that if what is beneath moves away so quickly that there is nothing to push off against and there is no resistance at all, the animal cannot move. . . . In the same way pentathletes who hold the *halteres* jump further than those who do not, and runners who swing their arms run faster, for there is a certain resistance in tension exerted toward the hands and wrists.

58 Pausanias 5.26.3   *ca.* A.D. 170

The *halteres* have the following form: they are made from an elongated circle or ellipse which is cut through but not exactly at the middle, made so that the fingers of the hand can pass through them just as they do through the handle of a shield.

59   Pausanias 5.7.10   *ca.* A.D. 170

Among the other victors [at Olympia in mythical times] it is said that Apollo beat Hermes at running and Ares in the *pyx*. They say that it is for this reason that the Pythikon flute-music is played during the jump in the *pentathlon*, because the flute-music is sacred to Apollo, and Apollo won Olympic victories.

60–61

The length which the ancient Greek athlete could jump in the halma, *thanks to the use of the* halteres, *has excited much controversy because of two groups of sources, one dealing with Phaÿllos of Kroton, the other with Chionis of Sparta. Note that, as in the case of the run from Marathon (above, nos.* **16–19**), *the sources that record the fabulous jumps are several centuries after the presumed fact.*

60a   Herodotus 8.47.5   *ca.* 430 B.C.

Of the Greeks who dwell outside Greece the only ones who helped Greece in its time of danger [480 B.C.] were the Krotoniates with one ship which was commanded by Phaÿllos, a man who won three Pythian victories.

60b   Pausanias 10.9.2   *ca.* A.D. 170

Most men take no account of the competitors in the musical contests, and I think that they are not worth much trouble. Moreover, I have already discussed those athletes who are famous in my account of Elis. At Delphi there is, however, a statue of Phaÿllos of Kroton. He had no victories at Olympia, but at Delphi he won twice in the *pentathlon* [482 and 478 B.C.?] and a third victory in the *stadion*. He fought against the Persians at sea [480 B.C.] in his own ship, which he equipped at his own expense and manned with fellow citizens from Kroton who were living in Greece. Such is the story of the athlete from Kroton.

60c   Zenobius 6.23   *ca.* A.D. 150

*Zenobius seems to have been a sophist educated in Rome at the time of the emperor Hadrian (*A.D. *117–138); to him is attributed a collection of* *proverbs, one of which is the following. It was believed in antiquity that his collection of proverbs was based on the work of Didymos and Tarrhaios, who seem to have been active in the first century B.C. If this is correct, the idea that Phaÿllos made a jump of 55 feet can be traced back to a date only (!) four hundred years after his time. But note the confusion in these sources about the origin of this athlete, and others with the same name.*

"Beyond the dug-up area": Phaÿllos was a pentathlete from Pontos who seems to have been a great *diskos* thrower and jumper. Since he jumped beyond the dug-up area 50 feet onto the hard ground, the event passed into the proverbial.

60d Scholion to Aristophanes, *Acharnians* 214

The following editorial comment on the text of Aristophanes cannot be dated. It certainly cannot be earlier than the third century B.C., is probably somewhat later, and could be several hundred years later. Note that Phaÿllos has now become an Olympic victor.

Phaÿllos was a first-class runner and an Olympic victor, famous as a *hoplitodromos,* and nicknamed the "odometer." He was also a pentathlete about whom the following epigram was written:

Five and fifty feet flew Phaÿllos,
But dished the *diskos* a hundred minus five.

There was also another Phaÿllos who was an athlete, victorious at the 8th Olympiad [748 B.C.], and a third Phaÿllos who was a thief.

60e The *Suda, s.v.* ὑπὲρ τὰ ἐσκαμμένα   tenth century A.D.

The following text comes from a lexicon compiled toward the end of the tenth century after Christ and based upon a variety of earlier material, some of which was primary, but most of which was itself secondary.

"Beyond the dug-up area": beyond measure. A metaphor from the *pentathlon.* It is said to come from the pentathlete Phaÿllos of Kroton who, when the *skammata* used to be 50 feet, first exceeded them with his jumps, as the epigram on his statue says: "Five and fifty feet flew Phaÿllos, but dished the *diskos* a hundred minus five." Plato also mentions this in the dialogue entitled *Kratylos* with regard to the correctness of names. It is also a proverb.

"Jumping beyond the dug-up area": Phaÿllos was a pentathlete from Pontos who seems to have been a great *diskos* thrower and jumper. Since he jumped beyond the dug-up area 50 feet onto the hard ground, the feat passed into the proverbial.

"To jump beyond the dug-up area": with reference to doing something hyperbolically, because Phaÿllos jumped more than 50 feet and tore up his leg.

60f   Plato, *Kratylos* 413a   ca. 385 B.C.

Plato does, indeed, use the metaphor as the Suda *tells us, but with no reference to Phaÿllos or any other athlete. Sokrates speaks:*

When I ask, "What is justice," I seem to them to ask too much and jump beyond the dug-up area.

61   Eusebius, *Chronika*   ca. A.D. 325

Eusebius was one of a series of chronographers of the Early Christian church who were concerned to establish early chronologies in the Judeo-Christian tradition by cross-references to other chronological schemes including that of the Olympiads. Under his name, although sometimes attributed to one Sextus Julius Africanus, is a list of the Olympiads, with some additional notes, in three languages: Armenian, Latin, and Greek. Under the entry for the 29th Olympiad (664 B.C.) is the following entry in Greek:

Chionis the Lakonian won the *stadion*. His *halma* was 52 feet.

The Armenian and Latin versions of this entry are the following:

Chionis the Lakonian won the *stadion*. A single jump of his was 22 cubits [33 feet].

The numeral for 52 in the Greek text is νβ; some have suggested that this is a corruption for κβ or 22. The bottom of the kappa *would have been lost.*

62   Ammonios, *On Similar
    and Different Words* 23   first–second century A.D.

Akontion is different from *dory*. The *akontion* is smaller than the *dory*, while the *dory* is the largest missile that is thrown by hand.

63 Pindar, *Pythian Ode* 1.43–45 476 B.C.

Modern scholars have sometimes debated whether the winner of the javelin was determined solely by distance of the throw, or whether accuracy was a part of the formula for victory. One source (no. 64) has been taken as evidence for the need for accuracy, but most seem to indicate that distance alone was the only criterion.

I hope that I shall not throw the bronze-tipped *akon* which I shake down with my hand outside the limits of the contest, but shall conquer my opponents with long throws.

64 Antiphon, *Second Tetralogy* 2.1–8 *ca.* 425 B.C.

An Athenian youth has been killed in the gymnasion *and another youth brought to trial for the homicide. This is one of the speeches prepared by Antiphon for the father of the accused boy to deliver to an Athenian court in the boy's defense. It reveals, in addition to some of the types of arguments which were used in the courts, some of the common practices in the* gymnasion *and, implicitly, a high degree of literacy in Athens. Does it also prove that accuracy was always a criterion in determining the winner in the javelin throw?*

It is now clear to me that misfortunes themselves and necessity can force those who dislike litigation into court, and those who are quiet to be loud and to say and do much which is contrary to their nature. I am not, nor do I want to be, the type of man who likes to appear in court, unless I have been fooling myself, but I have now been forced by misfortune to change my habits and appear as a defendant, and this in a case where I am hard pressed to understand the exact truth, and even more hard pressed to know how to present it to you. But I am forced by sheer necessity, gentlemen of the jury, and I must take refuge in your mercy. . . .

I thought that, by educating my son in those subjects which especially benefit the state, both the state and I would be rewarded. The result has not been what I had thought it would be. The lad, not because of insolence or mischief, but because he was practicing the *akon* with the boys in his age category in the *gymnasion,* did hit someone, but killed no one if the truth be known. He has been blamed for the mistake of another.

We would not be able to show that my son had not caused the boy's death had the *akontion* struck him outside the area marked for its flight.

But the boy ran into the path of the *akontion* and thus put his body in its way. Hence my son was unable to hit that for which he had aimed, and the boy was hit because he ran under the *akontion*, and the cause of the accident which is attributed to us was not one of our own making. The running into the path was the cause of the boy being hit, and my son is unjustly accused. He did not hit anyone who stayed away from his target. Moreover, since it is clear to you that the other boy was not struck while standing still, but only after moving of his own volition into the path of the *akontion*, it should be quite clear to you that he was killed because of his own error. He would not have been killed had he remained still and not run across.

Now both sides in this trial are agreed that the boy's death was accidental, and the guilt of the death must belong to the one who was guilty of the error. My son was guilty of no error. He was practicing not what he had been forbidden, but what he had been instructed to do. He was not among those who were practicing other exercises when he threw the *akontion*, but among the *akontion* throwers. He did not hit the other boy because he missed his target and threw into the bystanders. He did everything properly and as he had intended. Thus he was not the cause of an accident, but the victim of one, for he was prevented from hitting his target.

On the other hand, the dead boy wished to run forward, but missed the opportunity when he could have crossed without being hit. The result may not have been what he had intended, but he was guilty of an error which had an effect upon his own person. He paid the price of his mistake and has already received justice which causes us no joy, but rather sympathy and sorrow.

65   Plutarch, *Perikles* 36.3   *ca.* A.D. 100

In his biography of Perikles, Plutarch describes some of the personal loss and unhappiness of the fifth-century Athenian leader, including abuse from his son Xanthippos.

A certain pentathlete accidentally hit Epitimos of Pharsalos with an *akontion* and killed him. Xanthippos said that Perikles wasted a whole day with Protagoras whether the *akontion*, or the one who threw it, or the *agonothetai* were responsible according to the most correct reasoning.

F. EQUESTRIAN

66   Aristophanes, *The Clouds* 1–118   423 B.C.

The purpose of this play by Aristophanes, beyond providing entertainment, was an attack upon the "education" of the Sophists. Later in the play,

Aristophanes will, unfairly, present Sokrates as the prime example of the Sophists. Such a representation does not seem to have affected adversely a real admiration and respect between the two men. Neither had any love for the Sophists who taught, once paid, the use of the power of logic in making a bad cause appear to be the right one. In his caricature of this Sophistical system, Aristophanes begins with a confrontation between a father, Strepsiades (the "Twisted One" or the "Crooked One") and his son, Pheidippides (the "Sparer of Horses"). The wealth necessary to compete in the equestrian events becomes clear.

STREPSIADES: O dear me, O lordy, O Zeus! How long these nights are. Will they never pass? Will the day never come? I was certain I heard the cock crow hours ago, but my servants still are snoring. These are new times with strange customs. There are many reasons for avoiding war, but the best is that one can't beat one's own servants in wartime. Look at that son of mine, wrapped up, snoring and sweating under five thick blankets. Oh well, I might as well bundle up and snore along . . . I can't sleep at all. I am being bitten and eaten up by ticks and bedbugs, and by bills and race-horses, all because of this son of mine. He curls his hair and shows off his horses and drives his chariot—even in his dreams he is riding. But I am being ruined now that the end of the month approaches and it's time to pay the interest on my loans. Light a lamp, boy! Bring my ledger! I'll tot up my creditors and see what I owe them. "$26,400 to Pasias." Why do I owe that? Oh, for that hack with the Corinthian brand. O dear, I wish my eyes had been hacked out . . .

PHEIDIPPIDES [talking in his sleep]: Philon, you cheat! Stay in your own lane!

STREPSIADES: That's it. That's what has ruined me. Even in his sleep he dreams of horses.

PHEIDIPPIDES: How many laps do the war chariots run?

STREPSIADES: Not as many as you've run your father. Now then, what debt comes down on my ears after Pasias'? "$6,600 for a racing cart and wheels to Amynias."

PHEIDIPPIDES: Give the horse a roll in the dust and take him home.

STREPSIADES: But you, my boy, have already rolled me out of house and home. Some of my creditors are taking me to court, and others swear that they will impound my property for the interest I owe them.

PHEIDIPPIDES [now awake]: Father, why do you toss and turn all night long?

STREPSIADES: There's a buggered bill-collector in my mattress.

PHEIDIPPIDES: Well, please let me get some sleep.

STREPSIADES: Okay, you go ahead and sleep. You can be sure that these debts will fall on your head some day. And may there be a curse on the head of that matchmaker who aroused me to marry your mother. My life in the country was so nice, untidy, easygoing, unrestrained, brimming with olives, sheep, and honeybees. And then I—a real country bumpkin—had to go and marry her, a fine city lady, a proud, luxurious lady of good family. That's the way we married, I stinking of wine dregs, and fig skins, and greasy bundles of wool, she all sweet smelling of saffron and feasting and expenses. But she was not idle, oh no, she spent money far too fast.

SERVANT: The lamp has burned up all its oil.

STREPSIADES: What? Why did you light that big lamp? Come over here and get a thrashing.

SERVANT: What for?

STREPSIADES: Because you put in a big, fat, oil-guzzling wick. Anyway, when this son was finally born to us, our heir, we began to argue about his name. She wanted to give him some knightly name: Kallippides (Good Rider), or Xanthippos (Roan), or Charippos (Horsy Pleasure). I wanted to call him Pheiodonides (Thrifty) after his grandpa. In the end we compromised on Pheidippides. She took the boy and spoiled him. She used to say: "Wait 'til you grow up and drive to the Acropolis in your purple robe like my father Megakles used to do." But I used to say: "Wait 'til you grow up and drive goats in from the fields dressed like your father in a sheepskin coat." He never listened to me, and soon my funds were caught by a galloping consumption. Now that I have been thinking all night long, I believe I know a way out of our problem if he will follow my instructions. First, I must wake him, but sweetly and gently so that he will go along with my scheme. Pheidippides, my sweet lovely boy, wake up and kiss me and shake my hand.

PHEIDIPPIDES: Okay, Dad. What's up?

STREPSIADES: Do you love me, my son?

PHEIDIPPIDES: Of course. I swear so by Poseidon, god of horses.

STREPSIADES: No, no! Not that! Leave him out of it. That god of horses is the cause of all my troubles. But if you love me with all your heart, my son, obey me.

PHEIDIPPIDES: I shall obey.

STREPSIADES: Then change your ways immediately and go and learn what I tell you to. You see that house next door beyond the hedge? That is the thinking school of sophistic souls. There dwell men who will teach, for a price, how to speak in court and win the case whether right or wrong. I can't quite remember their names, but they are deep thinkers and fine gentlemen.

PHEIDIPPIDES: Not those cheats! I know whom you mean. Those pedants, those palefaced, barefoot tramps, Sokrates and his ilk.

STREPSIADES: Sssh! Hush! Don't say those foolish things. If you care about your future estate, leave the race track, go there and learn.

PHEIDIPPIDES: What do you want me to learn?

STREPSIADES: It's well known that they keep two Logics in their school, the Better and the Worse. This second logic, the Worse, is what I want you to learn. They will teach you to speak unjustly and win. Just think, if you learn that Unjust Logic, I will never pay all the bills and debts which have been due to you and your horses, not a penny of them.

67 Isokrates, *Team of Horses* 32–35   *ca.* 397 B.C.

The following is a part of the defense prepared by Isokrates for the younger Alkibiades, son of the famous Athenian of the same name. The son has been sued, upon coming of age, because of an alleged theft by his father of a team of horses, perhaps as long as 19 or 20 years earlier, from a certain Teisias. The younger Alkibiades is here both showing that his father was so wealthy that he had no need to steal horses and also reminding an Athenian jury of his father's services to the state. Both points emerge from the elder Alkibiades' participation in the Olympic Games of 416 B.C. See also nos. 116, 219.

During the same years when my father married my mother he saw that the festival at Olympia was beloved and admired by all men, and that it was there that the Greeks made display of wealth and strength of body and training, and both that the athletes were envied and that the cities of the victors became renowned. In addition, he believed that public services here were to the credit of the individual in the eyes of the citizens, but that services at that festival were to the credit of the city in the eyes of the whole of Greece. He thought these things through and, though in no way untalented nor weaker in his body, he held the gymnic games in contempt since he knew that some of the athletes were lowborn and from small city-states and poorly educated. Therefore he tried his hand at horse breeding, work of the uppermost crust and not possible for a poor man, and he beat not only his competitors, but all previous winners. He entered a number of teams which not even the biggest city-states, as public entities, had ever entered in the competitions, and their *arete* was such that he came in first, second, and third.

Beyond this, his outlays for the sacrifices and the other expenses of the festival were so lavish and so magnificent that it seemed the public outlays of all the others were less than the private outlays from his own pocket. In short, he completed the *theoria* making even the successes of his predecessors seem small potatoes next to his, and depriving his contemporary victors of their bragging rights, and leaving to future horse-breeders no chance of surpassing him.

I am ashamed to speak about his public services here as producer for dramatic competitions, as *gymnasiarchos,* and as sponsor of *triremes* because they so far surpassed those of any other citizen.

68 Sophokles, *Elektra* 681–756   *ca.* 415 B.C.

The setting of this play is Mycenae where Elektra plots revenge upon Klytaimnestra (her mother) and Aigisthos who had murdered her father, Agamemnon. Elektra's great hope lies with her brother, Orestes, who has, unknown to her, devised the stratagem of spreading the rumor of his own death and thus lowering the defenses of the murderers. Orestes' faithful paidagogos, disguised as a messenger, enters and relates the circumstances of the supposed tragedy:

Orestes went to the great festival of Greece, the Pythian Games, and when the *keryx* announced the first contest, the footrace, he stepped forward, a radiant figure admired by all who beheld him. Like an arrow he sped from the *aphesis* to the *termata,* and took away the crown of glorious victory. To make a long story short, I never heard of such prowess. I will add this much: the judges of the games announced no contest—*diaulos, pentathlon,* and the other competitions—that he did not win, and each time happy cheers hailed the proclamation of the *keryx:* "An Argive wins, Orestes son of Agamemnon, king of men and leader of the hosts of Hellas." And so things went, but when some angry god intervenes, even the strongest man is foiled.

Toward sunset the next day, he entered the chariot race. There were many charioteers: one was from Sparta, one from Achaia, two from Libya both skilled in guiding the yoked team. Orestes was the fifth in line with Thessalian mares, and an Aeolian was sixth with chestnut fillies. A Megarian was seventh; the eighth, with milk-white steeds, was an Ainian and the ninth was from Athens, city built by the gods. Last came a Boeotian, making the field of ten. They stood by while the judges cast the lots and arranged the order of the chariots. Then, at the brazen trumpet blast, they were off. All shook their reins and urged their horses on with shouts. The whole track was filled with the noise of rattling cars and the dust rose to heaven. All were bunched together and none spared the whip as each tried to break out of the pack and leave behind the whirling wheels and snorting steeds, for each saw his wheels splattered with foam and felt the breath of horses on his back. Orestes as he turned the farther *stele* held close and grazed it with the hub of his wheel, giving rein to his right horse but pulling in the nearer one. For a time all were safe and sound, but at the turn between the sixth and the seventh lap, the Ainian's horses took the bit and crashed head-on with the Libyan chariot from Barkaia. Then one after another fell into this single crash and smashed up and the whole Krisaian plain was filled with wreckage. The shrewd Athenian charioteer noted this and pulled off and slackened his pace to let the surge of panic-stricken horses pass him on the inside. Then came Orestes who had stayed behind the pack, for he trusted in a final burst at the finish. But when he saw that the Athenian was the one remaining rival, he shouted shrilly in the ears of his horses and drove them on until his yoke was even with that of the Athenian. Then the two raced on, first one, then the other, ahead by a nose. Until now Orestes, ill-starred youth, had taken his laps in safety, but at the last turn he loosed the left-hand rein too soon and, without noticing it, his axle struck the *stele*. The axle box was shattered and he was thrown over the chariot rail and, caught in his fall by the tangle of reins, he was dragged along while his frightened team dashed wildly over the track. As the crowd saw him somersault, there rose a wail of pity for the youth—for his daring deeds and his disastrous end—while he was now bounced into the ground, now flung head-over-heels into the sky. At last the charioteers caught his steeds and freed the blood-stained corpse, disfigured and marred past the recognition of his best friend.

69   Pausanias 6.20.10–19   *ca.* A.D. 170

If you leave the stadium [at Olympia] by the place where the *Hellanodikai* sit, you will find the region set aside for the horse races and the *aphesis* for the horses. This *aphesis* has a shape like the prow of a ship with its point toward the track. The prow continues up to the stoa of Agnaptos where it has broadened. A bronze dolphin on a rod has been made at the very tip of the point of the prow. Each side of the *aphesis* is more than 400 feet in length and has stalls built into it. Those entering the horse races are assigned stalls by lot. In front of the chariots, or of the horses in the *keles*, is stretched a cord instead of the *hysplex*. For each Olympiad an altar of unbaked brick, plastered on the exterior, is made right in the middle of the prow, and a bronze eagle with its wings stretched to the fullest extent rests upon the altar. The official appointed for the track sets in motion the mechanism which is inside the altar, and the eagle jumps so that it becomes visible to the spectators, and the dolphin falls to the ground. The first *hyspleges* on either side, those nearest to the stoa of Agnaptos, let loose and the first horses stationed by them take off. As they run they come to those who have been allotted to stand at the second position, and at that time the second *hyspleges* let loose. The same thing happens for all the horses so that at the tip of the prow they should be even with one another. From this point it is up to the drivers to show their skill and to the horses to show their speed. Kleoitas was the first to devise this *aphesis*, and he seems to have been proud of it, for he inscribed the following on a statue at Athens:

> He who first invented the horses' *aphesis* at Olympia,
> Kleoitas son of Aristokles, made me.

They say that after Kleoitas, Aristeides added some refinement to the mechanism.

One side of the hippodrome is longer than the other. The longer side is a bank of earth and, by the passageway exit through the bank, there is Taraxippos, the terror of horses. It has the shape of a circular altar, and as the horses run by it a great fear with no apparent cause seizes them. From the fear comes confusion, and in general the chariots crash and the charioteers are injured. For this reason the charioteers make sacrifices and pray that Taraxippos be kind to them. The Greeks have different views about Taraxippos. . . . It seems to me that the most probable of the stories is that Taraxippos is a surname of Poseidon of the Horses. At Isthmia Glaukos son of Sisyphos is a kind of Taraxippos. They say that he was killed by his horses when Akastos held funeral games for his father. At Nemea of the Argives there was no hero who hurt the horses, but a red rock rose up above the *kampe* of the horses, and the glare from this, as if from fire, wrought fear in the horses. But the Taraxippos at Olympia is the worse for frightening horses. On one *nyssa* is a bronze statue of Hippodameia holding a ribbon and about to crown Pelops with it for his victory.

The other side of the hippodrome is not a bank of earth, but a low hill.

---

70 Pausanias 6.10.7   *ca.* A.D. 170

There is the chariot of Kleosthenes of Epidamnos. This is the work of Ageladas . . . Kleosthenes was victorious at the 66th Olympiad [516 B.C.], and he dedicated a statue of himself and of his charioteer together with his horses. There are inscribed the names of his horses, Phoinix and Korax

(Raven), and on either side are the yoke horses, on the right Knakias (Prickly) and on the left Samos.

71 Pausanias 6.13.9   *ca.* A.D. 170

As the Corinthians relate, the mare of the Corinthian Pheidolas was called "Breeze." At the beginning of her race, she threw her rider, but nonetheless ran on in good order and turned the *nyssa* and, when she heard the trumpet, she ran faster, finished first at the *Hellanodikai,* and, recognizing her victory, stopped running. The Eleans awarded the victory to Pheidolas and allowed him to dedicate a statue of his mare [512 B.C.].

72 Pausanias 5.9.2   *ca.* A.D. 170

The *kalpe* was a race for mares. In the last lap they jumped off them and ran alongside the horses holding the reins just as the so-called *anabates* still do today. The *anabatai,* however, have different signals in the race than the *kalpe* and their horses are male. There was nothing ancient or dignified about the *apene,* and the animal itself, even if born in Elis, was accursed for the Eleans from olden times—for the *apene* was pulled by a team of mules rather than horses.

G. HERALD AND TRUMPETER

73 Pausanias 5.22.1   *ca.* A.D. 170

Competitions for the keryx *and the* salpinktes *became part of the Olympic Games in 396 B.C., and the winners of these competitions were regarded as Olympic victors with all rights and privileges appropriate to them, even if they had to work after their victories in making the public announcements for the remainder of the Games. These are obviously not part of the* gymnikoi agones, *and do not fit very comfortably with the* mousikoi agones *either.*

Within the *Altis* near the entrance leading to the stadium is an altar. The Eleans do not sacrifice on it to the gods, but the *salpinktai* and the *kerykes* stand on it when they compete.

74 Athenaeus, *The Gastronomers* 10.414F–415A   *ca.* A.D. 228

*Athenaeus is quoting Amarantos of Alexandria, an older contemporary of Galen (no. **177**), to show the prodigious talents of Herodoros, some of whose exploits are reminiscent of those of Milo the wrestler (nos. **163a–b**).*

... Herodoros the *salpinktes* from Megara was 5'3" tall, but strong in the ribs. He was accustomed to eat thirteen pounds of bread and twenty pounds of whatever meat he could put his hands on, to drink a gallon and a half of wine, and to play two trumpets at the same time. He had the habit of sleeping only on a lion's skin. His trumpet blast was very loud. When Demetrios Poliorketes was besieging Argos [303 B.C.] and his soldiers were not able to bring the siege-machine close to the walls because of its weight, Herodoros gave the signal with his two trumpets and forced the soldiers who were encouraged by the force of his blast to bring up the machine. He was a *periodonikes* ten times and he dined sitting up ...

H. MUSIC

75 Pausanias 10.7.2–7   *ca.* A.D. 170

*One of the major differences between the Olympic Games (and the Nemean originally) and the Pythian Games (and the Isthmian) was the inclusion of musical competitions in the Pythian and Isthmian. Pausanias gives us the nature of the events, and his opinion of their importance is to be seen in the entry (no. **6ob**) where he refuses to discuss the victors in the musical events. Even though these did not exist as events at Olympia, several sources make it clear that poetry, prose, and painting were on display there (e.g. nos. **82** and **166**), and the following entry (no. **76**) indicates that flute players were honored at Olympia with the privilege of accompanying the* pentathlon.

They record that the oldest competition, and the one for which they first established prizes, was the singing of a hymn to the god with the accompaniment of the *kithara*. ... In the third year of the 48th Olympiad, when Glaukias of Kroton was victorious in the *stadion* [586 B.C.], the Amphiktyones set up prizes for *kithara*-singing as from the beginning, but they added competitions in *aulos*-singing and in *aulos*-playing. ... They then also for the first time set up prizes for athletes in the same competitions as at Olympia except the *tethrippon*, and they themselves decreed the races for the boys' category in the *dolichos* and the *diaulos*. In the 2nd Pythiad [582 B.C.] they did not invite competitors for prizes, but established the games as *stephanitic* from then, and they then abolished the *aulos*-singing the sound of which they thought not auspicious, for the notes of the *aulos* itself were most brooding and the words sung with the *aulos* were funereal. ... At the 8th Pythiad [558 B.C.] they added a competition in playing the *kithara* without singing.

76 Pausanias 6.14.9–10   *ca.* A.D. 170

. . . a little man holding *auloi* is carved out on a *stele*. He was the second after Sakadas of Argos to win Pythian victories, for Sakadas won the games set up by the Amphiktyones which were not yet *stephanitic* [586 B.C.], and then he won two *stephanitic* victories [582 and 578 B.C.]. But Pythokritos of Sikyon won the next six Pythiads [574–554 B.C.]—he was the only *auletes* to do so. It is also clear that he played the flute to accompany the *pentathlon* six times at the Olympic Games. For these reasons the *stele* was set up at Olympia to honor Pythokritos and this inscription was put on it:

> This is the monument of the *auletes*, son of Kallinikos,
>   Pythokritos

I. POETRY AND PROSE COMPOSITION

77 Plutarch, *Moralia* 674D–675B   *ca.* A.D. 100

There was a discussion at the Pythian Games about the added competitions and whether they ought to be eliminated. Once there had been added to the original three competitions (Pythian *aulos*, *kithara*, and *kithara*-singing) the tragic actor, it was as if the gate had been left open and the massed attacks and invasions of all sorts of ear-pleasing events could not be repelled. Because of this the contest had a variety which were not unpleasant and a festive air, but its austerity and strict musicality were not preserved, and there were problems and many natural animosities toward the judges from the many who did not win.

Some thought that, most of all, the prose-writers and poets ought to be withdrawn from the contest, not because of a dislike for literature, but because of the unhappiness of having so many good and worthy competitors not all of whom could win. During the council I tried to change the minds of those who wanted to upset the established practices and to treat the contest like a harp with too many strings and too many notes. And during dinner, which was hosted by Petraios the *agonothetes*, when similar discussions arose I defended the musical competition. I showed that poetry was not a recent or new arrival in the sacred contests, but had long before received crowns of victory . . . [Plutarch goes on to cite many ancient authorities for his position, including Polemon's account of the Treasuries where it is noted] . . . that in the Treasury of the Sikyonians at Delphi was a gold book, dedication of Aristomache of Erythraia, twice winner in Epic Poetry at Isthmia.

"Nor is Olympia to be marvelled at," I said, "as if it had never changed nor added to its competitions. For the Pythian Games have only three or four additional musical contests, while the gymnic are essentially the same now as they were at the beginning. Olympia, on the other hand, has added everything except the *stadion*, and many were added only to be dropped, like the competition in the *kalpe* and the *apene*. Also the crown for the *pentathlon* for boys was abolished."

78   Vitruvius, 7 *praef.* 4–7   ca. 28 B.C.

The Roman architect Vitruvius, in his discussion of the foundations and histories of the great libraries of antiquity, recounts the story of how Ptolemy III Euergetes (246–221 B.C.) founded the library at Alexandria and, in celebration of that event, also founded literary competitions. The method by which winners were selected is of interest; perhaps something of the sort was used in the musical competitions as well.

Ptolemy consecrated games for the Muses and Apollo, and established prizes and honors, in the same way as for victorious athletes, for victorious authors.

When these arrangements had been made and the games were approaching, learned judges had to be selected to test the competitors. When the King had already picked six judges from the citizen body and still could not find a seventh, he referred the matter to the supervisors of the library and asked whether they knew someone for the job. They proposed Aristophanes [257–180 B.C.] who, with the utmost studiousness and the greatest diligence every day, was reading every book in the catalogue. And so at the start of the games when special seats were assigned to the judges and when Aristophanes had been summoned with the others, he took his assigned seat. The competition for the poets was first on the schedule and when their poems were recited the reaction of the crowd warned the judges which should be awarded the prize. And so, when each judge was asked his opinion, six awarded the first prize to the poet who had most pleased the audience . . . but when Aristophanes was asked for his opinion, he voted for the poet who had least pleased the crowd. When the King and everyone else were vehemently indignant, he rose and asked if he might be allowed to speak. In the ensuing silence Aristophanes showed that only one of the competitors was a true poet and that the others were all plagiarizers, and that the judges were to consider not stolen, but original writings. The crowd was wonderous and the King was dubious, but Aristophanes relied upon his memory and produced many volumes from specific bookcases and by comparing them with what had been recited he forced the plagiarizers to admit that they were thieves. And so the King ordered that they be tried and, when convicted, he dismissed them in disgrace, but he rewarded Aristophanes with high offices and appointed him head-librarian.

J. ACTING

79 *SIG*[3] 1080   276–219 B.C.

The following inscription is on a stone block discovered at Tegea and it celebrates the career of an actor (and sometime athlete) whose name is not preserved. Although none of the Panhellenic games is mentioned, the inscription still provides clear evidence that competitions in acting had become a normal part of other festivals by the 3rd century B.C. (see no. 104), and must soon have become a part of the Pythian festival itself (see above, no. 77).

> [He won]:
> the Great Dionysia at Athens with the *Orestes* by Euripides,
> the Soteria at Delphi with the *Herakles* by Euripides, and the
>   *Antaios* by Archestratos,
> the Ptolemaia in Alexandria in the *pyx* for men,
> the Heraia with the *Herakles* by Euripides and the *Archelaos* by
>   Euripides,
> the Naia in Dodone with the *Archelaos* by Euripides and the
>   *Achilles* by Chairemon,
> and a total of 88 Dionysia or acting competitions in cities and/or
>   various festivals which the cities organized.

K. PAINTING

80 Pliny, *Natural History* 35.58   A.D. 77

Pliny the Elder provides considerable information about ancient art and artists, and the following passage comes in the midst of a listing of painters. His reference to Corinth should be understood as a reference to the Isthmian Games, as emerges from a later reference to the painter Zeuxis whom Pliny dates to the fourth year of the 95th Olympiad—a date which most probably derived from the date of the Isthmian Games in 397/396 B.C. (i.e. the spring of 396). Pliny's reference to the "chronicles" must be to the Pythian victor's list (perhaps that of Aristotle).

While Panainos was in his prime [440s B.C.] a competition in painting was established at Corinth and at Delphi, and at the very first of these when he competed against Timagoras of Chalkis he was beaten by him at the Pythian Games, as is clear from an ancient poem of Timagoras himself—the chronicles no doubt being in error.

IV
Organization of a Panhellenic Festival

A. PREPARATIONS AT THE SITE

81 *CID* 2.139 246 B.C.

This inscription records contracts which were let for the preparation of Delphi for the Pythian Games. Each entry has the name of a contractor, a definition of the work which he was paid to do, and the sum paid him. Broken areas on the stone where the text is not preserved are indicated within brackets. The expenses, which total nearly $43,000 as preserved on the stone, are largely of a type which must have been typical of the costs of preparing Delphi every four years for the Pythian Games (and, more or less, all the other sites for their games).

Agazalos: digging and leveling the *xystos* and the peristyle: $814.

Agazalos: digging and leveling the *paradromis*: $726.

Agazalos: 270 bushels of white earth for the *xystos* at $6.42 per bushel: $1,732.50.

Kritolaos: fencing the *xystos*: $1,628.

Olympichos: maintenance work on the *xystos* and the *paradromis* and the *sphairisteria* and the *gymnasion*: $1,584.

Kritolaos: repairs to the drain alongside the shrine of Demeter: $909.26.

Sochares: for six picks: [?].

Eucharos: roping off the peristyle: $66.

Kleon: repairs to the wall of the *sphairisterion:* $1,320.

Asandros: sifting the mortar: $220.

Euthydamos: 201 bushels of black earth on the *sphairisterion* at $3.67 per bushel: $737.

Kleon: repairs to the wall by the shrine of Demeter: $1,298.

Pasion: plastering the *apodyterion* and the wall by the shrine of Demeter: $352.

Lyson: 15 bushels of white earth for plastering the *apodyterion* and the wall at $6.42 per bushel: $96.25.

Smyrnaios: cleaning out the Pythian stadium and repairing the "ridges": $462.

Smyrnaios: digging the Pythian stadium and digging and leveling the jumping pits: $4,840.

Nikon: construction of the *odeion:* $1,969.

Xenon: 600 bushels of white earth in the Pythian stadium at $6.11 per bushel: $3,666.70.

Melission: a pedestal in the Pythian theater: $1,232.

Euthydamos: fencing the Pythian stadium: $440.

Nikon: setting up the *proskenion* in the Pythian stadium: $264.

Nikon: the platform in the Pythian stadium at [?] per foot for [?] feet: $220.

Euthydamos: construction of the vaulted entrance in the Pythian stadium: $880.

Smyrnaios: cleaning out the [?]: $352.

Anaxagoras: construction of the 36 *kampteres:* $528.

Agazalos: that for the pentathletes: $396.

[?]: for 280 [?] at $9.17 each: $2,566.74.

Damastratos: [?] for the boxers: $3,410.

Melission: repair to the [?] in the vaulted entrance: $66.

[Smyrnaios]: cleaning out the hippodrome: [?].

Dionysios: digging around the *kampteres* in the hippodrome: [?].

Euthydamos: [leveling] around the *kampteres* in the hippodrome: $440.

Kallon: provision of the [?] in the hippodrome: $3,916.

Dion: the [?] in the hippodrome: $1,672.

Dion: the [?] of the houses: $1,056.

Pleistos: for the prizes: $2,200.

Euthydamos: for plating the [?] with bronze: $407.

Kleon: cleaning out and fencing the Kastalian spring with the Gorgon's head spout: $396.

Agazalos: cleaning out the [?]: $53.17.

[?]: cleaning out the smithy . . . : [?]

[?]: . . . the water channel of the *paradromis* and the pool: [?]

82 *IG IV². 1. 98*   early third century B.C.

An inscription from the Sanctuary of Asklepios at Epidauros records the following:

In the month of Apellaios during the priesthood of Thiokydes the contractor of the *hysplex*, Philon the Corinthian, owes to the God the penalty, against the contract price of $11,000, which the *agonothetes* of the *gymnikoi agones*, Trityllos, and the *Hellanodikai* assessed him and which the *boule* confirmed on appeal that he justly pay; of this, with what he has already been paid ($4,400) set aside, he owes the remainder [i.e. $6,600], plus a 50% penalty, since the contract was not fulfilled, or a total of $9,900; he and his guarantor, Nikon the banker from Corinth [are liable].

B. PREPARATIONS OF THE ATHLETES

83 Pausanias 6.23–24   *ca.* A.D. 170

The following description of the town of Elis gives many insights into the setting for, and some of the practices of, the month-long training period before the athletes set out for Olympia and the actual competition.

In Elis the noteworthy include an old *gymnasion* in which all the athletes have to train as much as is required before leaving to go on to Olympia. Tall plane trees grow among the tracks within a wall. . . . There is a separate track for the actual footraces, called the Sacred Track by the natives, and another track where the runners and the pentathletes practice. In the *gymnasion* is the Hundred Foot Room [see no. **147**] where the *Hellanodikai* match the wrestlers by age and then by ability. . . . There is another lesser enclosed *gymnasion* next to the larger and called the Square Gymnasion because of its shape. Here the athletes practice wrestling and they match those who are no longer wrestling to box with the softer *himantes*. . . . There is a third enclosed *gymnasion* which has the name Soft because of the softness of its floor. It is reserved for the *epheboi* during the time of the Olympic festival. . . . In this *gymnasion* is also the *bouleuterion* of the Eleans, and in it are exhibitions of off-the-cuff speeches and recitations of all kinds of written works. . . .

One of the two roads from the *gymnasion* leads to the *agora* and to the so-called *Hellanodikaion* . . . and the *Hellanodikai* are accustomed to take this road to the *gymnasion*. They enter before sunrise to match the runners, and at midday to match those in the *pentathlon* and in the competitions which are called heavy.

The *agora* of Elis is not in the Ionian style but in the older style, with stoas separated from one another and alleys between them. The contemporary name of the *agora* is Hippodrome, and the natives train their horses therein. The stoa toward the south is of the Doric order and its columns divide it into three aisles. The *Hellanodikai* spend most days there. In front of its columns and in the open part of the *agora* they make altars to Zeus which are only a few in number since they are do-it-yourself constructions and easily destroyed. The *Hellanodikaion* is on the left of one who enters the *agora* by the end of this stoa, and is separated from the *agora* by an alley. Those who have been elected *Hellanodikai* live for ten consecutive months in the *Hellanodikaion* while the Guardians of the Law teach them about their duties at the festival.

84 Philostratos, *Life of Apollonius* 5.43   ca. A.D. 230

*This Philostratos, probably the same as the author of the treatise on gymnastics (see above, nos. **12**, **20**, **24**, and **29**), wrote in the early third century after Christ a biography of Apollonius of Tyana, a religious and philosophical leader who was teaching slightly later than Christ. Indeed, both holy men were worshipped, together with Orpheus, Abraham, and Alexander the Great by the Emperor Alexander Severus (A.D. 205–235). The setting for this passage is Alexandria, which Apollonius is about to leave for a visit to a sect of "naked prophets" on the upper Nile, perhaps around A.D. 70. As a part of his preparations for the journey, Apollonius calls together his followers and addresses them:*

This undertaking requires an Olympic exordium, my men, which might be as follows. When the Olympic festival is approaching, the Eleans train the athletes for thirty days in Elis itself. Likewise, the people of Delphi collect the athletes when the Pythian festival approaches, and the Corinthians for the Isthmian festival, and they say to the athletes: "Go now into the stadium, and be men worthy of winning." When they are going to Olympia, however, the Eleans say to the athletes: "If you have worked so as to be worthy of going to Olympia, if you have done nothing indolent nor ignoble, then take heart and march on; but those who have not so trained may leave and go wherever they like."

85 Polybius 4.73.6–10   *ca.* 150 B.C.

Polybius describes Elis at the point in his narrative when it was captured by Philip V of Macedon in the winter of 219/218 B.C., but the picture is clearly generally correct for much of antiquity.

It happens that the country of the Eleans is more thickly settled and full of people and equipment than the rest of the Peloponnesos. Some of them are actually so wed to country life that, even for two or three generations, they have not appeared in the people's assembly. . . . It seems to me that they have adopted and legislated such a system from olden times partly because of their large territory, but even more because of the sacrosanct life which they got when a holy and inviolate Eleia was conferred on them by the Greeks because of the Olympic Games. Thus they were inexperienced in all danger and every kind of military incursion.

86 Pausanias 5.16.8   *ca.* A.D. 170

Neither the Sixteen Women [see no. **158**] nor the *Hellanodikai* perform their established rituals until they have purified themselves with a pig which is suitable for purification and with water. This purification takes place at the spring called Piera which is by the plain going from Olympia to Elis.

C. THE TRUCE

87 Pausanias 5.4.5–6   *ca.* A.D. 170

For the diskos seen by Pausanias at Olympia with the truce of Iphitos inscribed on it, see below no. **114**. *The dates of Iphitos, and of Lykourgos, are* *not agreed upon now, nor were they in antiquity, but Pausanias (5.8.5–6) seems to have accepted the games of Iphitos as those of the 1st Olympiad in 776 B.C. by our reckoning.*

Iphitos . . . a contemporary of the Lykourgos who wrote the laws for the Lakedaimonians, organized the Olympic festival in Olympia from the start and established the *ekecheiria.* . . . At that time Greece was especially worn by civil strife and by plague, and it came to Iphitos to ask the god at Delphi for a solution to those evils. And they say that it was proscribed by the Pythia that Iphitos himself and the Eleans had to renew the Olympic Games.

88   Thucydides 8.9.1–10.1   412 B.C.

During the Peloponnesian War, in the spring of 412 B.C., the Lakedai-monian allies under Agis gathered at the Isthmos of Corinth to prepare for a campaign together with the Chians, who were eager to revolt against Athens.

The Corinthians, even though the others were impatient to sail, had no pre-disposition to sail with them before they celebrated the Isthmian Games which were to take place then. Agis was prepared for them not to lose the Isthmian *spondai*, and he was going to make the expedition his own respon-sibility. But since the Corinthians did not agree and a delay took place, the Athenians sensed the plans of the Chians. . . . In the meantime the Isthmian Games took place and the Athenians (for the proclamation had been made) sent *theoroi* to them, and the plans of the Chians became crystal clear to them.

89   Demosthenes, *De falsa legatione, Hypoth.* 335   348 B.C.

A certain Athenian named Phrynon was going to the Olympic Games either as a competitor or as a spectator when he was seized by some troops of Philip [of Macedon] during the Sacred Month and robbed of everything. Phrynon went to Athens and asked that the Athenians appoint him ambas-sador so that he could approach Philip to get back his stolen items. The Athenians were persuaded and appointed him and Ktesiphon. When they went to Macedonia, Philip received them in a kindly and friendly way and returned to Phyrnon everything that his soldiers had robbed and more in addition from his own pocket, and apologized that his soldiers had not known that it was the Sacred Month.

D. PRELIMINARIES: REGISTRATION AND CERTIFICATION

90 Pausanias 5.24.9–10   *ca.* A.D. 170

Of all the images of Zeus, the Zeus in the *bouleuterion* [at Olympia] is the one most likely to strike terror into the hearts of sinners. This Zeus is surnamed Horkios [of the Oath], and he holds a thunderbolt in each hand. Beside this statue it is established for the athletes, their fathers and brothers, and their trainers to swear an oath on slices of the flesh of wild boars that they will do nothing evil against the Olympic Games. The athletes in the men's category also swear in addition that they have adhered strictly to their training for ten successive months. Those who judge the ages of the *paides* and of the *poloi* entered in the competition also swear that they will judge fairly and without taking bribes, and they will guard in secrecy everything about the examinee. I did not remember to ask what has to be done with the wild boar's meat after the oath of the athletes, although in more ancient times it was established with regard to sacrificial victims that a human being might not eat of that upon which an oath had been sworn.

91 Demosthenes, *Against Aristokrates* 40   352 B.C.

The list of places where a murderer may not go includes "the Games."

Why is he excluded from the Games? Because the Games in Greece are open to all, and the victim took part in them because everyone takes part in them. Therefore the murderer must absent himself.

92 Herodotus 5.22   *ca.* 430 B.C.

These descendants of Perdikkas [the Macedonians] are Greek, as they say themselves, and I happen to know this and will prove it later on. In addition, the *Hellanodikai* who organized the Games at Olympia have also shown this. When Alexander [I, king of Macedon, *ca.* 492–450 B.C.] decided to compete and appeared for that purpose, his Greek competitors wanted to exclude him, maintaining that the Games were for Greeks and not for barbarians. But when Alexander proved that he was an Argive, he was certified as a Greek and competed in the *stadion* and tied for first.

93 Artemidoros, *Interpretation of Dreams* 5.13   *ca.* A.D. 180

A boy wrestler, worried about his certification, dreamed that Asklepios was the judge and that, as he marched in procession with the other *paides*, the god disqualified him. Shortly thereafter, before the Games, he died. For that god is not the judge of games, but of life.

94 Pausanias 6.14.1–2   *ca.* A.D. 170

Pherias from Aigina, at the 78th Olympiad [468 B.C.], was thought to be very young and not yet ready to wrestle, and therefore was prohibited from competing. At the next Olympiad he was admitted to the *pale* for *paides,* and won it.

What happened to this Pherias was the exact opposite to that which happened to Nakasylos from Rhodes. Since he was 18 years old, the Eleans did not allow him to compete with the *paides,* but announced him among the *andres,* and he won . . .

Artemidoros from Tralles lost in the *pankration* for *paides* at Olympia because he was very young. When, however, the time came for the Games organized by the Smyrnaians of Ionia, his strength had so increased that, in the *pankration* and on one and the same day, he beat the *paides* against whom he had competed at Olympia, and then the so-called *ageneioi,* and thirdly the best of the *andres.*

E. SCHEDULE, HEATS, AND PAIRINGS

95 Pausanias 6.15.4–5   *ca.* A.D. 170

Although there must have been a regular schedule of the order of the events, this and the following passage show that modifications at the last moment were possible.

Kleitomachos of Thebes was the first after Theagenes of Thasos [see nos. **166, 167**] to win victories at Olympia in both the *pankration* and the *pyx.* He won a victory in the *pankration* at the 141st Olympics [216 B.C.; see no. **140**]. At the next Olympics Kleitomachos competed in both the *pankration* and the *pyx,* and meanwhile Kapros of Elis wanted to compete in the *pale* and the *pankration* on the same day. After Kapros had won in the *pale,* Kleitomachos suggested to the *Hellanodikai* that it would be fair if they announced the *pankration* before he was wounded in the *pyx.* His request seemed just and so the *pankration* was announced but he was beaten by Kapros. Nonetheless, Kleitomachos went on against the boxers with a stout heart and an unwearied body.

96 Dio Cassius 80.10   A.D. 217? or 221?

Aurelius Helix was so superior to his opponents that he wanted to compete in the *pale* and the *pankration* at the same time at Olympia, and in the Capitoline games at Rome he actually did win both events. But the Eleans were jealous of him, lest he become the so-called "Eighth from Herakles," and they called no wrestler into the stadium despite having programmed this competition on the whitened board.

97 Lucian, *Hermotimos* 40   *ca.* A.D. 170

The system for pairing opponents in the "heavy" events which Lucian here describes may go back to a time much earlier than his own day. Certainly such a system could fit with the evidence of the inscription of Cornelius Ariston given below.

A silver pitcher, sacred to Zeus, is set out. Into this are tossed small *kleroi*, about the size of beans and with inscriptions. On each of a pair is inscribed an *alpha*, on another pair a *beta*, on another a *gamma*, and so forth depending on the number of athletes. Two *kleroi* always have the same letter. Each of the athletes comes forward praying to Zeus and puts his hand into the pitcher, and one after another picks out one of the *kleroi*. A *mastigophoros* stands next to each athlete and holds his hand and thus does not allow him to know the letter which he has picked out. When they all have *kleroi*, the chief or another one of the *Hellanodikai*—I don't remember anymore—goes around the athletes who are standing in a circle and inspects their *kleroi*. Thus he matches one who has an *alpha* with the other who has picked out an *alpha* to compete with one another in the *pale* or the *pankration*, and then he matches the *beta* with the *beta* and the other letters in sequence. This is the way when the competitors are of an even number like eight or four or twelve, but when they are odd in number—five or nine or seven—an odd letter which has no duplicate inscribed on a *kleros* is added to the others. Whoever picks this one out remains *ephedros* until the other athletes have competed, for he has no corresponding letter, and this is no small stroke of good fortune for the athlete who will be able while still fresh to fall on those who have tired.

98 *IvO* 225   A.D. 49

The following inscriptions, on three sides of a statue base from Olympia, were intended to glorify the Olympic victor, but they give us details about pairings and byes which, presumably, were in operation for at least the "heavy" events.

On the front:

> Publius Cornelius Ariston, son of Eirenaios, of Ephesos, victor in
> the boys' *pankration* at the 207th Olympiad, to Olympian Zeus.

On the left side:

> He, though still a boy, but with the prowess of a man, he, where
> beauty and strength unite,
> Where does he come from? Who is he? Speak! You stand before
> the house of Zeus boasting of victories over what labors?
> Eirenaios is my father, stranger, and my name is Ariston; both sides
> of my family come from Ionic Ephesos.
> I was crowned *anephedros* at Olympia in the boys' *pankration*,
> having dusted off three opponents.

On the right side:

> I am heralded through all Asia, I am Ariston who was crowned
> with wild olive in the *pankration*.
> Whom Greece said was perfect when she saw me, though still a
> boy, with the *arete* of men, victorious with my blows.
> A winner not by the luck of the *kleros*, but without a bye, I was
> greeted by Zeus and the Alpheios.
> I alone of seven boys had no rest from their tricks, but always
> paired I beat them all.
> Thus do I glorify my father Eirenaios, and my fatherland Ephesos
> with immortal garlands.

99 Pausanias 6.13.4   *ca.* A.D. 170

Evidence for the number of competitors at the games and for elimination heats is scarce. The following passage from Pausanias shows that some system was used, although details are not clear. At the least, since there were 17 lanes in the balbis at Olympia, there must have been more competitors than that in the stadion mentioned here.

Polites was from Keramos in Karia, and he displayed every sort of *arete* in his feet at Olympia [A.D. 69]. From the race of greatest length in distance and time he went on, after a brief interval, to the shortest race, and having won the *dolichos* and the *stadion,* he added a third victory in the *diaulos.* In fact, Polites won a fourth time during the second race, for the competitors are grouped by the *kleros,* and they do not run all together. Rather those who win in their heat run again for the prize. And thus the victor in the *stadion* actually wins twice.

F. PROHIBITIONS AND PENALTIES

100   *CID* 1.3   *ca.* 450 B.C.?

The following regulation is inscribed on the side of the retaining wall of the stadium at Delphi about 50 feet from the southeast entrance. The forms of the carved letters suggest a date in the late fifth century B.C. There are difficulties with a few details, but the general significance of the regulation is clear.

Wine is prohibited in the vicinity of the *dromos.* If anyone breaks this rule, he shall make amends to Apollo by pouring a libation, making a sacrifice, and paying a fine of $110, half to Apollo and half to the informer.

101   *SEG* 48.541   525–500 B.C.

*This inscribed bronze tablet from Olympia is frustratingly broken and tantalizingly elliptical. But it reveals a number of important details from a very early time of the ancient Games and raises several questions. Were the tactics of Leontiskos of Messene (no. **34**) legal? Why is there clear reference to women if they were not allowed at the games (no. **149**)?*

The wrestler is neither to break a finger [nor————
the *diaitater* is to punish except upon the head [————
those who are stained are to be rounded up and noted [————
the Olympic Games he shall begin as worthy of victory again [————
neither an ally nor a woman. And if he knowingly does wrong [————
he is not to support a man of Elis nor of an ally [————
[?] drachmas are to be paid if he does an injury or [————
are to be given. A *theoros* is not with another's money to [————

102   Herodotus 8.59   430 B.C.

The assembled Greeks have to decide if and where they will take a stand in the face of the invasion of the Persian army and navy in 480 B.C.

Themistokles, who is determined that they should defend Salamis, speaks out of turn to the generals. A Corinthian, Adeimantos, chides him:

At the games, Themistokles, those who start too soon are flogged with switches.

And Themistokles responds:

But those who wait too long receive no crown of victory.

103   Pausanias 5.21.2–4   *ca.* A.D. 170

Going toward the stadium [at Olympia] from the *Altis* there is, on the left at the foot of Mt. Kronios, a stone platform with steps across it and leading up the hill. In front of this platform are bronze statues of Zeus. These have been made from the monies of fines levied against athletes who have mocked the games, and they are called *Zanés* by the locals. The first six were set up in the 98th Olympiad [388 B.C.] when Eupolos of Thessaly bought off with money those who had entered the *pyx:* Agenor of Arkadia and Prytanis of Kyzikos, as well as Phormion of Halikarnassos who had won in the Olympiad before this. They say that this was the first violation of the games by an athlete, and that the first who were fined by the Eleans were Eupolos and those who took money from him. . . .

Except for the third and the fourth, their bases have elegiac inscriptions on them. The first attempts to make clear that an Olympic victory is to be won not by money but by swiftness of foot or strength of body. The second says that the statue stands for honor to the god both by means of the reverence of the Eleans and by frightening athletes who would break the laws. The meaning of the epigram on the fifth is praise for the Eleans and not least for fining the boxers, and on the sixth that the statues are a lesson to all Greeks not to buy an Olympic victory.

104   *IG* IV².1.99   third century B.C.

When Kleaichmides the son of Aristokles was the *agonothetes* of the Games of Asklepios [at Epidauros] the athletes judged guilty of damaging the festival were fined $44,000 each: Taurides son of Telesios from Soloi in the men's *stadion*, Philistos son of Kallisthenes from Argos in the men's *pentathlon*, and Simakos son of Phalakrion of Epiros in the men's *pankration*.

When Sostratos son of Patrokleides was the *agonothetes* of the Games of Asklepios and of Apollo the actor judged guilty of not competing had his salary of $5,280 revoked: the comic Dionysios son of Dionysios of Rhodes.

G. OFFICIALS

105   Herodotus 2.160   *ca.* 430 B.C.

During the reign of Psammis as king of Egypt [*ca.* 590 B.C.] messengers came from Elis, boasting that they had organized the Olympic Games as the most just and the best of all mankind and claiming that not even the Egyptians, even though they were the wisest of men, could do better. Nonetheless, they were willing to listen to advice. The Egyptians, after putting their heads together, asked whether citizens of Elis were allowed to compete. The messengers responded that any Greek, including the Eleans, who wanted to compete could do so. The Egyptians said that this rule was certainly not just, for the Eleans could not help showing favoritism to the hometown player at the expense of the visitor, and that if they wanted to be just they should allow only non-Eleans to compete.

106   Lucian, *Hermotimos* 39   A.D. 165?

Recently I sat to the left of the *Hellanodikai* at Olympia thanks to Euandrides of Elis who kept a seat for me among his fellow citizens. I wanted to see near at hand everything that happened among the *Hellanodikai*.

107   Pausanias 6.1.4–5   *ca.* A.D. 170

While Troilos of Elis was serving as *Hellanodikes* he won two equestrian victories—one in the *synoris* for full-grown horses and one in the *tethrippon* for *poloi*. This was in the 102nd Olympiad [372 B.C.], and after this the Eleans passed a law that no one who was serving as *Hellanodikes* could enter the equestrian events.

108   Pausanias 6.3.7   *ca.* A.D. 170

Daidalos of Sikyon wrought the statue of Eupolemos of Elis. The inscription on it records that Eupolemos won the *stadion* for men at Olympia [396 B.C.] and that he had two Pythian crowns for victories in the *pentathlon* and another at Nemea. The following is also said about Eupolemos: that three *Hellanodikai* were stationed on the race track and that two of them gave the victory to Eupolemos, but the third to Leon of Ambrakia, and that, by an appeal of Leon to the Olympic *boule,* each of the *Hellanodikai* who judged Eupolemos the winner was fined.

109 Pausanias 5.9.4–6 (see no. **158**)   *ca.* A.D. 170

They acknowledge that the rules today for the *agonothetai* of the Olympic Games are not those which were established at the beginning. Iphitos organized the games by himself as did the descendants of Oxylos. But at the 50th Olympiad [580 B.C.] two men were appointed by lot from all the Eleans and entrusted to organize the Olympics, and for a long time thereafter the number of *agonothetai* remained at two. At the 95th Olympiad [400 B.C.] they established nine *Hellanodikai.* The equestrian events were entrusted to three of them, and the *pentathlon* was to be supervised by another three, and the rest of the events were the concern of the remaining *Hellanodikai.* In the second Olympiad after this [392 B.C.] the tenth *athlothetes* was established. At the 103rd Olympiad [368 B.C.] the Eleans had twelve tribes, and one *Hellanodikes* was chosen from each, but in the 104th Olympiad they were pressed by the Arkadians and lost some of their territory and the *demes* in that land so that they had eight tribes and, therefore, eight *Hellanodikai.* At the 108th Olympiad [348 B.C.] they returned again to the number of ten men, and that has remained down to our day.

H. REWARDS FOR VICTORY

110 Scholion to Euripides, *Hecuba* 573

The scholiast is explaining the phrase "to throw leaves" by citing Eratosthenes, head librarian at Alexandria in the late third century B.C., known as "the pentathlete" for his all-round knowledge.

Eratosthenes says concerning *phyllobolia* that in olden times men competed without prizes but that each spectator contributed and threw to the winner according to his ability. . . . Those who were sitting nearby offered crowns while those at a greater distance threw flowers and leaves.

111 Thucydides 4.121.1   423 B.C.

[The Skionaians] not only welcomed Brasidas with other beautiful things, but they also publicly honored him with a golden crown as the liberator of Greece, and privately put a *tainia* on him and paid tribute to him as if to an athlete.

112   Pausanias 8.48.2–3   *ca.* A.D. 170

I explained in my description of Elis the reason why a crown of olive is given to the victor at Olympia, and I will explain later why a crown of laurel is given at Delphi. The pine at the Isthmus and the celery at Nemea commemorate the misfortunes of Palaimon and of Archemoros, respectively. Many games have a crown of the palm, and everywhere the palm is placed in the right hand of the victor.

113   Lucian, *Anacharsis* 9–14   [*ca.* 590 B.C.]

See above, no. 35.

ANACHARSIS: What are these prizes for which you compete?

SOLON: A crown of olive at Olympia, a crown of pine at Isthmia, a crown of wild celery at Nemea, the laurel-berries sacred to Apollo at Delphi, and the oil of the olive at the Panathenaia. Why are you laughing, Anacharsis? Do you think that these prizes are insignificant?

ANACHARSIS: Oh no, Solon, the prizes which you are listing are most imposing. I am sure that those who offer them take pride in their generosity, and that the contestants are most eager to carry them off. So much so that they are willing to undergo these preliminary pains and to risk getting choked and broken in two by one another in order to get some laurel-berries and celery, as if it were not possible for anyone who wants them to get laurel-berries in large quantities, or to wear a crown of celery or of pine without getting his face smeared with mud or his belly kicked by the opposition.

SOLON: But my good man, we do not look at the prizes which are handed out. They are tokens of victory and a way to recognize the victors. Together with them goes a reputation which is worth everything to the victors, and getting kicked is a small price to pay for those who seek fame through pain. It cannot be acquired without pain, and the man who wants it must endure many hardships in the beginning before he can even start to see the profitable and sweet end of his efforts.

ANACHARSIS: When you speak of a "profitable and sweet end," Solon, you mean that everyone will see them wearing crowns and congratulate them on their victory after having pitied them for a long time during their pains, and that they will be fortunate to have traded in their pains for laurel-berries and celery?

SOLON: You are still ignorant of our customs, I tell you. In a little while you will change your mind when you go to the games and see that huge crowd of people gathering to see such things, and the theaters filled with thousands, and the contestants cheered, and he who wins thought equal to the gods.

ANACHARSIS: That is just the worst of it, Solon, if they have to endure these things not in front of a few, but before so many spectators and witnesses of the brutality. The latter probably congratulate the contestants upon seeing them streaming with blood or being strangled by their opponents, for these are the companions of their victories. With us Skythians, Solon, anyone who strikes a citizen or throws him down or tears his clothing gets a severe penalty from the elders even if the offense was witnessed by just a few, not to speak of the huge crowds which you describe at Isthmia and Olympia. I cannot but pity the competitors for what they endure, and I am amazed at the spectators who you say come from everywhere to the festivals, and are noble and prominent men but neglect their own urgent business for such things. I am unable to understand what pleasure it is to them to see men beaten, and slapped around, and smashed to the ground, and crushed by one another.

SOLON: If it were the time, Anacharsis, for the Olympic or Isthmian or Panathenaic Games, the events there would have taught you that we have not wasted our time on this subject. I cannot, just by telling you about it, convince you of the pleasure of what happens at such a festival as well as you would learn for yourself, sitting in the middle of the crowd, watching the *arete* of men and physical beauty, amazing conditioning and great skill and irresistible force and daring and pride and unbeatable determination and indescribable passion for victory. I know that you would not stop praising and cheering and applauding.

ANACHARSIS: No doubt, Solon, and laughing and jeering as well. I see that all these things—*arete* and conditioning and beauty and daring—are a waste since there is no purpose to them. It would be different if your country were in danger or your farmlands being raided or your friends and family being brutally kidnapped. Thus the competitors are all the more ridiculous if, as you say, they are the flower of the country and yet endure so much for nothing, making themselves wretched and marring their great big beautiful bodies with sand and black eyes in order that they might get a laurel-berry and an olive branch. I like to keep mentioning the prizes because they are so wonderful. But tell me, do all the contestants receive them?

SOLON: Not at all. Only one among them—the victor.

114   Pausanias 5.20.1   *ca.* A.D. 170

There are also other dedications here [in the Temple of Hera at Olympia]: . . .
The *diskos* of Iphitos and a table upon which are placed the crowns for the victors . . . The *diskos* of Iphitos has upon it the truce which the Eleans proclaim
for the Olympic Games, and this is not inscribed in a straight line, but the letters run around the *diskos* in the form of a circle. The table is made of gold and
ivory, and is the work of Kolotes [ca. 430 B.C.]. They say that Kolotes was from
Herakleia, but those who study sculpture say that he was from Paros.

115   Pausanias 5.15.12   *ca.* A.D. 170

The Eleans also have a *hestiatorion*. This is inside the *prytaneion*, opposite
the room of the hearth of Hestia, and in this room they give a banquet for
the Olympic victors.

116   [Andokides], *Against Alkibiades* 29   early fourth century B.C.

*Although the author of this speech is unknown, the date of its composition
seems clear. The activities described occurred in 416 B.C. after Alkibiades'
victory in the tethrippon (see above, no. 67).*

Alkibiades asked the leaders of the Athenian *theoria* to loan him the processional objects for him to use in his victory celebration the day before the
sacrifice, and then he cheated and refused to return them, because he wanted
to use the golden basins and censers before the city did. Thus all the foreigners who did not know that they belonged to us, saw the grand procession later and thought that we were using Alkibiades' processional objects.

117   Lucian, *Portraiture Defended* 11   *ca.* A.D. 165

*Panthea, favorite of the emperor Verus, responds to a flattering portrayal of
her:*

I hear it said by many—you men know if it is true—it is not permitted at
Olympia for the victors to set up statues that are larger than their bodies,
and that the *Hellanodikai* are especially careful that they are truthful, and
that this examination is even more accurate than that of certification [see
above, no. 90]. So be careful lest we get out of scale and the *Hellanodikai*
overturn our image.

118   Aischines, *Against Ktesiphon* 179–180   330 B.C.

Men of Athens, do you believe that anyone would want to suffer through the *pankration* or any other of the heavier events at Olympia, or any other of the *stephanitic* Games, if the crown were awarded not to the best but to the craftiest? No one would want to compete. Now, I believe, because it is rare and highly competitive and has an eternal fame for the victory, some are willing to put their bodies at risk and to undergo tremendous troubles. Suppose yourselves, then, to be the *agonothetes* of civic *arete* and reckon this—that if you give the prizes to a few who are worthy and in accordance with the laws, you will have many competitors for *arete*, but if you pass them out to whomever wants and to those who plot for them, you will corrupt even good natures.

V
Local Festivals

A. THE PANATHENAIC GAMES OF ATHENS

119 Aristotle, *Constitution of the Athenians* 60   *ca.* 325 B.C.

The Athenians also select by lot ten *athlothetai*, one from each tribe. Once these men have been tested, they hold office for four years, and they administer the Panathenaic procession and the *mousikos agon*, the *gymnikos agon*, and the *hippodromia*, and they have the *peplos* made, and together with the *boule* they have the amphoras made, and they pass out the olive oil to the athletes. The olive oil is collected from the sacred trees; it is assessed by the *Archon* from those who are working the fields where the sacred trees are located at the rate of three half-cups per tree. . . . The Treasurers safe-guard the olive oil in the Akropolis at all times except at the time of the Panathenaic Games when they dole it out to the *athlothetai*, and the *athlothetai* to the victors. Gold and silver are the prizes for the *mousikos agon*, shields for the *euandria*, and olive oil for the *gymnikos agon* and the *hippodromia*.

120 *IG* II² 2311   400–350 B.C.

This inscription contains a list of the prizes awarded in the Panathenaic Games at some point during the first half of the fourth century B.C. Although much of the original text is broken away, enough remains to reveal many of the prizes. Because of the differing nature of these, the estimated dollar value is given in parentheses next to the actual prize. Before the heading "For the

Warriors," all competitions were open to any Greeks; all listed after that heading were open only to Athenian citizens competing as individuals or as members of their tribe's teams. It may be noted that the total of the estimated value of the prizes, in excess of $570,000, does not include many parts which are broken away, especially including the prizes for nearly all of the equestrian events. Broken areas on the stone where the text is not preserved are indicated with brackets; note that a large section dealing with prizes for the men's and the ageneioi categories can be restored with certainty (see D. C. Young, The Olympic Myth of Greek Amateur Athletics *[1984] 116 n. 12).*

PRIZES FOR THE *KITHARA*-SINGERS

First place: a crown of olive in gold weighing 1,000 drachmas ($22,000) and 500 silver drachmas ($11,000).

Second place: 1,200 drachmas ($26,400).

Third place: 600 drachmas ($13,200).

Fourth place: 400 drachmas ($8,800).

Fifth place: 300 drachmas ($6,600).

For the *Aulos*-singers in the Men's Category:

First place: a crown weighing 300 drachmas ($6,600).

Second place: 100 drachmas ($2,200).

For the *Aulos* players:

First place: a crown weighing [?].

. . . Several lines missing on the stone . . .

For the Victor in the *Stadion* in the Boys' Category: 50 amphoras of olive oil ($19,800).

Second place: 10 amphoras of olive oil ($3,960).

For the Victor in the *Pentathlon* in the Boys' Category: 50 amphoras of olive oil ($19,800).

Second place: 6 amphoras of olive oil ($2,376).

For the Victor in the *Pale* in the Boys' Category: 30 amphoras of olive oil ($11,880).

Second place: 6 amphoras of olive oil ($2,376).

For the Victor in the *Pyx* in the Boys' Category: 30 amphoras of olive oil ($11,880).

Second place: 6 amphoras of olive oil ($2,376).

For the Victor in the *Pankration* in the Boys' Category: 40 amphoras of olive oil ($15,840).

Second place: 8 amphoras of olive oil ($3,168).

For the Victor in the *Stadion* in the *Ageneios* Category: 60 amphoras of olive oil ($23,760).

Second place: 12 amphoras of olive oil ($4,752).

For the Victor in the *Pentathlon* in the *Ageneios* Category: 40 amphoras of olive oil ($15,840).

Second place: 8 amphoras of olive oil ($3,168).

For the Victor in the *Pale* in the *Ageneios* Category: 40 amphoras of olive oil ($15,840).

Second place: 8 amphoras of olive oil ($3,168).

For the Victor in the *Pyx* in [the *Ageneios* Category: 50 amphoras] of olive oil ($19,800).

[Second place: 10 amphoras of olive oil ($3,960).]

For the Victor [in the *Pankration* in the *Ageneios* Category: 50 amphoras of olive oil ($19,800).

Second place: 10 amphoras of olive oil ($3,960)].

. . . Several lines missing on the stone . . .

[For the Victor in the *Stadion* in the Men's Category: 100 amphoras of olive oil ($39,600).

Second place: 20 amphoras of olive oil ($7,920).

For the Victor in the *Pentathlon* in the Men's Category: 60 amphoras of olive oil ($23,760).

Second place: 12 amphoras of olive oil ($4,752).

For the Victor in the *Pale* in the Men's Category: 60 amphoras of olive oil ($23,760).

Second place: 12 amphoras of olive oil ($4,752).

For the Victor in the *Pyx* in the Men's Category: 60 amphoras of olive oil ($23,760).

Second place: 12 amphoras of olive oil ($4,752).

For the Victor in the *Pankration* in the Men's Category: 80 amphoras of olive oil ($31,680).

Second place: 16 amphoras of olive oil ($6,336).]

. . . Several lines missing on the stone . . .

For the Two-Horse Chariot Race in the *Polos* Category: 40 amphoras of olive oil ($15,840).

Second place: 8 amphoras of olive oil ($3,168).

For the Two-Horse Chariot Race in the Full-Grown Category: 140 amphoras of olive oil ($44,440).

Second place: 40 amphoras of olive oil ($15,840).

PRIZES FOR THE WARRIORS

For the Victor in the *Keles:* 16 amphoras of olive oil ($6,336).

Second place: 4 amphoras of olive oil ($1,584).

For the Victor in the Two-Horse Chariot Race: 30 amphoras of olive oil ($11,880).

Second place: 6 amphoras of olive oil ($2,376).

For the Victor in the Processional Two-Horse Chariot: 4 amphoras of olive oil ($1,584).

Second place: 1 amphora of olive oil ($396).

For the Spear Thrower from Horseback: 5 amphoras of olive oil ($1,980).

Second place: 1 amphora of olive oil ($396).

For the Pyrrhic Dancers in the Boys' Category: A bull and 100 drachmas ($2,200).

For the Pyrrhic Dancers in the *Ageneios* Category: A bull and 100 drachmas ($2,200).

For the Pyrrhic Dancers in the Men's Category: A bull and 100 drachmas ($2,200).

For the Winning Tribe in *Euandria:* A bull and 100 drachmas ($2,200).

For the Winning Tribe in the *Lampadephoros:* A bull and 100 drachmas ($2,200).

For the Individual Victor in the *Lampadephoros:* A water jar and 30 drachmas.

PRIZES FOR THE BOAT RACE

For the Winning Tribe: 3 bulls and 300 drachmas ($6,600) and 200 free meals.

Second place: 2 bulls and 200 drachmas ($4,400).

. . . The rest of the stone is broken away . . .

121   Lysias 21.1 and 4–5   403/2 B.C.

A defendant, whose name is not known, presents a litany of his services to Athens including a list of the amounts he expended in productions at various festivals. This should be understood as the sponsorship of teams of young men whose training, as displayed in these competitions, was important to the survival of the state. His sponsorships include the following:

. . . I spent 800 drachmas ($17,600) for Pyrrhic Dancers at the Great Panathenaic Games in the archonship of Glaukippos [409/8 B.C.] . . . 700 drachmas ($15,400) for Pyrrhic Dancers in the *ageneios* category at the Little Panathenaic Games [in the archonship of Eukleides (404/403 B.C.)]. I won a *trireme* race at Sounion where I spent 1500 drachmas ($33,000). . . .

122   Athenaeus, *The Gastronomers* 13.565F   *ca.* A.D. 228

But even I myself praise beauty. And in the *euandria* they judge the most handsome and permit them to be the first of the bearers of sacred objects in the procession.

123   Pausanias 1.30.2   *ca.* A.D. 170

There is an altar of Prometheus in the Akademy, and they run from this to the city holding burning torches. The contest is to run and keep the torch burning at the same time. The torch and the victory are extinguished together for the front runner, and the victory passes on to the second place runner. But if his torch goes out, the third place runner takes the victory; and if everybody's torches go out, nobody wins.

B. THE ELEUTHERIA OF LARISSA IN THESSALY

124 *IG IX*, 2, 531   time of Christ

The following inscription preserves the names of the victors—all local citizens of Larissa—in the renewed Games in honor of Zeus Eleutherios. It also shows some of the competitions unique to this land which was known for its horsemanship.

Taurotheria: Markos Arrontios

Old style recitation: Philon the Younger, son of Philon

Cavalry charge: Demetrios, son of Demetrios

Infantry charge: Demetrios, son of Xenon

Synoris charge: Teimasitheos, son of Gorgopas

Torch race on horseback: Markos Arrontios

Salpinktes: Lysikles, son of Leptinos

Keryx: Petalon, son of Dionysios

Stadion in the Boys' Category: Gaios Klodios, son of Gaios

Stadion in the Men's Category: Demetrios, son of Demetrios

Diaulos in the Boys' Category: Neomenes, son of Ariston

Diaulos in the Men's Category: Aristomachos, son of Hermios

Torch race in the Boys' Category: Empedion, son of Homer

Pyx in the Boys' Category: Demoneikos, son of Eudemos

Pyx in the Men's Category: Demetrios, son of Demetrios

Pankration in the Boys' Category: Philon the Younger, son of Philon

Pankration in the Boys' Category, second trial: Eupalides, son of Themistogenes

Pankration in the Men's Category: Asklepiades, son of Asklepiades

Hoplites: Kteson, son of Pausanias

Aphippodroma: Aristomenes, son of Asandrides

Apobates: Ladamos, son of Argaios

Infantry marksmanship: Alexander, son of Kleon

Archery: Onomarchos, son of Herakleides

Cavalry marksmanship: Aristomenes, son of Asandrides

Enkomion speech: Kointos Okrios, son of Kointos

Enkomion epic: Amometos, son of Philoxenides

New style recitation: Philon the Younger, son of Philon

Epigram: Amometos, son of Philoxenides

---

125 *Anthologia Graeca* 9.543   ca. A.D. 40

The Anthologia *preserves epigrams collected by Philippos of Thessalonike in his* Garland—*an updated version of an earlier collection but including several dozen of his own poems. This one gives a description of the taurotheria mentioned in the victors' list above (no. **124**). The competition could have been witnessed by Philippos himself.*

> The well-horsed crew of Thessalian bull-drivers
>   Armed against the beasts only with their bare hands
> Spur their ponies to yoke them to the frightened charging bull,
>   Hastening to throw their arm-lasso around his head.
> At the same instant sliding this slip-knot noose to the limit
>   They roll even this mighty beast to the ground.

---

126 Heliodoros, *Aithiopia* 10.28–30   A.D. 250?

In the course of this romantic adventure story the hero, Theagenes of Thessaly, finds himself tied to the altar of the sun as an intended sacrificial victim. A bull tied to the adjacent altar of the moon suddenly breaks loose and charges around the arena causing chaos.

At that moment Theagenes, either impelled by his native courage or instigated by some god, saw that the guards posted around him had scattered by the impact of the chaos. He stood bolt upright . . . snatched a piece of split wood from the altar, seized hold of one of the horses that had not fled, vaulted onto its back, and grasping its mane used it for a bridle. Spurring his horse with his heel and goading it with the stick instead of a whip, he rode after the runaway bull. . . . He quickly caught up to the bull and drove it along from behind for a little while, prodding it and forcing it to run ever faster. Wherever it turned, he followed, being cautious to avoid its lunges to attack him.

    Once the bull became used to seeing him and to his actions, he began to ride next to it, flank touching flank so that horse and bull mixed breath and sweat together. His pace so nearly matched that of the bull that people at a distance could believe that the heads of the two animals grew from a single body, and they cheered Theagenes for his skill in driving this strange hippotauric *synoris.* . . . Now Theagenes spurred his horse to the limit in order to get a little ahead of the bull with the horse's breast next to the bull's head. Then he let the horse run free while he threw himself onto the bull's neck. Sticking his face down between its horns and locking his fingers together on its forehead, he made a crown and a noose of his arms on the bull's head. The rest of his body hung down on the right shoulder of the bull, slightly swinging to and fro from the animal's leaping about.

When he felt the bull beginning to reel under his weight and the muscle begin to fail, and when they reached the place where the King sat, he swung into the front and kicked at the bull's legs with his own feet, constantly hindering its motion. Hampered in its progress and succumbing to the young man's strength, its knees suddenly buckled and it lurched and rolled over its shoulders onto its back and lay for a long time on its back with its horns stuck in the ground so that its head was immobilized while its legs beat the air in futility.

C. THE *BOMONIKAI* OF SPARTA

127   Lucian, *Anacharsis* 38   *ca.* A.D. 170

The Spartan system of preparation for citizenship was legendary for its rigors. Lucian, already using Greek athletics as that part of the culture that would appear strangest to a foreigner (see no. 35), turns to the Spartan as the strangest of the strange, especially the voluntary blood-letting at the Altar (bomos) of Artemis Orthia.

Since you say, Anacharsis, that you will visit the rest of Greece, remember that when you get to Lakedaimonia not to laugh at them or to think that they are suffering in vain when they run together and hit each other for a ball in the theater, or go onto an island surrounded by water and chose sides and—naked, too—begin hostilities against one another until one team drives the other into the water. . . . Most of all, [do not laugh] when you see them being flogged at the altar and dripping with blood while their fathers and mothers stand by and are not only not distressed by the event, but actually threaten them if they do not endure the lashes, and beg them to bear the pain as long as possible and to be brave before the torture. Indeed, many have died in this *agon* because they gave no value to giving up under the eyes of their relatives while life was still in them. Their statues are set up at public expense; you will see honors paid to them.

VI

The Role of the Games in Society

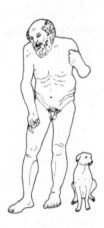

128 Cicero, *Tusculan Disputations* 5.3.9   45 B.C.

Cicero, in his presentation of Greek philosophy to a Roman audience, re-
counts a story about Pythagoras that Cicero had found recounted by a
pupil of Plato, Herakleides of Pontos. Pythagoras visited Leon, the ruler of
Phlious, at a date not far from 480 b.c. and displayed great learning during
their discussions. We see the various types of people who went to the
Games. The passage also shows that the Games were so well known that
they could be used for allegorical purposes.

Leon admired Pythagoras' genius and eloquence and asked him on which
art he relied the most. Pythagoras said that he knew no arts, but was a
philosopher. Leon marvelled at the novelty of the term and asked what was
a philosopher and what was the difference between them and the rest of
mankind. Pythagoras is said to have responded that the life of man seemed
to him like that festival which was held with the most magnificent games
with all of Greece assembled. There some, with their bodies trained, competed for the glory and the fame of a crown, others were motivated by the
profit potential of buying or selling, but there was yet another type, the best
of all, who sought neither applause nor profit, but came to observe and to
study what was done and how. So we, as if we have come to some festival

from another city, have come to this life from another life and another character where some served glory and others served money. But these are rare men who hold everything else as nothing but study the nature of things, these are called lovers of wisdom, for that is the meaning of the word "philosopher." So, as there at the games the most noble man watches without seeking any gain for himself, so in life the contemplation and recognition of the nature of things was far ahead of all other activities.

129 *POxy* II.222   *ca.* A.D. 250

This document is a fragment of papyrus which was found in Egypt late in the nineteenth century. Although written in the third century A.D., *it contains a list of the victors in the Olympic Games from the fifth century* B.C. *Where it can be checked against other evidence, it reveals itself to be very accurate. It shows not only the nature of the Olympic victors' list, but also how widespread and easily attainable such information was in antiquity, and it reminds us that the Olympiad was the single most frequently used and universally accepted form of chronological reckoning in the Greek world. We can only regret that we do not have more of it. Areas where the papyrus is torn away and the text not preserved are indicated in brackets. The top of the papyrus as preserved begins in the middle of the entry for the 75th Olympiad in 480* B.C.

Xenopithes of Chios, the *stadion* in the boys' category.

[. . .]kon of Argos, the *pale* in the boys' category.

[. . .]phanes of Heraia, the *pyx* in the boys' category.

[Ast]ylos of Syracuse, the *hoplites*.

[. . .]tondas and Arsilochos of Thebes, the *tethrippon*.

[Arg]os public, the *keles*.

[The 76th Olympiad—476 B.C.]

[Ska]mandros of Mitylene, the *stadion*.

[Da]ndis of Argos, the *diaulos*.

[?] of Sparta, the *dolichos*.

[?] of Taras, the *pentathlon*.

[?] of Maroneia, the *pale*.

[Euthymos of Lok]roi in Italy, the *pyx*.

[Theagenes of Th]asos, the *pankration*.

[? of Sp]arta, the *stadion* in the boys' category.

[Ag]esi[da]mos of Lokrai in Italy, the *pyx* in the boys' category.

[Ast]ylos of Syracuse, the *hoplites*.

[Ther]on of Akragas, the *tethrippon*.

[Hier]on of Syracuse, the *keles*.

[The 77th Olympiad—472 B.C.]

[Dan]dis of Argos, the *stadion*.

[..]ges of Epidauros, the *diaulos*.

[Erg]oteles of Himera, the *dolichos*.

[. . .]amos of Miletos, the *pentathlon*.

[. . .]menes of Samos, the *pale*.

[Euth]ymos of Lokrai in Italy, the *pyx*.

[Ka]llias of Athens, the *pankration*.

[. . .]tandridas of Corinth, the *stadion* in the boys' category.

[. . .]kratidas of Taras, the *pale* in the boys' category.

[Tel]lon of Mainalos, the *pyx* in the boys' category.

[. . .]gias of Epidamnos, the *hoplites*.

[Arg]os public, the *tethrippon*.

[Hier]on of Syracuse, the *keles*.

[The 78th Olympiad—468 B.C.]

[P]armeneides of Poseidonia, the *stadion*.

[Par]meneides, the same, the *diaulos*.

[. . .]medes of Sparta, the *dolichos*.

[..]tion of Taras, the *pentathlon*.

[Epha]rmostos of Opous, the *pale*.

[Me]nalkes of Opous, the *pyx*.

[..]titimadas of Argos, the *pankration*.

[Lyk]ophron of Athens, the *stadion* in the boys' category.

[..]emos of Parrhasia, the *pale* in the boys' category.

[. . .]los of Athens, the *hoplites.*

[..]nymos of Syracuse, the *tethrippon.*

> *. . . the papyrus breaks off . . .*

130 Aelian, *Varia Historia* 10.7   ca. A.D. 220

*Ancient Greek calendars were based on lunar months of about 29 1/2 days
which quickly got out of synchronization with the solar year. Attempts
were made to discover cycles of the lunar and the solar calendar that could
be co-ordinated, and it was at Olympia that the results of such research
were "published."*

The astronomer Oinopides of Chios dedicated at Olympia the bronze tablet
on which he inscribed the astrology of fifty-nine years, saying that this was
the big year. But the astronomer Meton [of Athens] erected *stelai* and wrote
on them the solstices and the big year, so he said, he discovered to be nine-
teen years.

131 Xenophon, *Memorabilia* 3.13.5   ca. 355 B.C.

*The distance from Athens to Olympia is given by Herodotus (2.7.1–2) as
1485 stadia, or roughly 170 miles.*

Sokrates said to someone who was afraid of the road to Olympia: "But why
do you fear the journey? Don't you walk around nearly all day at home?
Don't you walk there to lunch? And again to have dinner? And again to
sleep? Don't you see that if you would string together all the walking you do
in five or six days anyway you could easily travel from Athens to Olympia?"

132 Plato, *Hippias Minor* 363c–364a   ca. 380 B.C.

*The writings of the sophist Hippias of Elis (ca. 485–415 B.C.; see no. 15) in-
cluded an edition of the list of Olympic victors. Here he is about to be inter-
viewed by Sokrates.*

HIPPIAS: It would be strange if I—who always go from my home in Elis
to the Olympic Games every time when they are celebrated; who enters the
sanctuary and am ready to speak, if someone asks, on any of the subjects I
have prepared; who answers any questions if someone asks—it would be
strange if I should now avoid the questions of Sokrates.

SOKRATES: O Hippias, you are blessed if at each Olympiad you arrive at the sanctuary with such optimism about the wisdom of your soul. I would be amazed if any of the athletes who go to the same place to compete were so fearless about their bodies and had as much confidence in them as you have in your intelligence.

HIPPIAS: Of course I feel this way, Sokrates. Ever since I began to compete in the Olympics, I have never met anyone better in any way than me.

133 *IvO* 64   28 B.C.

This inscription is one of several lists of officials for the Sanctuary of Zeus at Olympia. They seem to have served for the entire four-year Olympiad, and not just during the festivals, and must have been particularly involved with religious and sacrificial activities as their titles imply. Some officials seem to have changed regularly, but others which were hereditary, such as the prophets, or which required specialized skills, such as the flutist, continued over many years. In addition to the officials listed in this inscription, other officials are known such as the "doctor" and the "architect," perhaps for specialized needs of limited duration. They remind us that Olympia was not only for athletes or athletics, and not only for the time of the Games.

SACRED TO ZEUS
THE ADMINISTRATION FOR THE 189TH OLYMPIAD

Sacred Attendants
Eudamos son of Euthymenes
Sophon son of Lykos
Aphrodeisios son of Euporos

Spondophoroi
Antiochos son of Antiochos
Herakleides son of Herakleides
Lykidas son of Lykidas

Prophets
Kallitos, Klytiad, son of Antias
Pausanias, Iamid, son of Diogenes

Bailiffs
Arkesos son of Harmodios
Kallias son of Pausanias
Hippias son of Karops

Moschion son of Dameas
Pausanias son of Diogenes

Flutist
Aristarchos son of Aristokles

Exegete
Polychares son of Aristokrates

On-Call Sacrificing Priest
Zopyros son of Olympichos

Secretary
Herakleides son of Herakleides

Wine-pourer
Alexas son of Sophron

Libation-dancers
Epiktetos son of Herakleides
Hilaros son of Antiochos
Epiktetos son of Aphrodeisios

Woodman
Euthymos son of Sotion

Parcher and Butcher-Cook
Alexas son of Lykos

134 Plutarch, *Demetrios* 11.1   *ca.* A.D. 100

Among the Athenians' attempts in 307/6 B.C. to curry favor with the Mace-
donians Antigonos and his son Demetrios was the motion by one Stratokles:

Those who were sent by public decree to Antigonos or Demetrios should be
called *theoroi* rather than ambassadors, just like those who went to Delphi
or Olympia to conduct the traditional sacrifices on behalf of their cities at
the Greek festivals.

135 Diogenes Laertius, *Empedokles* 8.53   A.D. 250?

The philosopher Empedokles of Akragas had many strong ties to Olympia,
including the victories of his grandfather in the keles and his father in the

pale *at the same Olympics in 496 B.C. Here Diogenes quotes Favorinus who was active in the first half of the second century after Christ.*

Empedokles sacrificed an ox made of honey and barley for the *theoroi*.

136 *BCH* 77 (1953) 389   third century B.C.

The following decree honors a foreign benefactor for his services to Argos. It is one of many examples which show the central and common role of the games in the political and diplomatic life of an ancient polis, as well as the highly organized administration that lay behind the successful festivals.

It is resolved by the people [of Argos] that Agathokles, son of Nikostratos, of Athens and his descendants shall be a *proxenos* and a benefactor of the city of the Argives and a *thearodokos* [of the festivals] of Zeus at Nemea and of the Argive Hera; that they shall be exempt from public duties and shall have the right of asylum even in financial matters on both land and sea, in both war and peace; that they shall have front-row seats in whatever festivals the city organizes; that this *proxenia* be inscribed in the Sanctuary of Apollo Lykeios.

137 Aelian, *Varia Historia* 4.15   *ca.* A.D. 220

Straton son of Korrhagos appears to have been ill toward an end. Although he was of a noble and wealthy family, he did not exercise. Since he had an illness of the spleen and was forced to take therapy from exercises, and at first he exercised as much as was necessary to regain his health, but as his technique improved he got further into the practice. Thus he won at Olympia on the same day both the *pale* and the *pankration* [68 B.C.], and at the next Olympiad, and at the Nemean and Pythian and Isthmian Games.

138 Aristotle, *Rhetoric* 1365a   *ca.* 330 B.C.

Since that which is more difficult or more rare is the better, seasons and ages and places and times and powers produce great things; that is, if one does something beyond his power or his age or his equals, and if he does them in such a way and place and time, he will have greatness and beauty and goodness and justice and oppositions. From such a situation came the epigram for the Olympic victor:

I used to carry on my shoulders with a bucket-yoke
fish from Argos to Tegea.

139   Plutarch, *Alexander* 4.9–11   *ca.* A.D. 100

Alexander loved neither fame of all kinds nor recognition from everyone,
unlike his father, Philip, who acted like a sophist in his pride in the power of
his speeches, and stamped his coins with his chariot victories at Olympia.
On the contrary, when his comrades asked if he wanted to compete at
Olympia in the *stadion* since he was fast afoot, Alexander responded, "Yes,
if my competitors are kings."

140   Polybius 27.9.3–13   *ca.* 130 B.C.

In the *gymnikoi agones* when a humble and very inferior boxer is matched
against a famous and unbeatable opponent, immediately the crowd splits off
its support to the inferior man and they call out encouragement and bob and
weave and punch together with him. And if he happens to land a punch on
the other guy and mark his face, they jump up and down in their excite-
ment. Sometimes they attack the other fellow with insults, not because they
hate or scorn him, but becoming curiously sympathetic toward and naturally supportive of the underdog. But if someone gets their attention at the
right time, they quickly change their position and resume their impartiality.
They say that Kleitomachos did this, for he appeared to be unstoppable in
the games, and his fame was worldwide. But King Ptolemy had ambitions of
demolishing his fame, and he prepared and sent off with great pride the
boxer Aristonikos who seemed naturally adapted for this sport.

   When Aristonikos arrived in Greece and was set up at the Olympic
games against Kleitomachos [216 B.C.; see no. **95**], the crowd came to be on
Aristonikos' side and cheered him, happy that someone had dared, even for
a little, to stand up against Kleitomachos. When, as the bout proceeded, he
appeared to be the equal of, and now and then wounded, Kleitomachos, there
was applause and the crowd shared in his attacks and shouted out encouragement to Aristonikos. At that point they say that Kleitomachos, who was
standing off and catching his breath, turned to the crowd to learn why they
wanted to cheer Aristonikos and take his side as much as they could. Did
they think that he was not following the rules of the games? Or did they not
understand that he, Kleitomachos, was fighting right now for the fame of
Greece, but that Aristonikos was fighting for the fame of King Ptolemy? Did
they want to see an Egyptian win the crown at Olympia from the Greeks?

Or did they prefer that a Theban and Boeotian be proclaimed as victor in boxing in the men's category? When Kleitomachos had spoken in this way, they say that there was such a change in the crowd's feelings that it rather than Kleitomachos finally beat Aristonikos.

141   Herodotus 6.127   *ca.* 430 B.C.

Kleisthenes of Sikyon had a daughter named Agariste. He wanted to give her as a bride to the best man he could find of all the Greeks. When he was at Olympia and had won the *tethrippon* [572 B.C.], Kleisthenes announced that whoever of the Greeks considered himself worthy of being the son-in-law of Kleisthenes should come to Sikyon on the sixtieth day (or sooner), and he would validate the marriage one year from that sixtieth day. Then all the Greeks who were puffed up with themselves came as suitors, and Kleisthenes made them work out in the *dromos* and the *palaistra*.

142   Plutarch, *Themistokles* 17.4   *ca.* A.D. 100

It is said that when Themistokles went to the next celebration of the Olympic Games [476 B.C., after the battle of Salamis] and entered the stadium, everyone there forgot the competitors all day long as they watched him and pointed him out to strangers, all the while admiring and applauding him.

143   Lucian, *Herodotus* 1–4 and 7–8   *ca.* A.D. 170

Lucian (see above, no. 7) presented this essay before an audience in Macedonia, which he compares and contrasts to Olympia. In so doing he provides us with a glimpse of some non-athletic activities which went on at Panhellenic festivals, at least in his own time and almost certainly at the time of Herodotus (ca. 430 B.C.), and reminds us that competitions such as prose composition and painting which were known at, for example, Delphi (above, no. 77) but never a part of the official program at Olympia, still were known even there in some form.

Would that some of the other qualities of Herodotus could be imitated. I do not mean all of them, for this would be too much to hope for, but just one of them, perhaps the beauty of his diction, or the harmony of his words, the aptness of expression native to Ionia, or his extraordinary judgement, or the countless diverse elements which he has brought together into a unity beyond hope of imitation. One quality, however, which you and I and everyone else can imitate, is in the handling of his composition and in the speed with which he developed his reputation throughout the whole Greek world.

When he had sailed from his home in Caria straight to Greece, he considered what would be the quickest and easiest route to fame and reputation for himself and his writings. He thought that it would be a long and tedious waste of time to travel around reading his works, now in Athens, now in Corinth or Argos, now in Sparta. He had no appetite for such a hit-and-miss proposition which would, moreover, delay his acquisition of a reputation, and he planned to win the hearts of all the Greeks at a single point in time if he could.

The time for the Olympic festival was approaching, and Herodotus thought that this was the opportunity for which he had been waiting. He kept an eye out at the festival until it was crowded and the most prominent men had assembled from everywhere. Then he went into the rear chamber of the Temple of Zeus not like a spectator, but like a contestant in the Olympic Games. He then recited his histories and so mesmerized those present that his books were called after the Muses, since they were also nine in number.

It was not long until he was better known than the Olympic victors. There was not a man who had not heard the name of Herodotus; some heard it at Olympia, others heard it from those returning from the festival. All he had to do was appear and someone would point him out: "That there is Herodotus who wrote in Ionic of the Persian Wars and celebrated our victories." Such were the rewards of his histories that in a single assembly he won the universal acclaim of the whole of Greece and he was proclaimed not just by a single *keryx*, but in every city-state which had some participant at the festival.

Those who followed learned the lesson of this shortcut to fame. Hippias the sophist, who was a native of Elis, and Prodikos of Keos and Anaximenes of Chios and Polos of Akragas and dozens of others always recited their works in person at the festivals and thus won quick recognition.

But there is no need for me to talk about those ancient sophists and authors since more recently Aëtion the painter displayed his own painting of the "Marriage of Roxane and Alexander" at Olympia. Proxenides, a *Hellanodikes* at the time, was so enthusiastic about his talent that he married his daughter to Aëtion. . . .

Herodotus, to return to him, thought that the Olympic festival was a suitable place for him, the displayer of Greek victories, to be displayed to the

Greeks. Please do not think that I am mad or that I compare my works to his, but he and I are similar. When I first came to stay in Macedonia, I wondered what to do. My first desire was to become known to all of you and to show off my works to the most Macedonians possible, but to go around at that time of year in person to each city seemed less than convenient. Rather, I thought to await your present festival and make my appearance to deliver my lecture. Thus, I thought, would my prayers be answered.

Now you are all assembled together, the heads of each city, the leaders of Macedonia, in the fairest of all cities which is not, thank goodness, like Olympia with its cramped quarters, its tents and shanties, and its stifling heat. Nor is my audience a crude crowd which would rather be watching athletes than hearing Herodotus. It is the best of orators and historians and sophists. If you compare me to Polydamas, or Glaukos, or Milo, you will think that I am a foolhardy man. But if you forget them and strip me and look at me alone, I shall not seem so deserving of the whip. But even such a judgement would be satisfactory in such a stadium.

144   Aelian, *Varia Historia* 4.9   *ca.* A.D. 220

Plato the son of Ariston shared a tent at Olympia with some men he did not know, nor did they know him. He so gained their affection with his comradery, eating with them simply and passing the days with all of them that the strangers felt fortunate that they had met this man. He made no mention of the Akademy, nor of Sokrates. He only told them that his name was Plato. Later when they visited Athens, he received them graciously, and the strangers said, "Plato, please take us to see your namesake, the student of Sokrates, take us to his Akademy, and introduce us to that man so that we can enjoy him."

He responded, quietly and with a smile as was his custom, "I am that man."

145   Dio Chrysostom 8.4–6, 9–12, 26, 36   A.D. 97

Dio the "Golden Mouthed" was an orator and philosopher who was no stranger to the Panhellenic games. In A.D. 97 he delivered a speech at the Olympic Games, and in this discourse he portrayed the Cynic philosopher Diogenes at the Isthmian Games in ca. 358 B.C. We cannot be certain whether the picture of the festival is to be taken as true to the time of Diogenes or to that of Dio four centuries later; perhaps there was little difference.

After the death of his friend Antisthenes, Diogenes moved from Athens to Corinth, and he lived there without either renting a house or staying with a friend. He camped out in a public park. The reason for his move was that he observed that most men visited Corinth at one time or another because of its harbors and prostitutes, and because the city was located at the crossroads of Greece. Thus, just as the good doctor will go to help where the largest number of sick people are, so Diogenes thought it was necessary for the wise man to go where fools proliferate.

When the time came for the Isthmian Games, and everyone was at Isthmia, he went too. It was his custom at the festivals to study the ambitions of men and why they went out in public and what it was that was a source of pride to them. . . .

That was also the time to hear crowds of wretched sophists around the Temple of Poseidon as they shouted and heaped abuse on each other, and their so-called students as they fought with one another, and many historians reading out their dumb writings, and many poets reciting their poetry to the applause of other poets, and many magicians showing their tricks, many fortune-tellers telling fortunes, countless lawyers perverting justice, and not a few peddlers peddling whatever came to hand. Immediately a crowd gathered around him too, but with no Corinthians since they saw him every day in Corinth and had grown accustomed to the novelty. Thus, the crowd consisted of strangers, and each of them would speak or listen for a short time and then leave, fearing his examination of their opinions. For this reason Diogenes said that he was like a Lakonian dog; many men would pet these dogs and play with them when they were displayed at the festivals, but no one would buy one because no one knew how to handle them.

When one man asked Diogenes if he too had come to watch the competition, Diogenes said, "No, but to participate." When the man laughed and asked him who his competitors were, Diogenes gave him his familiar glowering glance and said: "The toughest and most difficult to defeat, ones which no Greek can stare down. Not those competitors who run or wrestle or jump, nor those who box and throw the javelin and the *diskos*, but those who chastise a man." "Who are they?" asked the other. "Hardships," said Diogenes, "which are severe and unbeatable for men who are gluttons and puffed with their own worth and snore at night, but which can be conquered by men who are thin and lean and have waists thinner than wasps. Or do you think that those pot-bellied bullies are good for something? I think that they are ripe candidates to serve as sacrificial victims and that they have less soul than swine. The man who is noble is the one who considers hardship as his greatest competitor and struggles with it day and night, and not, like some goat, for a bit of celery or olive or pine, but for the sake of happiness and *arete* throughout his whole life."

Diogenes continues with this theme for some time, explaining more fully his meaning and drawing upon mythology, especially upon the labors of Herakles, to illustrate his point.

While Diogenes was saying these things, many people collected around him and listened with great pleasure. Then, perhaps with the thought of Herakles and the Augean stables in mind, he stopped speaking, squatted on the ground, and took a crap. At this the crowd scattered, saying that he was crazy, and the sophists raised their din again.

146   Epiktetos 1.6.23–28   *ca.* A.D. 120?

The Stoic philosopher Epiktetos, in lecturing on the natural gifts which man possesses but which are denied to animals, touches on man's ability to endure hardships and annoyances in his quest for knowledge and understanding. He chooses as an example the experiences of a visitor to Olympia.

There are unpleasant and difficult things in life. But don't they happen at Olympia? Don't you suffer from the heat? Aren't you cramped for space? Don't you bathe badly? Don't you get soaked by rains? Don't you get your fill of noise and shouting and other annoyances? But I suspect that you compare all this to the value of the show and endure it?

147   Lucian, *Peregrinus* 19–21, 31–32, 35–37   A.D. 165

The following is excerpted from a letter in which Lucian describes to a friend an extraordinary happening at the Olympic Games of A.D. 165. This involved one Peregrinus, or Proteus as he was also known, a Cynic philosopher who had converted to Christianity in his early life, reverted to Cynicism, and then became enamoured of Indian mysticism. Lucian clearly had no great love for him. These passages show, of course, the lengths to which some were willing to go to attract attention to themselves, but they also reveal something of the activities which went on, at least in the Roman period, before and after the Olympic festival proper. The opening scene is set in a gymnasion at Elis and the speaker (perhaps Lucian himself) is rebutting one of Peregrinus' disciples who had just previously spoken. He recounts the career of Peregrinus.

Coming at last to Greece when he had been sent packing from Rome, he arrived at Olympia [A.D. 153] where at one moment he abused the Eleans, the next he tried to incite the Greeks to rebel against Rome, and the next he libelled a man who was not only outstanding in literary achievements but also prominent because of his many benefactions to Greece [Herodes Atticus]. Peregrinus attacked him particularly because he had brought water to Olympia and prevented the visitors to the festival from dying of thirst. Peregrinus accused him of making the Greeks soft, for the spectators of the Olympic Games ought to endure their thirst and—yes by Zeus—even die on account of the dryness of the place. And he said these things while he drank the very same water.

When the crowd stoned him with one accord and nearly killed him, Peregrinus—stout chap—managed to escape death by hiding in the Temple of Zeus. Afterwards, at the next Olympiad [A.D. 157], he delivered to the Greeks a speech which he had composed during the intervening four years. In this he praised the man who had brought in the water and defended himself for running away at that time.

Finally, he came to be scorned by all and no longer admired, for his stuff was all old-hat and he could find no further novelty with which to surprise those who came his way, and make them marvel and stare at him. So he concocted this ultimate bit of recklessness about the pyre and spread a story among the Greeks immediately after the last Olympic festival [A.D. 161] that he would burn himself up at the next festival. And now, they say, the faker is actually doing this, digging a pit, collecting firewood, and promising some fantastic endurance.

The speaker goes on for some time, disparaging Peregrinus and his follow-ers, and inciting the crowd against them. He then leaves the platform at the approach of one of those disciples.

When Theagenes heard the shouting, he came at once, got up, and began to rant and shout countless terrible things about the man who had just got down—I do not know the name of that excellent man. I left him busting his gut and went off to the athletes, for the *Hellanodikai* were said to be already in the Hundred Foot Room (see no. **83**) where they matched the athletes by lot.

That is what happened at Elis. When we reached Olympia, the rear chamber of the Temple of Zeus was full of people either criticizing Proteus or praising his goal, and most of them came to blows. Finally, Proteus himself, together with a huge crowd, appeared after the contest for the heralds. He had, of course, something to say about himself, telling of his life and the risks which he had run and of all the difficulties which he had endured for the sake of philosophy. He had a great deal to say, but I heard little of it due to the number of bystanders. In the end I was afraid of being crushed in the confusion, and I left, bidding a long farewell to the sophist who was so enamoured of death as to be delivering his own funeral oration.

Lucian goes on to recount a little of Peregrinus' speech and something of his satisfaction at the admiring crowd which he had excited.

The end of the Olympic Games soon came—the best Olympics which I have seen, incidentally, of the four which I have attended as a spectator. It was not easy to get a carriage since so many were leaving at that time, and so I stayed on against my will. Meanwhile, Peregrinus kept delaying, but finally announced a night upon which he would cremate himself. One of my companions invited me to go along, and so I rose at midnight and took the road to Harpina where the pyre was. This is nearly three and a half miles from Olympia as you leave by the hippodrome toward the east. As soon as we arrived we found a pyre laid in a pit about six feet deep. It was made mostly of the pitchy wood of torches, with brush in the gaps so that it would ignite quickly. When the moon was rising (she also had to see this greatest of deeds) he approached, dressed as usual, and with him were the leaders of the Cynics. Proteus, and some of the others, held a torch. Coming forward from all sides, they lit a huge fire. Peregrinus, laying aside his wallet, his cloak, and that Herakles' club, stood there in an absolutely filthy shirt. Then he asked for incense to throw on the fire. When someone produced it, he threw it into the burning pyre, and then faced south and said: "Shades of my mother and father, receive me kindly." Having said this, he jumped into the fire. He was not, however, visible for he was surrounded by the flames which had risen to a considerable height.

I did not criticize him for calling upon the spirit of his mother, but I could not restrain my laughter when he called upon the spirit of his father, for I remembered the stories that he had killed his father. The Cynics stood around the pyre, not weeping, but their silence showing some grief as they watched the fire. Finally choked with rage at them, I said: "Let's leave, you fools. It's no fun to look at a roasted old man nor to pick up that vile odor on ourselves. Or are you waiting for some painter to come along and portray you as the companions of Sokrates in prison are portrayed?" They were beside themselves and reviled me and some even went for their walking sticks. But then, after I threatened to gather up some of them and throw them into the fire so that they could follow their teacher, they shut up and kept quiet.

148   Euripides, *Hecuba* 28–30 and Fragment 868   *ca.* 424 B.C.

Given the all-pervasive character of athletics in the ancient world, it is not surprising that athletic metaphors are present in literature, including tragedy. Two of the many examples are presented here. In the first the ghost of Polydoros speaks of his own corpse. In the second the negated form of diaulos is used.

A. Now I lie on the shore, now in the surf of the sea, unmourned, unburied, washed back and forth by the many *diauloi* of the waves.

B. The gods of the underworld have a gloomy, *adiaulos*, seat for lost souls on the Acherontian lake.

VII
Women in Athletics

149 Pausanias 5.6.7–8   *ca.* A.D. 170

As one goes from Skillos down the road to Olympia, but before one crosses the Alpheios River, there is a mountain with high and very steep cliffs. The name of the mountain is Typaion. The Eleans have a law to throw off these cliffs any women who are discovered at the Olympic festival, or even on the Olympia side of the Alpheios on the days which are forbidden to women. They say that no woman has ever been caught except Kallipateira. (Some say that the name of the woman was Pherenike, not Kallipateira.) She had been widowed and, disguised like a male trainer, she took her son to Olympia to compete. When her son Peisirodos won, Kallipateira jumped over the fence with which the trainers were restrained, and exposed herself. She was thus discovered to be a woman, but they released her unpunished out of respect for her father [Diagoras of Rhodes; see below, nos. **170** and **248**], her brothers, and her son, all of whom had been victors at Olympia. They passed a law, however, that in the future trainers would have to attend the competition in the nude.

150 Pausanias 6.20.8–9   *ca.* A.D. 170

The stadium is a bank of earth on which is a seat for the sponsors of the competition. Opposite the *Hellanodikai* is an altar of white marble. Seated on this a woman watches the Olympic Games, the priestess of Demeter Chamyne; this office is bestowed on a woman from time to time by the Eleans. They do not prevent virgins from watching the games.

151a Pausanias 3.8.1 *ca.* A.D. 170

The Spartan king Archidamos had a daughter whose name was Kyniska. She was extremely ambitious to enter the competition at Olympia, and was the first woman to breed horses and the first woman to win an Olympic victory. Other women, especially Lakedaimonian women, won Olympic victories after Kyniska, but none is so famous as she.

151b *IvO* 160 396 B.C.?

A fragmentary circular statue base of black marble found at Olympia has the following inscriptions:

(on top): Kings of Sparta were my fathers and brothers. Kyniska, victorious at the chariot race with her swift-footed horses, erected this statue. I assert that I am the only woman in all Greece who won this crown.

(on front): Apelleas, son of Kallikles, made it.

151c Plutarch, *Agesilaos* 20.1 396 B.C.?

When Agesilaos noted that some of the citizens of Sparta thought that they were important because they were breeding horses, he pressured his sister Kyniska to enter a chariot in the Olympic Games [in 396 B.C.?]; he wanted to show the Greeks that an equestrian victory was the result of wealth and expenditure, not in any way the result of *arete*.

152 Xenophon, *Constitution of the Lakedaimonians* 1.4 *ca.* 375 B.C.

In his description of the constitution of Sparta Xenophon describes the work of the legendary lawgiver, Lykourgos.

Lykourgos, thinking that the first and foremost function of the freeborn woman was to bear children, ordered that the female should do no less body building than the male. He thus established contests for the women in footraces and in strength just like those for the men, believing that stronger children come from parents who are both strong.

153 Plutarch, *Lykourgos* 14.2–15.1   *ca.* A.D. 100

Lykourgos exercised the bodies of the virgins with footraces and wrestling and throwing the *diskos* and the *akon* so that their offspring might grow forth from strong roots in strong bodies, and so that they might be patient and strong in childbirth and struggle well and easily with its pains. He removed from them all softness and daintiness and effeminacy and accustomed the girls no less than the boys to parade in the nude and to dance and sing at certain religious festivals in the presence of the young men as spectators. . . .

The nudity of the virgins was not shameful, for modesty was present and intemperance was absent, but it implanted plain habits and an eager rivalry for high good health in them, and it imbued them with a noble frame of mind as having a share in *arete* and in pride. Whence it came to them to speak and to think as it is said that Gorgo the wife of Leonidas did. When some woman—a foreigner it would appear—said to her, "Only Spartan women rule men," she answered, "Only Spartan women bear men."

These customs were also a stimulant for marriage—I mean the parades of undressed virgins and their games in the view of young men who were led on by an axiom "not geometric, but erotic," to quote Plato. Moreover, Lykourgos prescribed dishonor for bachelors.

154 Euripides, *Andromache* 595–601   426 B.C.

Euripides, reflecting a common Athenian attitude toward the place of Spartan women in athletics, has Peleus chide Menelaos specifically for the behavior of Helen and then continue on to say:

A Spartan girl could not be chaste even if she wanted. They abandon their houses to run around with young men, with naked thighs and open clothes, sharing the same racetracks and *palaistrai*—a situation which I find insufferable. And if your girls are so trained is it any wonder that your Spartan women grow up without knowing what chastity is?

155 Thucydides 3.104   423 B.C.

The Athenians first celebrated their quadrennial festival at Delos after the purification [540–530 B.C.]. There had been a great gathering at Delos in olden times by the Ionians and the surrounding islanders. They made *theorias* together with their wives and children, even as the Ionians now celebrate the Ephesian Games. There had been a *gymnikos agon* and a *mousikos agon,* and the cities sent groups of dancers.

156 Pollux 4.120 (see no. **178**) *ca.* A.D. 180

Bibasis *was a type of Lakonian dancing competition which was established not only for boys but also for girls. The dancers jumped up and touched their buttocks with the heels of their feet, and they counted the jumps whence came the epigram of one woman:*

A thousand kicks in the *bibasis,* I kicked most of all the girls.

157 Pausanias 6.24.9 *ca.* A.D. 170

In the *agora* of Elis there is also a building for the Sixteen Women, and there they weave the *peplos* for Hera.

158 Pausanias 5.16.2–7 (see no. **109**) *ca.* A.D. 170

Every fourth year at Olympia the Sixteen Women weave a *peplos* for Hera, and they also sponsor the Heraia competition. This contest is a footrace for virgins who are of different ages. They run in three categories: the youngest first, the slightly older ones next, and then the oldest virgins are the last to run. They run as follows: their hair hangs down on them, a *chiton* reaches to a little above the knee, and the right shoulder is bared as far as the breast. They also use the Olympic stadium, but the track is shortened by one-sixth. The winners receive a crown of olive and a portion of the cow sacrificed to Hera, and they have the right to dedicate statues with their names inscribed upon them. Those who serve the Sixteen Women are, like the sponsors of these games, women. They trace the competition of the virgins also back to antiquity. They say that Hippodameia, out of gratitude to Hera for her marriage to Pelops, collected Sixteen Women and, with them, sponsored the first Heraia. . . . The Sixteen Women also arrange two choral dances; they call one that of Physkoa, the other that of Hippodameia. . . . The Eleans are now divided into eight tribes, and from each they choose two women.

159 Pausanias 3.13.7 *ca.* A.D. 170

. . . there is a shrine of a hero who they say led Dionysos on the road to Sparta. The so-called Daughters of Dionysos and the Daughters of Leukippos sacrifice to this hero before they sacrifice to the god. Footraces have been established for the other eleven so-called Daughters of Dionysos.

160 Pausanias 5.8.11   *ca.* A.D. 170

Afterwards they added the *synoris* for *poloi* . . . the victor was Belistiche, a woman from the coast of Macedonia . . . at the 128th Olympiad [264 B.C.].

161 Athenaeus 13.609E–610A   *ca.* A.D. 228

I know of a women's beauty contest that was once established. Nikias, in his *Arkadika*, says that it was established by Kypselos [650–625 B.C.], who founded a city in the plain by the Alpheios River. In this city he settled some Parrhasians and set up a precinct and an altar to Eleusinian Demeter and in her festival he held his beauty contest; the first winner was his wife Herodike. This *agon* is still held today, and the women competitors are called "gold-bearers." Theophrastos [*ca.* 319 B.C.] says that there is a beauty contest for men at Elis which is judged with all seriousness and the winners get weapons as prizes. Dionysios of Leuktra says that these are dedicated to Athena, and the victor, beribboned by his friends, comes along with the procession to her temple. Myrsilos, in his *Historical Paradoxes*, testifies that the crown is made of myrtle. This same Theophrastos says that in some places women's judgings of sobriety and housekeeping take place, just as among the barbarians, and in other places there are beauty contests as at Tenedos and Lesbos.

162 *SIG*³ 802   A.D. 47

The following inscription was found at Delphi on a limestone statue base which originally supported the statue of three sisters.

Hermesianax son of Dionysios, citizen of Kaisarea Tralles as well as of Athens and Delphi, dedicates this to Pythian Apollo on behalf of his daughters who hold the same citizenship:

For Tryphosa, who won the Pythian Games when Antigonos and Kleomachidas were *agonothetai*, and the following Isthmian Games when Iouventios Proklos was *agonothetes*, in the *stadion*, first of the virgins.

For Hedea, who won the chariot race in armor at the Isthmian Games when Cornelius Pulcher was *agonothetes*, and the *stadion* at the Nemean Games when Antigonos was *agonothetes* and at Sikyon when Menoitas was *agonothetes*. She also won the *kithara*-singing in the boys' category at the Sebasteia in Athens when Nouios son of Philinos was *agonothetes*.

For Dionysia, who won the Isthmian Games when Antigonos was *agonothetes*, and the games of Asklepios at sacred Epidauros when Nikoteles was *agonothetes*, in the *stadion*.

VIII
Athletes and Heroes

163a   Pausanias 6.14.5–8   *ca.* A.D. 170

Dameas of Kroton made the statue of Milo, son of Diotimos, also of Kroton.
Milo won six victories in the *pale* at Olympia, including one in the boys' category [536 B.C.]. At Delphi he won six times in the men's category and once
in the boys'. He came to Olympia to wrestle for the seventh time [in 512
B.C.], but he could not best his fellow citizen Timastheos who was younger
than he and who refused to come to close quarters with him. It is also said
that Milo carried his own statue into the *Altis,* and there are stories about him
concerning the pomegranate and the *diskos.* He would grip a pomegranate so
that no one could wrest it away and yet not squeeze it so hard as to bruise it.
He would stand upon a greased *diskos* and make fools out of those who would
rush at him and try to knock him off the *diskos.* There were other things
which he did to show off. He would tie a cord around his forehead as if it were
a ribbon or a crown. He would then hold his breath until the veins in his head
were filled with blood and then break the cord by the strength of those veins.
Another story is that he would let his right arm hang down along his side to
the elbow, but turn his forearm out at right angles with the thumb up and the
fingers in a row stretched out straight so that the little finger was the lowest,
and no one could force the little finger away from the other fingers. They say
that he was killed by wild beasts. In the land of Kroton he happened upon a
dried-up tree trunk into which wedges had been placed to split it. Milo, in his
vanity, stuck his hands into the trunk, the wedges slipped, and Milo was
caught in the trunk until wolves discovered him.

163b   Athenaeus, *The Gastronomers* 10.412F   *ca.* A.D. 228

Milo of Kroton used to eat twenty pounds of meat and twenty pounds of bread and wash it down with eight quarts of wine. At Olympia he hoisted a four-year-old bull on his shoulders and carried it around the stadium, and then butchered it and ate it all alone in one day.

164   Pausanias 6.9.6–7   *ca.* A.D. 170

It is said that at the Olympic festival in 492 B.C. Kleomedes of Astypalaia killed Ikkos of Epidauros during the *pyx*. When he was convicted by the *Hellanodikai* of foul play and stripped of his victory, he went out of his mind with grief and returned to Astypalaia. Once there he attacked a school with about sixty children in it and pulled down the column which supported the roof which fell on the children. When the townspeople came after him with rocks and stones, he took refuge in the sanctuary of Athena where he hid in a box with the lid closed over him. Try as they might, the Astypalaians could not open the box. Finally, they smashed the boards of the box, but found neither Kleomedes nor his corpse. Puzzled by this, they sent representatives to Delphi to ask what had happened to Kleomedes. The Pythia, they say, responded in the following way:

> Kleomedes of Astypalaia is the last of heroes.
> Honor with sacrifices him who is no longer mortal.

From that time the Astypalaians worshipped Kleomedes as a hero.

165   Lucian, *Assembly of the Gods* 12   *ca.* A.D. 170

Apollo, you are no longer popular, but already every stone and every altar that is drenched in oil and covered with wreaths and provided with a swindler—and there are plenty of them—deliver oracles. And already the statue of the athlete Polydamas cures those who have fevers at Olympia and so does Theagenes on Thasos.

166a   Pausanias 6.6.4–6   *ca.* A.D. 170

Euthymos was born in the land of the Lokrians in Italy; they live near the Zephyrian cape. His father was called Astykles, but the locals say that he was the son, not of this man, but of the Kaikinos River, which divides the territory of Lokris from that of Rhegion. Although Euthymos won the victory in the *pyx* in the 74th Olympiad [484 B.C.], he was not successful at the next Olympiad. The reason was that Theagenes of Thasos wanted to win at one Olympiad both the *pyx* and the *pankration*. He beat Euthymos in the *pyx*, but did not have enough strength left to win the olive in the *pankration* because he was already exhausted by his fight with Euythmos. For this the *Hellanodikai* penalized Theagenes with a fine of $132,000 to be paid to Zeus, and another $132,000 to be paid to Euthymos. They judged that Theagenes had entered the *pyx* merely to spite Euthymos. At the 76th Olympiad [476 B.C.] Theagenes paid in full the fine to Zeus, and did not enter the *pyx* competition, as compensation to Euthymos. In this Olympiad, and again in the next [472 B.C.], Euthymos won the crown in the *pyx*.

*(See above, no. **129**.)*

166b   *IvO* 144   472 B.C.

A statue base of white marble found at Olympia has the following inscription:

Euthymos of Lokroi, son of Astykles, having won three times at Olympia, set up this figure to be admired by the mortals. Euthymos of Lokroi Epizephyrioi dedicated it. Pythagoras of Samos made it.

167a   Pausanias 6.11.2–9   *ca.* A.D. 170

The next statue at Olympia is that of Theagenes the son of Timosthenes of Thasos. The Thasians, however, say that Theagenes was not the son of Timosthenes, who was a priest of the Thasian Herakles, but of a phantom of Herakles which, disguised as Timosthenes, had intercourse with Theagenes' mother. They say that when Theagenes was nine years old, as he was going home from school, the bronze statue of some god which stood in the *agora* caught his fancy, so he picked up the statue, put it on his shoulders, and carried it home. The citizens were outraged by what he had done, but one of their respected elders convinced them not to kill the boy, but to order him to go home immediately and bring the statue back to the *agora*. He did this and quickly became famous for his strength as his feat was shouted through the length and breadth of Greece. I have already related the most famous of Theagenes' achievements at Olympia [no. **166a**]. It was then for the first time in the records that the *pankration* was won *akoniti*; the victor was Dromeus of Mantineia. At the next festival [476 B.C.], Theagenes won the *pankration*. He also won three times at Delphi in the *pyx*. His nine victories at Nemea and ten at Isthmia were divided between the *pyx* and the *pankration*. At Phthia in Thessaly he ceased training for the *pyx* and the *pankration*, but concentrated upon winning fame among the Greeks for his running, and he defeated those who entered in the *dolichos*. He won a total of 1,400 victories. After he died, one of his enemies came every night to the statue of Theagenes in Thasos, and flogged the bronze image as though he were whipping Theagenes himself. The statue stopped this outrage by falling upon the man, but his sons prosecuted the statue for murder. The Thasians threw the statue into the sea, following the precepts of Drako who, when he wrote the homicide laws for the Athenians, imposed banishment even upon inanimate objects which fell and killed a man. As time went by, however, famine beset the Thasians and they sent envoys to Delphi. Apollo instructed them to recall their exiles. They did so, but there was still no end to the famine. They sent to the Pythia for a second time and said that, although they had followed the instructions, the wrath of the gods still was upon them. The Pythia then responded to them:

> You do not remember your great Theagenes.

The Thasians were then in a quandary, for they could not think how to retrieve the statue of Theagenes. But fishermen, who had set out for fish, happened to catch the statue in their nets and brought it back to land. The Thasians set the statue back up in its original position, and are now accustomed to sacrifice to Theagenes as to a god. I know of many places, both among the Greeks and among the barbarians, where statues of Theagenes have been set up. He is worshipped by the natives as a healing power.

167b   BCH 64–65 (1940–41) 175 *ca.* A.D. 100

This inscription was discovered at Thasos outside the shrine of the heroized Theagenes. It is inscribed upon a circular marble block which has a large cavity hollowed out of its center with a slit connecting to the top surface of the block; in other words, it is an offering box with the slit representing the place for deposit of money.

Those who sacrifice to Theagenes are to contribute not less than $3.66 in the offering box. Anyone who does not make a contribution as written above will be remembered. The money collected each year is to be given to the High Priest, and he is to save it until it has reached a total of $22,000. When this total has been collected, the *boule* and the *demos* shall decide whether it is to be spent for some ornamentation or for repairs to the shrine of Theagenes.

168   Pausanias 6.5.1–9   *ca.* A.D. 170

The statue on a high base is the work of Lysippos, and it is of the tallest of
all men except those called heroes. . . . Other men have won glorious victories in the *pankration,* but Polydamas the son of Nikias of Skotoussa has
other feats to his credit in addition to his crowns for the *pankration* [includ-
ing one at Olympia in 408 B.C.]. The mountainous region of Thrace which
lies on this side of the Nestos River as it flows through the land of Abdera
breeds many wild beasts including lions. The lions frequently roam as far
south as the region around Mt. Olympos, one side of which faces north
toward Macedonia, the other south toward Thessaly and the Peneios River.
On this part of Mt. Olympos Polydamas killed a lion, a huge and powerful
wild beast, without the use of a weapon. His ambition to rival the labors of
Herakles drove him to do this, for Herakles thus killed the lion of Nemea
according to the legend. Polydamas also went into a herd of cattle and
grabbed the largest and strongest bull by one of its hind feet. Polydamas
held the hoof fast despite the bull's leaps and struggles until it finally put
forth all its strength and escaped, but left its hoof behind in the hand of
Polydamas. It is also said of him that he stopped a charioteer who was
driving his chariot at a high speed. Seizing the back of the chariot with one
hand, he brought both horses and driver to a halt. . . . But in the end, as
Homer says, those who glory in their strength are doomed to perish by it,
and so Polydamas perished through his own might. He entered a cave
together with his best friends to escape the summer heat. As bad luck would
have it, the roof began to crack and it was obvious that the cave could not
hold up much longer and would fall in quickly. Recognizing the disaster that
was coming, the others turned and ran out; but Polydamas decided to stay.
He held up his hands in the belief that he could prevent the cave from
falling in and that he would not be crushed by the mountain. His end came
here.

*A part of the base of the statue of Polydamas by Lysippos has been found
at Olympia (inv. no. A 45). On the front Polydamas wrestles with one of
the Immortals—the bodyguards of the king of Persia—while the king
watches. On the left side of the base Polydamas wrestles with the Lion,
while on the right he is seated on the Lion's skin, but the top part is broken away and one cannot know his specific action. In addition, there is a
portrait in Copenhagen (inv. no. 542) that has been identified as that of
Polydamas. Neither base nor head show any traces of oil; see above,
no. 165.*

169   Pausanias 7.17.13–14   *ca.* 170 A.D.

The tomb of the runner Oibotas is also in the territory of Dyme. He
received nothing special from the Achaians although he was the first of
them to be an Olympic victor [756 B.C.]. Oibotas therefore made a curse that
no other Achaian should win an Olympic victory. Some god took care that
the curse of Oibotas would be effective, but the Achaians ultimately sent to
Delphi to learn why the crown of the Olympics was eluding them. So they
paid other honors to Oibotas and dedicated a statue of him at Olympia when
Sostratos of Pellene won the *stadion* for *paides* [460 B.C.]. Even still in my
time those Achaians who are about to go to compete in the Olympics sacrifice to Oibotas as to a hero and, if they win, place a crown on the statue of
Oibotas at Olympia.

170   Pausanias 6.7.1–5   *ca.* 170 A.D.

Next one comes to the statues of the Rhodian athletes, Diagoras and his family [nos. **149** and **248**]. They were set up one after another in the following
order. Akousilaos won a crown for the *pyx* in the men's category. Doreius, the
youngest, won at Olympia in the *pankration* three times in a row. Even earlier than Doreius, Damagetos beat the entrants in the *pankration*. These
were all brothers and the sons of Diagoras, and next to them is the statue of
Diagoras who won a victory for the *pyx* in the men's category. . . . In addition, the sons of the daughters of Diagoras practiced the *pyx* and won
Olympic victories, Eukles the son of Kallianax and Kallipateira—daughter of
Diagoras—in the men's category, and Peisirodos, whose mother came to
Olympia dressed as a male *gymnastes,* in the boys' category. The statue of
this Peisirodos stands in the *Altis* next to that of his maternal grandfather.
They say that Diagoras came to Olympia together with his sons Akousilaos
and Damagetos. When the young men won, they carried their father
through the crowd at the festival while the Greeks pelted him with flowers
[see no. **110**] and called him fortunate in his sons. . . . In addition to his
Olympic victories, Doreius the son of Diagoras had eight Isthmian and seven
Nemean victories, and it is said that he won a Pythian victory *akoniti.* . . . Of
the obvious friends of the Lakedaimonians, Doreius was the most obvious,
for he fought against the Athenians with his own ships until captured and
taken alive by an Attic *trireme* to Athens. The Athenians, before Doreius was
brought to them, were angry with him and always threatening him, but
when they met in the *ekklesia* and saw such a great and famous man brought
to them as a prisoner, they changed their mind and let him go free even
though they could, in justice, have done him real damage.

171a Pausanias 7.27.7   *ca.* A.D. 170

The people of Pellene will not even mention the name of Chairon who won twice in the Isthmian Games and four times in the Olympics [356–344 B.C.] in the *pale*. This is because he overthrew the constitution of Pellene and received from Alexander the Great the most invidious of all gifts—to be established as tyrant of one's own fatherland.

171b Athenaeus, *The Gastronomers* 9.509B   *ca.* A.D. 228

Some of the philosophers of the Academy today live wickedly and disgracefully. They are famous although they have gained fortunes by means of sacrilege and trickery; they remind me of Chairon of Pellene who attended the lectures of Plato and Xenokrates. He became the bitter tyrant of his city and not only drove out the best citizens of the city, but also gave their property to their slaves and forced their wives to marry their slaves. Such were the benefits which he derived from the beautiful *Republic* and the illegal *Laws*.

172a Diodorus Siculus 17.100–101   *ca.* 30 B.C.

Alexander the Great held a huge banquet for his friends [325 B.C.]. During the drinking something occurred which is worth mention. Among the companions of the king was a Macedonian named Koragos who was very strong in body and who had distinguished himself frequently in battle. The drink made him pugnacious, and he challenged to a duel one Dioxippos of Athens, an athlete who had won several glorious victories [including one in the *pankration* at Olympia in 336 B.C.]. As might be expected of those in their cups, the guests egged them on and Dioxippos accepted the challenge. Alexander set the day for the battle, and when the time came for the duel thousands of men assembled for the spectacle. Because he was one of them, the Macedonians and Alexander rooted for Koragos, while the Greeks favored Dioxippos. Koragos came onto the field of honor clad in the finest armor, while the Athenian was naked with his body oiled and carrying a well-balanced club.

Both men were marvellous to see in their magnificent physical conditions and their desire for the fight. The spectators anticipated a veritable battle of gods. The Macedonian looked like Ares as he inspired terror through his stature and the brilliance of his weapons; Dioxippos resembled Herakles in his strength and athletic training, and even more so because he carried a club.

As they approached each other, the Macedonian hurled his spear from the proper distance, but Dioxippos bent his body slightly and avoided it. Then the Macedonian poised his long pike and charged, but when he came within reach, the Greek struck the pike with his club and splintered it. Now Koragos was reduced to fighting with his sword, but as he went to draw it, Dioxippos leaped upon him, grabbed his swordhand in his own left hand, and with his other hand he upset his opponent's balance and knocked his feet from under him. As Koragos fell to the ground, Dioxippos placed his foot on the other's neck and, holding his club in the air, looked to the crowd.

The spectators were in an uproar because of the man's incredible skill and superiority. Alexander motioned for Koragos to be released, then broke up the gathering and left, clearly annoyed at the defeat of the Macedonian. Dioxippos released his fallen foe and left as winner of a resounding victory. His compatriots bedecked him with ribbons for the victory which he had won on behalf of all the Greeks. But Fortune did not permit him to boast of his victory for very long.

The king became increasingly antagonistic toward Dioxippos, and Alexander's friends and indeed all the Macedonians about the court, envious of Dioxippos' *arete*, persuaded one of the servants to hide a gold drinking cup under the pillow of his dining couch. During the next *symposion* they pretended to find the cup and accused him of theft. This placed Dioxippos in a shameful and disgraceful position. He understood that the Macedonians were in a conspiracy against him, and he got up and left the *symposion*. When he had returned to his own quarters, he wrote a note to Alexander about the trick which had been played on him, gave this to his servants for delivery to the king, and then committed suicide. He may have been ill-advised to accept the duel, but he was even more foolish to have done away with himself, for it gave his critics the chance to say that it was a real hardship to have great strength of body, but little of mind.

172b   Aelian, *Varia Historia* 12.58   *ca.* A.D. 220

Dioxippos the Athenian athlete was victorious at Olympia and was celebrating his *eiselasis* into Athens in accordance with athletic custom. A crowd gathered from all around and was watching him, hanging on his every move. In the crowd was a woman particularly distinguished by her beauty who had come to see what was going on. The moment Dioxippos saw her he was beaten by her beauty. He could not look away from her and kept turning to keep her in sight. Since he was blushing, it became clear to the crowd that he was not idly staring at her. Diogenes of Sinope understood what was happening and said to his neighbors: "Look at your great big athlete, throttled by a little girl."

173   Aelian, *Varia Historia* 10.19   *ca.* A.D. 220

Eurydamas of Cyrene won the *pyx*, even though his opponent knocked out his teeth. To keep his opponent from having any satisfaction, he swallowed them.

174   *Anthologia Graeca* 11.82

Charmos once ran the *dolichos* against five competitors, but came in seventh. You will probably ask, "Since there were six contestants, how could he come in seventh?" The reason was that a friend of his ran onto the track shouting "Go Charmos!" Thus he came in seventh, and if he had five more friends he would have finished twelfth.

175   *Anthologia Graeca* 11.85

Once while running the *hoplitodromos*, Marcus was still running at midnight. The custodians mistook him for one of the honorary stone statues which line the track, and locked up the stadium. The next day they opened the stadium and found that Marcus had finished the first lap.

IX
Ball Playing

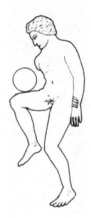

176 Athenaeus, *The Gastronomers* 1.14F–15A   *ca.* A.D. 228

In this passage Athenaeus quotes from Antiphanes who was a comic poet of the fourth century B.C., and from Juba of Mauretania who wrote in the early first century after Christ.

The so-called *folliculus* was invented by Atticus of Naples, the *paidotribes*, for the exercises of Pompey the Great. The game which is called, on account of the ball, *harpaston* used to be called *phaininda*. I like this game best of all.

Ball games produce considerable exertion and fatigue, and severe twistings of the neck. Thus Antiphanes says: "Ouch, what a pain in the neck I've got." Antiphanes depicts the game of *phaininda* as follows: "He caught the ball and laughed as he passed it to one player at the same time as he dodged another. He knocked another player out of the way, and picked one up and set him on his feet, and all the while there were screams and shouts: 'Out of bounds!' 'Too far!' 'Past him!' 'Over his head!' 'Under!' 'Over!' 'Short!' 'Back in the huddle!'"

The game was called *phaininda* either from the feinting of the ball players, or the name of its inventor who was, according to Juba of Mauretania, Phainestios the *paidotribes*.

177 Galen, *On Exercise with the Small Ball*   ca. A.D. 180

Galen began his career as an obscure gladiator and medical trainer, but rose to become the court physician of the emperor Marcus Aurelius. He does not hark back to an earlier period, but reflects the practices of his own day. In these we can see a change to a more scientific system of physical education which had evolved from the teachings of generations of gymnasium trainers.

The most eminent philosophers and physicians of antiquity have discussed adequately the benefits to health of gymnastic exercises and diet, but no one has ever set forth the superiority of exercises with the small ball. I am thus justified in setting forth my thoughts on the subject.

I believe that the best of all exercises is the one which not only exercises the body, but also refreshes the spirit. The men who invented hunting were wise and well acquainted with the nature of man, for they mixed its exertions with pleasure, delight, and rivalry. Of course, there is a refreshment common to all exercises, but there are special advantages to the exercises with the small ball as I will now show.

First is its convenience. If you think of how much equipment and time is needed for hunting, you know that no politician or craftsman can participate in such sports, for they require a wealthy man with plenty of equipment and leisure time. But even the poorest man can play ball, for it requires no nets nor weapons nor horses nor hunting dogs, but only a ball and a small one at that. It does not interfere with a man's other pursuits and causes him to neglect none of them. And what could be more convenient than a game in which everyone, no matter his status or career, can participate?

You will also find that it is the best all-around exercise if you stop to think about the possibilities and the natures of the other exercises. You will find that one is violent, another gentle; that one exercises the upper part of the body, or some part of the body such as the hips or the head or the hands or the chest, instead of the whole body. None keeps all the parts of the body equally in motion; none has a pace which can be speeded up and slowed down again. Only the exercise with the small ball achieves all this.

When the players line up on opposite sides and exert themselves to keep the one in the middle from getting the ball, then it is a violent exercise with many neck-holds mixed in with wrestling holds. Thus the head and the neck are exercised by the neck-holds, and the sides and chest and stomach are exercised by the hugs and shoves and tugs and the other wrestling holds. In this game the hips and legs are violently stretched and strained, for they provide a base for such exertion. The combination of running forward, backward, and jumping sideways is no small exercise for the legs; if the truth be told, this is the only exercise which puts all parts of the leg in motion. There is exertion on one set of tendons and muscles in running forward, upon another set in running backward, and upon yet another in jumping sideways. The man who moves his legs in only one motion, as for example the runner, exercises them irregularly and unevenly.

Just as ball playing is a good exercise for the legs, so it is even better for the arms, for it is customary to catch the ball in every sort of position. The variety of positions will strain different muscles to varying degrees at different times. You will also understand that ball playing trains the eye if you think about how the player will not catch the ball if he has not judged its flight accurately. The player will also sharpen his critical abilities by planning how to catch the ball and stay out of the middle, and how to snatch the ball if he happens to be in the middle. Thinking alone will keep weight down, but if it is mixed with some exercise and rivalry which ends in pleasure, it promotes health in the body and intelligence in the mind. This is an important benefit if an exercise can aid both the body and the mind toward the *arete* which is inherent in each.

You can easily understand that ball playing trains for the two most important maneuvers which a state entrusts to its generals: to attack at the proper time and to defend the booty already amassed. There is no other exercise so suited to training in the guarding of gains, the retrieval of losses, and the foresight of the plan of the enemy. Most exercises produce the opposite effects by making the mind slow, sleepy, and dull. Even those who compete in the wrestling at the *stephanitic* games tend more toward fleshiness than toward the practice of *arete*; at least most of them have grown fat and have difficulty in breathing. Such men are of no use as generals in war or as administrators of imperial and civil business. It is better to give a job to pigs than to them.

You may think that I favor running and other weight-reducing exercises. That is not so, for I condemn a lack of moderation in anything. Therefore I do not approve of running, for it reduces the weight too much and provides no training in courage. Victory in war does not belong to those who can run away the fastest, but those who are able to prevail in close encounters. The Spartans did not become the most powerful because they could run the fastest, but because they had the courage to stand and fight. As far as health is concerned, any exercise is unhealthy in direct proportion to its unequal development of all parts of the body. Thus in running some parts of the body are overly exerted, while other parts are not exercised at all. This is not good, for it nourishes the seeds of disease and weakens strength.

I especially favor that exercise which promotes sufficient health for the body, harmonious development of its parts, and *arete* in the spirit. All of these are to be found in exercise with the small ball. It can benefit the mind in every way, and it exercises all parts of the body equally. It thus contributes to health and to moderation in physical condition, for it causes neither excessive corpulence nor immoderate thinness. It is also suitable for actions which require strength and for those demanding speed. Thus the most strenuous form of ball playing is in no way inferior to other exercises.

Let us consider its most gentle form. There are times when we need this form due to our age which is either not yet ready for severe exertion, or no longer able to exercise strenuously, or due to a desire for relaxation or for recuperation from an illness. I believe that in this form ball playing is also superior to all the other exercises. No other exercise is so gentle if you wish to practice it gently. You need only to move in moderation at some times, and to stay put at others. Afterwards one should have a soft rubdown with oil and a hot bath. This is the most gentle of exercises, and it is thus beneficial for one who needs rest, for restoring ill health, and for old and young alike.

Moderate exercises between the extremes which I have already described can also be practiced with the small ball. One should be aware of this in order to take full advantage of the game. If, as happens to all of us, some necessary work has overtaxed some parts of the body, they can be rested while the parts which were idle can be exercised until the whole body has been equally exercised. Throwing from a distance and with vigor requires little or no exertion by the legs, and thus rests the lower part of the body while exercising the upper parts rather strenuously. Running swiftly over a large area while throwing only occasionally from a distance exercises the lower parts more than the upper. Quickness and speed in the game, without heavy exertion, exercise the lungs. Vigor in tackling, throwing, and catching, but without speed, stretch and strengthen the body. When vigor and speed are both present, both the body and the lungs will be exercised. The proper amount of stretching and relaxing cannot be written. This cannot be predicted, but must be learned for each individual by experience. Even the correct exercise is ruined if it is not used in the proper amounts. This should be the business of the *paidotribes* who is in charge of the exercises.

Let me now conclude this discussion. I do not want to omit from my list of the advantages of ball playing that it does not have the dangers which most other exercises have. Sprinting has killed many men by rupturing important blood vessels. So too a loud and prolonged shouting has caused serious injuries to many men. Violent horseback riding has ruptured the kidneys and injured the chest and sometimes the testes. I do not even mention the stumblings of horses which have frequently thrown riders from their seats and killed them. So too the *halma* and the *diskos* and exercises in digging have injured many. Do I even need to speak of wrestlers? They are all lame or sprained or bruised or permanently disabled in some part of their bodies. If, in addition to the advantages already discussed, there is also present in ball playing a freedom from danger, then this must be the best exercise of all.

178   Pollux 9.103–107 and 119   *ca.* A.D. 180

Pollux, who was a rhetorician and held a professorship at the University of Athens, wrote a thesaurus of terms and names. Although his work survives to us only in the form of a ninth-century A.D. abridgement, even this abbreviated form contains much of interest. The following passage is part of a section concerned with the names of children's games.

The names of children's ball games were *episkyros, phaininda, aporrhaxis, ourania*. *Episkyros* was also called *ephebike* and commonball. It was usually played with opposing teams of equal number. In the middle a line was drawn with a chip of stone which they called a *skyros*. They set the ball on this line, and each team drew another line behind the opposition. The team which got the ball first threw it over the opposition whose job it was to grab the ball while it was still moving and throw it back the other way. This would continue until one team had pushed the other over the back line.

   Phaininda got its name either from its inventor, Phainindos, or from the word for feinting, since the player fakes a throw to one player, but actually throws to another, and thus deceives the player who expected the ball. This resembles the game with the small ball which is called *harpaston* from the word for snatching away. One might call *phaininda* the game with the soft ball.

   Aporrhaxis has the form of bouncing the ball vigorously on the ground, and dribbling it again and again with the hand. The number of bounces is counted.

   Ourania is played with one player bending backward and throwing the ball up into the sky. The others compete in snatching the ball before it falls back to the ground. . . . When they dribbled a ball against a wall, they counted the number of bounces. The loser was called the donkey and had to do whatever he was told. The winner was called the king and gave the orders. . . .

Ephedrismos is played by setting up a stone at a distance and trying to hit it with balls or with stones. The one who does not knock it over has to carry the one who did knock it over, with his eyes held shut by the other one, until he happens upon the stone which is called the *dioros*.

X

Gymnasion, Athletics, and Education

179 Vitruvius, *On Architecture* 5.11   *ca.* 28 B.C.

Vitruvius was a practicing architect whose treatise on architecture is the only one of many in antiquity which has survived. In this passage he describes the layout of a Greek athletic complex, and his description corresponds very well to the third-century B.C. palaistra-gymnasion *buildings at Olympia.*

Although the construction of a *palaistra* is not common in Italy, its plan has been handed down and it therefore seems worthwhile to explain the *palaistra* and to show how it is planned among the Greeks.

In *palaistrai* square or oblong peristyle courts are to be made with a perimeter of two *stadia,* a distance which the Greeks call *diaulos.* Three sides of the court are to be single colonnades; the fourth side is to be the one which faces south and it is to be a double colonnade so that, when there are rain storms with heavy winds, the rain will not reach the interior of the colonnade.

On the three sides of the court with single colonnades there are to be planned spacious *exedrai* with seats where philosophers, rhetoricians, and others who delight in studies can sit and discuss their subjects. In the double colonnade, however, the following elements are to be located: in the middle there is to be an *ephebeion* (this is an especially large *exedra* with seats) the length of which is to be one-third greater than its width. Next to this on the right as we face it is to be the *korykion*. Next after this room is to be a *konisterion*, and next to the *konisterion* at the corner of the colonnade is to be a cold bath which the Greeks call a *loutron*. To the left of the *ephebeion* is to be an *elaiothesion*, and next after the *elaiothesion* is to be the *frigidarium*, and from this room is to be the entrance to the furnace room at the corner of the colonnade. Next behind the furnace room toward the interior from the *frigidarium* is to be placed a vaulted sweating room with its length twice its width. Part of the space behind this room is to be for the *laconicum* and the other part, at the corner of the building, is to be for a warm bath. These are the arrangements within the *palaistra*.

Outside the *palaistra* three colonnades are to be arranged. One of these is to be entered from the peristyle of the *palaistra*. The other two colonnades are to have running tracks and be located to the left and to the right of the first colonnade. Of these colonnades, the one which faces north is to be double and especially wide; the others are to be single colonnades. Within these colonnades there are to be walkways at least ten feet wide along the back wall and along the columns. The central area is to be excavated down to a level track a foot and one-half below the walkways with steps down from the walkways to the track which is to be at least twelve feet wide. Thus the clothes of those on the walkways will not be stained by the oil of those who are exercising. This sort of colonnade is called a *xystos* by the Greeks whose athletes exercise during the winter in covered tracks a *stadion* in length. Next to the *xystos* and to the double colonnade are to be open-air walkways which the Greeks call *paradromides*. Here the athletes exercise even in the winter when the weather is good. The *xystoi* are to be laid out so that there are groves of plane trees between the two colonnades, and walkways are to be made of cement among the trees. Behind a *xystos* the stadium is to be planned so that large crowds can watch the athletes in comfort.

180   *ID 1417AI.118–154*   155 B.C.

The following is one of a series of inventories from the island of Delos, listing the valuable moveable articles which were handed from one set of annual officials to those of the next year. The list is organized by building, one of which is of particular interest in providing an idea of the various "furnishings" which were to be found in ancient athletic buildings. We know from other inscriptions that most of the dedicators of the statues listed below (e.g. Tlepolemos and Hegeos) were either gymnasiarchs or vice-

gymnasiarchs. The various dedicatory torches, shields, and other similar gear should be recognized as trophies from victories in local festivals.

IN THE *GYMNASION*. Bronze items: ON THE RIGHT OF ONE ENTERING THE PERISTYLE: an Eros, about two feet high on a column, holding a lion skin and a club, a dedication of Tlepolemos and Hegeos; a torch on the wall, a dedication of Eukleides the Athenian; an archaic helmet box with copper inlay, without inscription. IN THE NEXT COLONNADE: a totally nude male statue. BY THE *APODYTERION* (on the right): a torch, dedication of Demokrates the Athenian; a two-foot-tall statue of Herakles on a base, dedication of Aphthonetos. ON THE LEFT OF THE *APODYTERION:* an Eros about two feet high and a water jar on a stone base, dedication of Oineos; on the right of the Eros a torch on the wall, dedication of Protogenes of Alexandria; another small statuette on the wall, dedication of Erasinos and Paches; a seated statue of Herakles about a foot tall, dedication of Apollodoros and Tlepolemos; a seated statuette of Apollo about a foot tall and holding a *kithara*, dedication of Mantitheos and Aristeas; another statuette about three feet tall, dedication of Autokles. IN THE NEXT COLONNADE: a totally nude male statue (in the *Exedra*) holding a staff, dedication of the Delians; another statuette (in the *Exedra*) about two feet tall built into the wall, without inscription; a statue of Herakles about two feet tall having a lion-skin mantle, without inscription; a statue of Pallas about two feet tall in a frame, dedication of Satyros of Kiphissia; and two torches and other small figures about two feet tall in a frame, without inscription; two small torches, one a dedication of Diotimos son of Berenikides, the other of Eumenes. IN THE *SPHAIRISTERA* on the sundial: a small statue of Triton. TOWARD THE *APODYTERION:* a female statue holding a drinking cup in her hands, dedication of Aristion son of Theodoros; ten bronze shields. IN THE CUSTODIAN'S OFFICE: (unweighed) two water jugs of which one is complete, the other without handles and with the neck broken through; a complete holy water basin; two jars without inscription; an urn; the handles of this are in the water jar; stone: forty-one herms. IN THE *LOUTRON:* three elevated tubs; ten tubs on the floor; a semi-circular stool. IN THE *EXEDRAI* AND THEIR DEPENDENCIES: a sundial on a column; sixty gilt shields with inscriptions; another five with gold edges; another thirteen without gold with inscriptions; many dedicatory plaques; ten more shields with gold edges; two amphoras, dedications of Euagion the Athenian; five bronze torches, one the dedication of Tharses the Athenian, another of Nikias the Athenian, another of Charios the Athenian, another of Diokles the Athenian, and the fifth torch the dedication of Metrodoros the Samian.

181   Athenaeus, *The Gastronomers* 13.561C–D   *ca.* A.D. 228

Zeno [335–263 B.C.] said in his *Republic* that Eros is a god who helps with the safety of the city-state. That other philosophers, older than Zeno, also recognized that Eros is holy and removed from all evil is shown by the fact that he is established in the *gymnasia* along with Hermes and Herakles, the former in charge of speech, the latter in charge of strength. When they are united, friendship and harmony are born, and through them the most beautiful freedom grows for their partakers.

182   Plato, *Lysis* 203a–211a   *ca.* 386 B.C.

This Platonic dialogue, a fine example of the "Socratic method," gives a vivid image of the Greek palaistra *and some of the activities which went on there.*

I was on my way straight from the Akademy to the Lykeion by the road that runs outside and alongside the city walls. When I came to the little gate at the spring of Panops I ran into Hippothales son of Hieronymos and Ktesippos from the deme Paianiea together with a group of other teenagers standing around. Hippothales saw me and said, "Hi, Sokrates! Where are you coming from and where you headed?"

"I'm going from the Akademy straight to the Lykeion."

"Why don't you turn in here and come straight to us?"

"Where?" I asked. "And who is with you?"

"Here," he said, showing me an enclosure opposite the city wall, and a door standing open. "We pass our time here—we and many other beautiful boys."

"What is this place?" I asked. "And how do you pass your time exactly?"

"It's a *palaistra*," he answered, "recently built, and we pass our time in discussions which we would be glad to share with you."

"Good show!" I said. "But who is the *didaskalos* here?"

"Your old buddy," he replied, "and admirer, Mikkos."

"By God, he is no dummy, but a proper sophist."

"Why don't you come along and see who all is here?"

"First I would prefer to learn the terms of entry and who is the local pretty boy."

"We each have our own favorite, Sokrates."

"And who is yours, Hippothales? Won't you tell me?"

He reddened at the question and I said, "Hippothales son of Hieronymos, there is no need to say whether or not you are in love—I see for myself that not only are you in love, but that the passion is already far advanced. I may be a dummy and useless in other things, but god has given me the ability to recognize immediately a lover and a beloved."

He reddened even more when he heard this and then Ktesippos said, "What a joke, Hippothales, that you blush and hesitate to tell Sokrates his name. If Sokrates spends another ten seconds with you he will be bombarded with the name by you in any case. Let me tell you, Sokrates, that our ears are numb from being hit with 'Lysis this and Lysis that'; and if Hippothales has had a bit to drink, we are apt to be roused from a deep sleep with the name 'Lysis' ringing in our ears. And his talk about Lysis is bad enough, but he drowns us with his poems and love letters. But worst of all is when we have to listen to him singing—in his fine voice—the praises of his boyfriend. And now he blushes at a question from you?"

"I guess this Lysis must be a newcomer," I said. "At least I don't recognize his name."

"They don't usually call him by his own name," said Ktesippos, "but still use his father's name. But I'm sure you know the boy by face—that alone is enough to recognize him."

"But tell me who his father is," I said.

"Demokrates from Aixone."

"Bravo, Hippothales," I said. "What a noble and dashing lover you have found. Now go and show me what you are showing these friends here so that I might see if you understand what a lover ought to say about his boyfriend to him and to others."

"Hang on, Sokrates," said Hippothales. "Do you place any weight in what this Ktesippos said?"

"Do you deny that you love that boy he mentioned?" I asked.

"No," he replied, "but I don't write poems and love letters to my boyfriend."

"He is not well," interrupted Ktesippos. "He babbles and raves."

And I said, "Hippothales, I don't want to hear your verses nor any song you may have composed for the boy, but to hear how you speak so that I can learn how you behave toward your boyfriend."

"Let Ktesippos tell you," he said, "since he must know and remember accurately if, as he says, he is constantly being talked deaf by me."

"Right on," said Ktesippos, "and it is a joke, Sokrates. Don't you agree that it is laughable to be a lover and have your mind set specially on a special boy, and yet have nothing special to say that any other boy couldn't say? Why anybody, indeed, the whole city, can sing about his father Demokrates and his grandfather Lysis and all his ancestors, and their wealth and horse breeding and victories in the *tethrippon* and the *keles* at Delphi and Isthmia and Nemea, and about things even staler than those—but that is what our friend here celebrates in verse and song."

The discussion continues for some time and a consensus is reached that Hippothales does not know how to carry on with Lysis, and that Sokrates should arrange to provide an example.

"That's what I will have to do," I said. And taking Ktesippos along, I entered the *palaistra*. We found that the boys had performed the sacrifices already and that the sacred rites were nearly done, and they were playing knuckle-bones and all dressed to the nines. Most of them were playing outside in the courtyard, but some in a corner of the *apodyterion* were playing odds and evens with quantities of *astragaloi* which they picked from some little baskets, while others stood around and watched. One of these was Lysis who stood among the boys and the young men wearing a garland on his head and of a distinct appearance, worthy to be called not just beautiful, but imbued with *kalokagathia*.

We went and sat down on the opposite side where it was quiet and began to talk to one another. Then Lysis kept turning to look at us, and it was clear that he wanted to come over, but he was hesitant to come by himself. Then Menexenos came in from playing in the courtyard and when he saw me and Ktesippos, he came to sit down beside us. Lysis saw the chance and came along to sit down with Menexenos, and the others came along too, including Hippothales. He saw that there were so many that he could hide behind them and be out of Lysis' sight, dreading that he might be hateful to him. So he stood and listened.

I looked at Menexenos and asked, "Son of Demophon, who is older, you or Lysis?"

"We argue about that," he replied.

"Do you also argue about who is the more noble?" I asked.

"Sure do," he said.

"And who is the more beautiful?"

They both laughed. I continued, "I shall not ask about who is the wealthier since you are friends, aren't you?"

"Sure are," they responded in unison.

"Then there can be no difference in wealth since they say that friends share everything."

They agreed, and I was going on to ask who was the more just and who the smarter, when someone came and took Menexenos away saying that the *paidotribes* was calling him. It seemed that he was involved in the sacred rites and had some chore to do. Once he had gone off, I asked Lysis, "Do your father and mother love you, Lysis?"

"Yes, they do," he responded.

"Do they want you to be as happy as possible?"

"Certainly."

"Do you think a man is happy when he is enslaved and not allowed to do anything he wants?"

"No, by Zeus, I don't."

"Well, then, if your father and mother love you, and want you to be happy, it must be clear in every way that they are constantly looking out for ways to make you happy."

"Of course," he said.

"Therefore," I said, "they allow you to do whatever you want, and they do not chastise you or prevent you from doing anything you might desire?"

"Ha! Fat chance, Sokrates. You should see my no-no lists."

"What's that?" I said. "They want you to be happy—and yet stop you from doing whatever you want? But tell me—if you wanted to ride on one of your father's chariots and take the reins in some race, would they permit you?"

"No way!"

"But who would they permit?"

"Some charioteer hired by my father."

"What's that? They would trust some hired hand rather than you, their own son, to do what he wants with the horses, and pay him hard cash on top of everything else?"

"You bet," he said.

"At least," I said, "they allow you to drive the team of mules, and they let you take the whip and beat them as you like."

"Not likely," he replied.

"Why not?" I asked. "Is no one permitted to beat them?"

"Of course," he said, "the muleteer is."

"And is he a slave or a free man?"

"A slave."

"Well," I said, "it seems that they have more faith in a slave than in their own son, and they trust him with their property more than you, and they allow him to do what he wants but prohibit you. And tell me this—do they allow you to control yourself, or do they not trust you with yourself?"

"No, they don't."

"But who controls you?"

"My *paidagogos* here."

"Is he a slave?"

"Certainly. He is our possession," Lysis said.

"Weird—a slave controls a free man," I responded. "What does this *paidagogos* do to control you?"

"He takes me to my *didaskalos.*"

"And do your *didaskaloi* control you?"

"Always."

"In other words," I said, "your father has deliberately set a large number of masters and controllers over you. But when you go home to your mother, does she let you do what you want so that you might be happy, as for example to play with her wool or her loom when she is weaving? Surely she doesn't stop you from touching her weaving or spinning tools?"

He laughed at that—"Sokrates, not only does she stop me, but I would get whopped if I dared to touch her things."

"By Herakles," I said, "have you wronged your father or your mother?"

"Of course not," he replied.

"But then why do they constantly prevent you from being happy and doing what you want and treat you like a slave all day long? You don't do anything you want. It seems to me that you have no benefit from all your wealth—which is under the control of everyone but you—or from your noble breeding—which someone else also leads and tends to. You, Lysis, you control nothing and you do nothing that you want to do."

"But Sokrates," he said, "I am not of age."

"No, no," I said. "That cannot be the reason. I imagine that your parents trust you with certain things without waiting for you to come of age. Don't they tap you, for example, first of all to read or write for them?"

"Yes, they do," he admitted.

"And you are allowed to write first whichever letter you choose, and then whichever second? And to read whichever you want first and second? And I'll bet that when you pick up your lyre your parents don't stop you from tightening or loosening whatever string you want, or from plucking with your nail or striking with a plectrum—or do they stop you?"

"Oh, no."

"Then, Lysis, why don't they stop you in these things since they do stop you with regard to those other things we mentioned before?"

"Perhaps because I understand these things, but not those?"

"Well, then," I said, "your father isn't waiting for you to come of age to entrust everything to you, but for the day when your knowledge is better than his—on that day he will entrust himself and all his belongings to you?"

"Yes, I guess so," he said.

"Okay," I said, "but what about this? Does your neighbor think about you in the same way as your father? When he thinks that your knowledge of management is better than his will he entrust the management of his property to you?"

"I think that he will entrust it to me."

"All right, but will the Athenians entrust their affairs to you when they feel that you are adequately knowledgeable?"

"They will."

"Very well," I said, "and what about the King of Persia? Would he trust his eldest son, heir to the whole of Asia, to put whatever he wants in the soup, or would he trust us if we were to show him that we were more knowledgeable than his son about the preparation of food?"

"Clearly he would choose us," said Lysis.

"And he wouldn't let his son add even a pinch of spice, but we could throw in even salt by the shovelful if we wanted?"

"Why not?"

"What if his son had something wrong with his eyes? Would he allow his son to touch himself, or not, given that his son is not a doctor?"

"Not!"

"But if he knew that we were doctors and well educated, he would not stop us from opening his son's eyes and sprinkling in ashes and dirt."

"Agreed."

"So he would trust us more than himself or his own son in whatever he thought that we were more knowledgeable?"

"Of necessity, Sokrates," he said.

"In other words, my dear Lysis," I said, "we are to be entrusted by everyone—Greeks and barbarians, men and women—with everything about which we have been educated and we will do what we want and no one will deliberately hinder us. In fact, we will be free in these matters and control other people who will, in effect, belong to us since we will derive benefit from them. But in those matters about which we have not acquired knowledge, not only will we not be entrusted to do what seems best but we will be hindered actively by everybody—and not only by outsiders but even by our parents. In such matters we shall be dominated by others, and will receive no benefit from them. Do you agree that this is the way the matter stands?"

"I agree," he said.

"And will anyone be our friend or love us in matters where we are useless?"

"No way," he replied.

"In other words, your father doesn't love you, nor does anyone love anyone else to the extent that he is useless?"

"So it seems," he said.

"But if you get smart, my boy, then everyone will be your friend because you will be useful. But if you don't get smart, no one—neither your father nor your mother nor your comrades—will be your friend. But see here, Lysis, can you be highly educated in those matters in which you have not yet had any education?"

"How could I be?"

"Then you need a *didaskalos* where you are not educated?"

"Indeed I do."

183   Aischines, *Against Timarchos 9–12*   345 B.C.

In a counter-suit against Timarchos, Aischines claims that Timarchos' moral conduct disqualifies him from participation in public life, including the right to bring suit against anyone (and especially Aischines himself, of course). One area of legal prohibition which Aischines presents shows laws were enacted to control conduct in the gymnasion. *As will emerge in the sources after this one (nos.* **184** *and* **185***) Athens was not alone, for conduct in the* gymnasion *seems to have been a frequent and widespread concern in antiquity.*

The lawgiver seems to have mistrusted *didaskaloi*—to whom we necessarily entrust our *paides*, and whose livelihood depends upon self-control, the lack of which means poverty for them—for he explicitly prescribes, first, the hours when a free-born *pais* may go to the *didaskaleion*, and then the number of *paides* who may be together in a group, and when they are to leave, and he forbids the *didaskaloi* to open the *didaskaleia* and the *paidotribai* to open the *palaistra* before the sun has risen, and he prescribes that they are to close up before the sun has gone down, for he has isolation and darkness very much in mind.

He also regulates who the *neaniskoi* ought to be in order to matriculate, and at what age, and for an official who is responsible for them and for the supervision of *paidagogoi*, and concerning the *Mouseia* in the *didaskaleia* and the *Hermaia* in the *palaistrai*, and finally the company which the *paides* may keep in their dances.

He also orders that the *choregos*, who is about to spend out of his own pocket on our behalf, be more than forty years of age in order that he might have reached the most self-controlled time of life when he encounters our *paides.*

Once you know these laws you will see that the lawgiver thought that the well-brought-up *pais* becomes, as a man, useful to the city. But when the nature of the man gets a wicked education early on, he thought that nearly all of the boys brought up in a bad way would become citizens like this Timarchos.

Mr. Clerk of the Court, read these laws to the jury.

THE LAWS

The *didaskaloi* of the *paides* shall not open the *didaskaleia* before sunrise, and they shall close them before sunset. Except for the son, brother, or son-in-law of the *didaskalos,* no one over the age of the *paides* is to enter when the *paides* are within. Anyone who disobeys and enters is to be punished with death.

And the *gymnasiarchos* shall in no way allow anyone outside the age limit to participate in the *Hermaia.* The *gymnasiarchos* who allows this and does not exclude an overage person from the *gymnasion* is to be subject to the law about the ruination of the freeborn.

The *choregoi* who are appointed by the *demos* are to be over the age of forty.

184   *SIG³* 578   third century B.C.

An inscription on a marble stele from Teos gives interesting details about the faculty of the palaistra. *The beginning of the decree is not preserved.*

. . . . after the election of the *gymnasiarchos* a *paidonomos* not younger than the age of forty is to be appointed.

In order that all the free *paides* be educated just as Polythrous, son of Onsemimos, instructed the *demos,* establishing with his forethought a most beautiful monument to his own good fame as he donated $748,000 toward this end:

1. At the end of the annual election of the magistrates and after the election of the secretaries there are to be appointed three grammar teachers who are to teach the *paides* and the girls; the annual salary of the one elected on the first round is to be $13,300; of the one elected on the second round $12,100; and of the one elected on the third round $11,000.

2. There are to be appointed two *paidotribai* whose annual salary is to be $11,000 each.

3. There is to be appointed either a *kitharistes* or a *psaltes* with an annual salary of $15,400 for the one elected, who is to teach those *paides* who might have been passed on to the next year, and of those whom he is to teach each year, the younger ones are to be taught music in general and either to be a *kitharistes* or a *psaltes,* but the *epheboi* are to be taught only music in general. The *paidonomos* is to decide about the ages of these *paides.* If there should be an intercalary month an additional month's salary is to be paid.

4. After notification to the *demos* the *paidonomos* and the *gymnasiarchos* are to hire an infantry drill master and a teacher of archery and the javelin. These are to teach the *epheboi* and those *paides* who have been enrolled in the music lessons. The salary of the teacher of archery and the javelin is to be $5,500 and that of the infantry drill master $6,600. The infantry drill master is to teach not less than two months each year.

The *paidonomos* and the *gymnasiarchos* are to see to it that the *paides* and the *epheboi* are carefully exercised in their lessons just as is prescribed for each of them in the laws. If the grammar teachers argue about the size of their classes, the *paidonomos* is to settle the dispute and they are to abide by his decision. The grammar teachers are to produce the customary exhibitions in the *gymnasion* and the music teachers in the *bouleuterion* [and the *paidotribai* in the stadium]. . . .

185 SEG 27.261   before 167 B.C.

A large marble stele found in Verroia in Macedonia gives a full, if legalistic, view of the workings of a gymnasion. *It is inscribed on both sides, although not all of the text on the front is preserved.*

Side A

In the generalship of Hippokrates son of Nikostratos, on the 19th of the month Apellaios with the *ekklesia* in session, the *gymnasiarchos* Zopyros son of Amyntas, together with Asklepiades son of Heras and Kallipos son of Hippostratos, proposed:

Since all other public offices are regulated by law, and since in those cities in which there are *gymnasia* with an associated *aleimma* gymnasiarchal laws are on public display, it would be good if we also followed this custom and established guidelines for the auditors in the *gymnasion* as well to be written on a *stele* for public display. By doing this the younger men will be ashamed and obedient to their leaders, and their revenues will not be wasted by those legally elected *gymnasiarchoi* who will always be responsible for their actions.

The city resolved to adopt the law introduced by the *gymnasiarchos* Zopyros son of Amyntas, Asklepiades son of Heras, and Kallipos son of Hippostratos, to make it public, to oblige the *gymnasiarchos* to adhere to it, and to write it on a *stele* for display in the *gymnasion*. It took effect on the 1st of the month Peritios.

THE GYMNASIARCHAL LAW

The city is to elect the *gymnasiarchos* at the same time as its other officials.

The *gymnasiarchos* shall be not younger than thirty years of age and not older than sixty.

The elected *gymnasiarchos* is to swear the following oath of office:

"I swear by [??] and by Herakles and by Hermes that I will be a *gymnasiarchos* in accordance with the gymnasiarchal law; and that I will do anything and everything not covered by the law in the most just manner I possibly can; and I will not do special favors for my friends nor unjust injuries to my enemies; and from existing revenues for the young neither will I myself steal, nor will I allow anyone else to steal in any way that I might know or that I might discover. If I am true to my oath, may all be well with me; if not, may the opposite be my fate."

When the elected *gymnasiarchos* begins his term of office he is to assemble the *ekklesia* on the 1st of Peritios in the *gymnasion* in order to select three men who, having been elected and having sworn the oath of office, are to supervise the youth in the manner which they arrange and the *gymn-* . . .

. . . *the remainder of this side of the stone is worn away* . . .

Side B

CONCERNING THE *NEANISKOI*

. . . No one under the age of thirty is allowed to disrobe without the permission of the leader when the signal is down; when the signal is up, no one at all is allowed to disrobe without the permission of the leader, nor is anyone allowed to oil himself in some other *palaistra* in the city. Whoever disobeys is to be stopped by the *gymnasiarchos* and fined $1,100.

All the regulars in the *gymnasion* are obliged to obey whomever the *gymnasiarchos* selects as leader just as if he were the *gymnasiarchos*. If not, the *gymnasiarchos* is to flog the disobedient one with a switch, and to fine the other boys.

The *epheboi* and those less than twenty-two years of age are to train in spear-throwing and archery every day at the time when the *paides* are to oil themselves, and to train as well in whatever other instruction seems necessary.

CONCERNING THE *PAIDES*

The *neaniskoi* are not to annoy the *paides* nor to natter at them, and the *gymnasiarchos* is to fine and punish the transgressions of these restrictions. The *paidotribai* are to be present twice every day in the *gymnasion* at the time designated by the *gymnasiarchos*, except in the case of illness or some pressing business. If not, let him appear before the *gymnasiarchos*. If the *paidotribes* seems to be cutting hours and not being present at the appointed time for the *paides*, he is to be fined $110 for every day. The *gymnasiarchos* is also to be in charge of flogging the *paides* who misbehave and the *paidagogoi* who are not free, and of fining those who are free. The *paidotribai* are to examine the *paides* three times a year, every quarter, and to establish standards for them, and the victor is to be crowned with an olive wreath.

CONCERNING THOSE WHO ARE NOT TO ENTER THE *GYMNASION*

No slave is to disrobe in the *gymnasion*, nor any freedman, nor their sons, nor cripples, nor homosexuals, nor those engaged in commercial craft, nor drunkards, nor madmen. If the *gymnasiarchos* knowingly allows any of the aforementioned to be oiled, or continues to allow them after having received a report of them, he is to be penalized $22,000. In order that this be exacted, the denouncer is to give a deposition to the city auditors, who are to pass it on to the city tax collector. If they do not pass it on, or the tax collector does not exact the penalty, they also are to pay the same penalty and a commission of 33% is to be given to the denouncer. If the *gymnasiarchos* thinks he has been indicted unjustly, he may appeal within ten days to be judged by the competent court. Future *gymnasiarchoi* are also to prevent those who seem to be oiled illegally. If not, they are subject to the same penalties.

No one is to talk back to the *gymnasiarchos* in the *gymnasion*. Whoever does so is to be fined $1,100. If anyone strikes the *gymnasiarchos* in the *gymnasion*, those present are to prevent and not allow it, and the striker is to be fined $2,200 without trial in accordance with common law. And if someone who is present is able but does not help, he is to be fined $1,100.

CONCERNING THE *HERMAIA*

The *gymnasiarchos* is to organize the *Hermaia* during the month of Hyperberetaios and to sacrifice to Hermes and to hold a *hoplitodromos* and three other contests of physical conditioning—*euexia, eutaxia, and philo-ponia*—for those under the age of thirty. The *gymnasiarchos* is to select seven local men as judges of physical conditioning. Three of these are to be selected by *kleros* and to swear to Hermes that they will judge fairly whoever seems to have built his body the best, and not be influenced by any favors nor by any enmity. If those selected do not judge or are unable to be sworn in, the *gymnasiarchos* is to be responsible for fining the disobedient one $220 and for allotting one of the remaining four men as a replacement for the absentee. With regard to the awards for coordination and training, the *gymnasiarchos* is to judge coordination on the basis of who seems to be the best coordinated of those under thirty years of age and training on the basis of who, of those under thirty years of age who were provided with *aleimma* during the same year, seems to be the best trained. The victors are to be crowned that same day and may, if they want, bind a ribbon around their heads.

A *lampadedromia* is also to be organized as a part of the *Hermaia* for the *paides* and another for the *neaniskoi*. The expense for the armor is to come from existing revenues. The sacral magistrates are to execute the *Hermaia* by taking from each of the regulars in the *gymnasion* not more than $44 and the same from the loiterers in the *gymnasion* except for those who can provide to the magistrates replacements for themselves.

The *paidotribai* are also to execute the sacrifice to Hermes at the same time when the priests do, taking from the *paides* not more than $22 each, and they are to divide up the portions of the raw meat of the sacrificial animals, but the magistrates and the *gymnasiarchos* are to prevent any degeneration into a drinking bout.

The victors are to dedicate the prizes which they received within eight months of the beginning of the term of office of the next *gymnasiarchos*. If not, the *gymnasiarchos* is to fine them $2,200. The *gymnasiarchos* is responsible for flogging and fining those who disrupt the games and those who do not compete legally in the games, as well as anyone who sells a victory.

CONCERNING ELECTIONS OF TORCH-LEADERS

The *gymnasiarchos* is to select three local torch-leaders in the month of Gorpiaios and each of those selected is to provide oil to the *neaniskoi* for ten days. Three torch-leaders are also to be selected from the *paides* and to provide oil on the same days. If any of those selected, or the father of one, or his brothers or the orphan-guardians, objects that he is not able to be a torch-leader, let him be excused five days after he was selected. If anyone fails to perform as torch-leader without having been excused, he is to be penalized $1,100 and must provide the oil and serve as torch-leader all the same. Similarly, if one appears to have been excused improperly, as proven by the *gymnasiarchos* and the young men, he is to be penalized $1,100 and forced to provide the oil and to serve as torch-leader all the same. In place of him who has been excused properly, the *gymnasiarchos* is to appoint another and he is to organize the *lampadedromia* of the *paides* from those regulars who seem to him best qualified, and the *lampadedromia* of the *neaniskoi* is to be organized in the same way.

CONCERNING JUDGES

The *gymnasiarchos* is to establish as judges those he thinks best qualified, one set for the *lampadedromia* of the *Hermaia* and for the long race, and one set for the remaining contests. If anyone accuses any of the judges saying that he has been cheated, let the case be heard in accordance with common law.

The *gymnasiarchos* is to be responsible for the current revenues for the young men and for expenditures from them; but when his term in office has expired, the whole of the revenues, any additional income from fines or penalties, and expenditures from those monies, are to be written on a board and displayed in the *gymnasion* in the month of Dios of the next year. The city auditors are to look at his books every quarter and anyone who wants may call him to account after their examination. Surplus revenue is to be handed over to the next *gymnasiarchos* within thirty days of leaving office. If he does not hand over either his accounts or the surplus itself, he is to be penalized $22,000 for the young men, and the city tax collector is to assess this penalty and the auditors to record it, and he is to hand over his accounts and the surplus all the same.

The one who buys the revenue of the *gloios* is to provide the services of a *palaistra* guard who is to be as much under the orders of the *gymnasiarchos* as those who belong to the *gymnasion*. If one is disobedient or misbehaves, he is to be flogged by the *gymnasiarchos*.

If anyone steals anything from the *gymnasion*, he is to be liable to a judgement of sacrilege before the competent court.

The *gymnasiarchos* is to write up the reason for which all fines were assessed and announce it in the *gymnasion* and display the names of those fined on a chalkboard and pass it on to the city tax collector, and the tax collector, having collected the fine, is to return it to the current *gymnasiarchos*. If anyone claims that he has been fined unjustly, he may appeal to be judged by the appropriate officials, and if he should win his appeal, the *gymnasiarchos* is to pay 150% of the fine to him, and a surcharge of 20% and 10% to the city.

Whoever wants may call the *gymnasiarchos* to account within twenty-four months after the end of his term in office, and such cases are to be judged by the competent court.

The law was passed by the city magistrates with one negative vote.

186   Aristotle, *Constitution of the Athenians* 42   *ca.* 325 B.C.

*We learn here something of the compulsory ephebic training of every potential Athenian citizen. In addition to the clear connections between athletics and this training, which was a prerequisite of the good citizen, we may infer that there was no compulsory education beyond the ephebic training. Aristotle expresses his opinions upon this system elsewhere (see below, no. **189**) but we can also infer, although Aristotle does not explicitly state as much, that a basic literacy for every Athenian citizen will have been assured during the ephebic training.*

Citizenship belongs to those whose parents were both citizens, and they are registered in their *demes* when they are eighteen years old. When they are about to be registered, the members of the *deme* vote upon them. They vote first as to whether the candidates have been shown to be of legal age. If not, the candidates are returned to the *paides*. Secondly, they vote as to whether the candidate is a free man and of legitimate birth. If they vote that he is not a free man, he appeals to a court of law, and the members of the *deme* select five of their members to argue the case against him. If the court decides that he has no right to be registered in the *deme*, the city sells him into slavery. After this the *boule* examines those who have been registered and if it finds anyone who is younger than eighteen, it fines the members of the *deme* who registered him. When the *epheboi* have been examined, their fathers meet in tribal divisions and select three men of forty years of age or more from each tribe whom they think are the best and most suitable to be the *sophronistes,* and one from all of the Athenians to be the *kosmetes* in charge of them all.

The *kosmetes* and the *sophronistai* then collect the *epheboi* and first make a tour of the temples and shrines. They then go to Peiraieus and some of them garrison Mounichia and others Akte. The *demos* also elects two *paidotribai* and *didaskaloi* for them who are to teach them infantry drills and the use of the bow, the javelin, and the sling. The *demos* gives a *per diem* of $22 to each of the *sophronistai* and a *per diem* of $14.75 to each of the *epheboi.* The *sophronistes* of each tribe takes the pay of his *epheboi* and buys their provisions in common, for each tribe eats together, and he is in charge of all the other supplies as well. This is the way that they spend the first year.

The following year there is an assembly in the theater and the *epheboi* march in review for the people. They receive a shield and a spear from the city, and they patrol the countryside and are garrisoned in the border guard posts. They are on guard for two years. They wear a *chlamys* and are completely tax exempt. They are allowed to be neither plaintiff nor defendant in law suits in order that they have no excuse for absences. There are exceptions in the cases of estates, of exercising the right to claim an heiress by marriage, and of priesthoods which may have been inherited. When the two years have passed, they have become full citizens.

187   *IG II². 1006*   122 B.C.

By the late Hellenistic period in Athens it had become common to make official note of especially worthy groups of epheboi or of the special efforts of their teachers. Although the following inscription is some two centuries later than the description by Aristotle (no. 186) many of the institutions described by him are to be seen in the following text, as well as details of the events of a specific ephebic year. This text is on a single slab of marble but consists of three basic parts. The first is a decree in honor of the epheboi of the year 123/122 B.C. and most of their teachers including the justification for the decree as well as the decree proper. The second part is a similar decree specifically in honor of the kosmetes of that year. The third is a list of the epheboi who are now Athenian citizens.

In the archonship of Nikodemos [122/121 B.C.]. . . . Since the ephebes in the archonship of Demetrios [123/122 B.C.] performed their registration sacrifices in the *prytaneion* at the common hearth of the *demos* together with the *kosmetes* and the priest of Demos and the Graces and the *exegetes* in accordance with the laws and decrees of the *demos,* and then paraded to the shrine of Artemis Agrotera, encountered the sacred objects and escorted them, including the image of Iacchos, and they brought the cattle in Eleusis for the sacrifice, and for those in the other shrines and the *gymnasia,* and they completed their races, paraded in the processions, and ran the *lampadedromia* as is customary, and led the image of Pallas out to Phaleron and thence led it back again by torchlight and with all proper deportment; they also led the image of Dionysos from the hearth to the theater by torchlight and they escorted at the festival of Dionysos a bull worthy of the god which they sacrificed at the shrine in procession (for which they were crowned by the *demos*); and since they also completed the sacrifice to Athena Nike, escorting with grace and dignity the cow which they then sacrificed on the Acropolis to the goddess; they also carried out the other customary sacrifices to the gods in accordance with the laws and the decrees; they also performed in the *gymnasia* throughout the whole year supporting and obedient to the *kosmetes,* and acknowledging that it is of greatest importance and most necessary to preserve the discipline of the lessons ordained by the *demos* they were blameless and obedient to the orders of the *kosmetes* and the *didaskaloi;* they were also faithful adherents of Zenodotos, attending his lectures in the Gymnasion of Ptolemy and in the Lykeion, as well as of the other philosophers who were in the Lykeion and the Academy during the whole year; they also guarded the *ekklesia* under arms in an orderly manner; and since they continually met the arrivals of those friends and benefactors, the Romans; and since on Memorial Day they ran a *hoplitodromos* from the Tomb of the Unknown and carried out the other customary duties, and they displayed their weapons at the festival of Theseus and on Memorial Day; they placed in the offering plate of the Mother of the Gods the $1,540 prescribed by the decree of the *demos* and they dedicated another in addition in the shrine in Eleusis; and since they went out under arms to the borders of Attika and became familiar with the countryside and the roads, and with the country shrines where they sacrificed and received good omens on behalf of the *demos;* and since they also visited Marathon and laid a wreath at the Tomb of the Unknown there and offered sacrifice to those who fell in war for the cause of freedom; and since they visited the Amphiareion and learned the history of the protection of the shrine by their forefathers from olden times and having sacrificed they returned on the same day to their own stations; and since they also sailed to the trophy and sacrificed to Zeus of the Trophy, and performed a boat race in the parade of the Great Gods; and since they also raced around Mounychion into the harbor of Mounychia; and since they did the same at the festival of the

Diïsoterioi; and since they also sailed out for the festival of Ajax and having held a boat race there and paraded and sacrificed to Ajax, the *deme* of Salamis commended them and crowned them with a golden crown for accomplishing the assignment with good discipline and elegance; and since they preserved harmony and friendship toward one another for the whole year being faction-free in accordance with the policy of the *kosmetes;* and since they also presented their receipts to the *boule* as required by law; and since, behaving bravely in all ways and willing to follow the precepts of the *kosmetes* and perform in the best interests of the city, and of their own dignity, they repaired an old stone-throwing catapult at their own expense, even furnishing the missing parts and renewing for many years to come the use of the instrument, even for instructional purposes, thus repairing as well an educational deficiency; inasmuch as they completed their other duties with blameless conduct and cared to repair deficiencies at their own expense it is fitting that the *boule* and the *demos* honor these worthy young men, obedient to the laws and decrees and to the *kosmetes* since they came of age.

GOOD FORTUNE

Resolved by the *boule* that those allotted chairmen for the next *ekklesia* consult about how the *demos* is to be presented with the opinion of the *boule* that the *epheboi* in the archonship of Demetrios be commended and crowned with a golden crown on account of their reverence for the gods and the discipline which they maintained for the whole year and their *philotimia* toward the *boule* and the *demos;* and that the crown be proclaimed at the new dramatic contests of the festival of Dionysos in the town and at the gymnic contests of the Panathenaic and the Eleusinian festivals; that the generals and the treasurer of military funds see to the purchase of the crown; that the *didaskaloi* be commended, and the *paidotribes* Timon son of Timarchos of Boutades and the swordsman Satyros son of Herakleides of the *deme* Kiphissia and the spearman Nikandros son of Demetrios of the *deme* Euonymea and the archer Askleipiades son of Aristokrates of the *deme* Marathon and the catapultist Kalchedon son of Kalchedon of the *deme* Perithoides and the assistants Satyros son of Apollonios of the *deme* Halimon, Hieron son of Herakleides of the *deme* Anagyra, and Athenaios son of Isidoros of the *deme* Halaiea, and to crown each of them with a crown of olive leaves; that the secretary inscribe this decree on stone *stelai* and set one up in the *agora* and the other wherever it seems appropriate; that the treasurer of military funds pay the expenses incurred by the inscription and the erection of the *stelai.*

In the archonship of Nikodemos. . . . Since the *demos* always takes the greatest pains with the education and discipline of the *epheboi*, desirous that they make the transition from childhood to manhood and become inheritors of the fatherland, and that they lawfully command the country and the guard posts and the borders of Attika, and that they become experienced in weaponry and practiced in the attributes of war, and educated in such a way that they crown the city with the best and most august trophy, for which reason the *kosmetes* is appointed from among those who have lived the very best lives, and from this group Dionysios son of Sokrates of the *deme* Phyle, appointed *kosmetes* for the year of the archonship of Demetrios, accepting the trust voted to him by the *demos* for the *epheboi*, performed the registration sacrifices together with them at the common hearth in the traditional way, and paraded them to the shrine of Artemis Agrotera; and since, considering that the greatest glory for the fatherland is their discipline and courage, he made himself worthy of the precepts of the *demos*, having first made his own education proper to and worthy of the *demos* and of the *epheboi*; and since he led them all year in the *gymnasia* and made clear to all of them his authority and dignity, keeping them free of accusations all year and obedient to the orders of the generals, his own, and those of the *didaskaloi*; and since he provided in every way for their education and soundness of mind, seating them next to the philosophers and attending all their lectures for the whole year. In the same way he took pains with their literacy, adhering to the precepts of Zenodotos concerning the practice of writing as well as to physical exercises, and similarly making them practice with the catapult he provided for their *philotimia* toward one another; and since he also accomplished their maneuvers under arms to the guard posts and the borders of Attika without a suspicion of distress and he sacrificed with good omens on behalf of the *demos* in the shrines throughout the countryside; and since he also performed all the other sacrifices to the gods together with them and received good omens, and he was commended by the *boule* and the *demos* for the sacrifices he performed reverently and honorably with them; and since he also sacrificed to the local heroes to whom it is customary to sacrifice; and since he led them to the Tomb of the Unknown at Marathon and laid a wreath there and offered sacrifice to those who fell in war for the cause of freedom. He led them to the Amphiareion and they learned the history of the protection of the shrine from ancient times by the *demos* and they sacrificed and returned on the same day to their own stations; and since he sailed to the trophy and sacrificed to Zeus of the Trophy; and since he accomplished a boat race during the sacrifices and parades which took place in Peiraieus; and since he sailed to the festival of Ajax on Salamis and, having paraded and sacrificed, was commended and crowned by the inhabitants of the island for accomplishing the assignment with good discipline and elegance; and since he encountered the sacred objects and escorted them including the statue of Iacchos; and since he completed the parades and the *lampadedromia;* and since he accomplished the races in the *gymnasia* and the encounters with those friends and allies, the Romans; and since he escorted the image of Pallas to Phaleron and thence led it back again by torchlight, and similarly he led the image of Dionysos into the theater; and since he guarded the *ekklesia,* keeping the *epheboi* under arms and in good order; and since he also presented their receipts to the *boule;* and since at the festival of Theseus and Memorial Day he completed the customary races, as also at the festival of the Diïsoterioi; and since he brought the cattle in a manly way at the sacrifice in Eleusis and for the other sacrifices; and since he gave, together with the *epheboi,* into the offering place of the Mother of the Gods the $1,540 prescribed by the decree of the *demos* and together with them dedicated another silver offering plate in the shrine in Eleusis; and since he renewed for many years to come the neglected instruction in and use of the instrument, persuading them in the best interest of the city and of their own dignity to repair at their own expense one of the ancient catapults and thus to repair an educational deficiency; and since he took pains to preserve their *philotimia* as they followed his lead and sat near him all year long, and attended lessons with them and having got them off to a well-disciplined start he led them well and justly through everything in the same way, and preserved their harmony and health and *esprit de corps,* employing patriotic goodwill to all—because of which the *epheboi* honored him with a gold crown and a bronze statue following their ancestors in the gratitude traditional to Athenians and exhibiting the *kalokagathia* and goodwill wrought in them throughout the whole year; and since he presented his accounts for audit in accordance with the law; thus the *boule* and the *demos* were ever open in honoring worthily those of the *kosmetai* who are righteous and those who lead justly and in accordance with the laws and those who exhibit their goodwill toward the *demos,* and they become an imitated example to others.

GOOD FORTUNE

Resolved by the *boule* that those allotted chairmen for the next *ekklesia* consult about how the *demos* is to be presented with the opinion of the *boule* that the *kosmetes* of the *epheboi* in the archonship of Demetrios, Dionysios son of Sokrates of the *deme* Phyle, be commended and crowned with a gold crown in accordance with the law on account of his *arete* and the righteousness which he has shown to the *boule* and the *demos*, and that this crown be proclaimed at the new dramatic contests in the festival of Dionysos in the town and at the gymnic contests of the Panathenaic and Eleusinian festivals; that the generals see to the purchase of the crown; that Dionysios be forgiven the manufacture and setting up of the image with which the *epheboi* honored him even though the laws forbid; and that he shall have some other benefit to be found by the *demos*—whatever seems worthy; that the secretary inscribe this decree on two stone *stelai* and erect one in the *agora* and the other wherever it seems appropriate; and that the treasurer of military funds pay the expenses incurred by the inscription and erection of the *stelai*.

Here follow depictions of the various crowns and a list of the names of the epheboi, *arranged by tribe, and other names, probably of the* didaskaloi. *Although not all the names of the* epheboi *are preserved, their total number was clearly fifty-eight; the total number of their instructors (kosmetes, didaskaloi, swordsman, archer, etc., but not including the philosophers) was at least thirty-two.*

188   Plato, *Laws* 794d–796d   *ca.* 350 B.C.

In constructing his ideal state Plato is much concerned with the education of the young. This education is to begin with the expectant mother keeping the fetus in a state of constant motion which is to continue until the child has reached the age of three. For the next three years the child is to be supervised in closely regulated play, and instruction proper is to begin at the age of six for boys and girls alike. This is to be under the supervision of elected officials of at least fifty years of age in three public gymnasia and exercise fields distributed around the city. The test of the validity of education is to be its service and utility to the state, and physical education plays a large role in the system as can be seen in the following.

It is a nearly universal and ignorant opinion that the right and the left hands are naturally different and adapted for different tasks. But the feet and legs are clearly equal to one another in abilities, and it is because of the stupidity of nurses and mothers that we have all become lame, so to speak, in our hands. For in natural ability the two limbs are equal, but we have made them different by constantly using them incorrectly. This makes no difference in trivial matters as, for example, whether a man uses the left hand for the fiddle and the right for the bow or vice versa. But it is something like mindlessness to follow these examples and set habits when it is not necessary. This is shown by the Skythian custom of using both hands interchangeably for the functions of drawing the bow and of fitting the arrow into it. There are numerous similar examples which teach us that the left hand is no weaker by nature than the right, and that those who think so are wrong. This matters little in the case of the fiddle and other such instruments, as we have already said, but it matters very much when we come to use weapons, especially at close quarters. There is a vast difference here between the trained and the untrained, between the practiced and the unpracticed. Just as the athlete who is thoroughly trained in the *pankration* or the *pyx* or the *pale* is capable of fighting with his left limbs and does not move the left side as if it were numb or lame, so too with weapons of war and everything else the man who possesses a pair of arms or a pair of legs should use them all to equal advantage and allow none of them to go untrained or without practice. Indeed, if a man had a hundred hands, he should be able to throw a hundred missiles at once. These matters must be the concern of the male and the female officers of instruction. The women must oversee the feeding of the infants and their games, and the men must oversee the lessons of the children, so that all the boys and girls may be sound of hand and foot and may not have their natural abilities lamed by their habits.

The lessons may be divided into two types: the gymnic which concern the body, and the musical which refresh the soul. There are two kinds of gymnic lessons: wrestling and dancing. There are two types of dancing: the free and noble, and that which aims at physical fitness, agility, and beauty by exercising the various parts of the body, when practiced with vigor and a graceful firmness and toward the end of strength and health, must not be omitted since these lessons are useful for all purposes.

When we reach this point in our legislation we should charge both the pupils and their teachers that the latter should impart these lessons gently, and the former receive them gratefully.

189 Aristotle, *Politics* 1337a–1339a   *ca.* 325 B.C.

Aristotle, like Plato, considers the question of utility as a primary test of education, but his system is at once both more pragmatic and more idealistic than Plato's. As he discusses contemporary theories and practices, and argues for his system, Aristotle raises basic questions about education, and many of them are familiar today.

No one would disagree that the lawgiver should give special attention to the education of the young. Inasmuch as there is one end for the whole state, it is clear that education must also be one and the same for all and that the supervision of this must be public and not private in the way that each man now supervises the education of his own children, teaching them whatever he thinks they should be taught. There ought to be public supervision for matters of public concern. At the same time one ought to think not that a citizen belongs to himself, but that all citizens belong to the state, for each is part of the state, and the supervision of each part ought naturally to have regard for the supervision of the whole. One might praise the Spartans in this respect, for they pay great attention to the education of their children and conduct it on a public system.

It is clear that there ought to be legislation about education, and that education ought to be conducted on a public system. But one must not forget what the nature of education is, and what ought to be taught. At present there are disagreements about these questions. Not everyone agrees about what the young ought to learn and whether the goals should be *arete* or the good life, nor is it clear whether studies should be directed toward the development of intellect or of character. Troublesome questions arise from the current status of education, and it is not clear whether the student ought to study those things which are useful for life, or those which lead toward *arete*, or those which are theoretical. Each of these has its supporters. Nor is there even agreement about what constitutes *arete*, which leads logically to a disagreement about training for *arete*.

It is at least clear that the young must be taught those utilitarian things which are absolutely necessary, but not everything which is utilitarian. A distinction must be made between those pursuits which are liberal and those which are not liberal; that is, the student ought not to participate in those utilitarian pursuits which lead to vulgarity. It is necessary to define as vulgar any pursuit or craft or science which renders useless the body or soul or mind of free men for the practice of *arete*. Thus we call vulgar those crafts which deteriorate the condition of the body and those employments which earn wages, for they make the mind preoccupied and degraded. Even liberal sciences are liberal only up to a point, for to devote oneself to them too rigorously and completely can have the damaging results of vulgarity. The purpose of one's pursuits or studies also makes a great difference. If the purpose is for the inherent joy of the project, or for friendship, or for *arete*, it is not illiberal. He who does the very same thing, however, because of other people would seem to be acting as a servant or a slave.

There are essentially four areas of normal education: reading and writing, physical exercises, music, and the fourth, according to some people, drawing. Reading and writing and drawing are important because they are useful in life and serviceable. Physical education is important because it contributes to manliness. But someone might question music. This is because, at present, most participate in it for the sake of pleasure. But those who include music in education from the beginning do so, as has often been said, because nature itself seeks not only to work properly, but also to relax nobly. For if both work and leisure are necessary, but leisure is more desirable as a goal than work, then one ought to ask what is the proper occupation of leisure. Certainly leisure must not be spent in playing, for it would necessarily follow that play is the goal of life. Since play ought not to occupy times of leisure, but rather times of work (for play gives rest, and the weary need rest, and work is accomplished by weariness), it follows that we must use play at the proper times since we are using play as a therapy due to its relaxation of the soul and its restfulness because of its pleasure. Leisure, on the other hand, seems to contain pleasure and happiness and the good life, and this belongs not to those who are working, but to those at leisure. The man who is working works for some goal which he does not possess, but happiness is a goal already reached. Hence it is clear that some subjects are to be learned and studied simply for the pleasure in the pursuit of them, and that these studies and lessons are goals in themselves, while those branches of learning which relate to work are to be learned and studied as a means to some other ends. For this reason our predecessors included music in education not as a necessity (for there is nothing necessary about it), nor as utilitarian in the way that reading and writing are useful for business and personal finances and learning and politics nor in the way that drawing is useful in making one a better judge of the works of craftsmen nor in the way that physical education helps with health and strength (for we do not see such results from music). Music therefore remains as a leisure pursuit which is a form of pastime appropriate to free men.

It is therefore clear that there is an aspect of education which ought to be taught to our sons not because it is useful or necessary, but because it frees the spirit and ennobles the soul. It is also clear that some of the useful things ought to be studied by the young not only because of their utility, such as reading and writing, but also because they can lead to the study of other things. In the same way drawing should be studied, not so that one might not be cheated in buying and selling equipment, but rather because this study makes a man observant of beauty. To seek utility in everything is not appropriate to men who are of great spirit and free.

Since it is clear that education by habit must precede education by reason, and that education of the body must precede education of the mind, it is clear that the children must be turned over to the *gymnastai* and the *paidotribai*, for the one works with the condition of the body, the other with its actions.

At the present time some of the states with the greatest reputation for attention to their children produce in them such an athletic condition as to detract from the form and growth of the body. The Spartans, although they have avoided this mistake, turn their children into little animals through their labors, which they think contribute to manliness. But, as has often been said, attention must be paid not just to one virtue, nor even to one virtue before all others. Indeed, they do not even consider whether their training leads to that virtue. For we see in these cases of animals and of foreign races that courage and manliness do not belong to the wildest, but rather to the more gentle and lion-like temperaments. There are many foreign races inclined toward murder and cannibalism which have no share in manly courage. Nobility and not animalism should play the leading role, for neither a wolf nor any other animal will risk a noble danger, but only a good man. Those who train their children in athletics to the exclusion of other necessities make their children truly vulgar and available to the state for only one kind of work, and actually train them worse for this one job than others do.

It is, then, agreed that we should make use of physical education and how we should make use of it. Until puberty lighter exercises should be applied, and forced diets and required works forbidden in order that there be no impediment to growth. There is no small proof that such training can stunt growth. In the list of Olympic victors one can find only two or three who have won in both the boys' category and the men's category. The strength of those who train too hard in youth is robbed by the required exercises. When the boys have spent three years after puberty on their lessons, then it is proper that the next period of their lives be spent on exercises with the required diets.

XI

The Spread of Greek Athletics in the Hellenistic Period

190 Athenaeus, *The Gastronomers* 12.539C   *ca.* A.D. 228

Among the many effects of the conquests of Alexander the Great was the spread of Greek culture, including athletics, throughout his empire. We read in the Anabasis *of Arrian that Alexander celebrated competitive games at many places along his route including sites in the modern states of Turkey, Lebanon, Egypt, Iraq, Iran, Afghanistan, Uzbekistan, Tajikistan, Pakistan, and India. Perhaps more telling, however, is the "sports-mania" of his men as revealed in the following mention of two of his comrades and their customary practices during the march of conquest to the East.*

Perdikkas and Krateros were such lovers of gymnic exercise that they brought along with them on the march a *stadion*-worth of goatskins beneath the shade of which—once they had grabbed a place in the encampment—they exercised. They also brought along many wagonloads of the kind of *konis* used in the *palaistra*.

191 *SIG³* 402   246 B.C.

The following text, from a marble stele discovered at Delphi, preserves the response of Chios to a delegation from the Aitolian League, which had recently come into control of Delphi. It shows that athletics were growing

as a business back at home as well as being spread through the known
world. For the date see Fouilles de Delphes *III.3.215.*

Inasmuch as the Aitolians have been kinsmen and friends of the *demos*
since the days of our forefathers, and have shown their reverence toward the
gods and their friendship toward us by sending as *theoroi* Kleon and
Herakon and Sotion to announce the Soteria games which they are establishing as a memorial to the salvation of Greece and of the victory over the
barbarians who were attacking the sanctuary of Apollo which is common to
all Greeks, and the Greeks themselves, and the Aitolian League and the general Charixenos have also written to the *demos* about these affairs, to
inquire whether we would accept the musical competition as *isoPythian*
and the gymnic and equestrian competitions as *isoNemean* with regard to
the age categories and the prizes, as they have been decreed, and whether
the *demos* would increase the honors of the gods, commemorating the kin-
ship and friendship which the Aitolians have for it.

GOOD FORTUNE

Resolved by the *demos,* that the announcement be accepted and that the
Soteria Games which the Aitolians have established on behalf of the sanctuary of Apollo in Delphi and of the salvation of Greece be *stephanitic,* just
as voted by the Aitolian League, with the musical competition to be
isoPythian and the gymnic and equestrian competitions to be *isoNemean*
with regard to the age categories and the prizes; that citizens who compete
and win at the Soteria have the same honors as those written in the law for
victors at the Pythia and Nemea; that the Aitolian League be commended
and crowned with a gold crown because of its *arete* and reverence toward
the gods and valor against the barbarians; that, in order that these honors be
seen by all, the Sacred Herald announce at the festival of Dionysos in the
theater, just when the contest in the boys' dance is about to take place, the
following announcement: "The *demos* of the Chians crowns the Aitolian
League with a gold crown because of its *arete* and reverence toward the
gods; it votes and accepts the games which the Aitolians are establishing,
with the musical competition as *isoPythian* and the gymnic and equestrian
competitions as *isoNemean* with regard to the age categories and prizes";
that the *agonothetes* is to include the announcement in his program; that
the next *theoroi* who sail off are to inscribe this decree on a stone *stele* and
erect it in the Sanctuary of Apollo in Delphi; that three *theoroi* are to be
selected from all the Chians forthwith when this decree has been voted; that
in the future the announcement of the *theoroi* will occur every four years

when the *theoroi* for the Olympic Games are selected; that $11,000 will be given to these *theoroi* for the sacrifice, but the amount to be given for expenses will be decided by the *demos*; that the appropriate officials pay the expenses for the inscription of the decree and for the *stele*; that $2,200 be given for the crown and the Aitolian *theoroi* be extended hospitality. . . .

192 *SIG³ 630*   182 B.C.

The following is a decree of the Amphiktyonic Council of Delphi in response to a delegation sent to it by Eumenes II, king of Pergamon. It was inscribed on a limestone block in front of the Temple of Apollo at Delphi.

Resolved by the Amphiktyones that King Eumenes son of King Attalos be commended and crowned with a crown of the laurel sacred to Pythian Apollo with which it is traditional to crown those who do good voluntarily, on account of his *arete* and goodwill toward the Greeks; to erect a bronze equestrian statue of him in Delphi; to agree that the shrine of Nikephoros in Pergamon be inviolate for all the time that King Eumenes might determine, and to not trespass on the defined area either in war or in peace; and also to accept the Nikephoria Games as *stephanitic* just as the king might think fit, and that they shall be with regard to the age categories and the prizes for the victors, the musical *isoPythian* on the one hand, and the gymnic and equestrian *isOlympic* on the other. Also that this decree be inscribed in Delphi on the base of the statue of the king in front of the temple, and in Pergamon in the shrine of Athena Nikephoros; and that the crown of the king and the inviolability of the shrine be proclaimed at the Pythian and the Soteria Games.

193 Maccabees 2.4.9–15 and 18–19   first century B.C.

After the ascension of Antiochos Epiphanes as King of Syria in 175 B.C., a certain Jason bribed his way into the position of high priest in Jerusalem and sought permission

. . . to set up a *gymnasion* and an *ephebeion* and to enroll those in Jerusalem as citizens of Antioch. When the king granted this and Jason became leader, he straightway changed his countrymen to Greek customs. . . . He happily founded a *gymnasion* right under the *akropolis* and organized the best of the *epheboi* to wear a *petasos*—such was the acme of Hellenism . . . that the priests were no longer willing to undertake liturgies at the altar, but despised the temple and neglected the sacrifices in their haste to participate in the illegal activities in the *palaistra* whenever the *diskos* invited them, and the leaders no longer set stock in their ancestral honors but wanted Greek glories. . . . When it was time for the quadrennial *agon* at Tyre and the king was to be present, the abominable Jason sent as *theoroi* from Jerusalem those who had turned into citizens of Antioch.

194   Polybius 2.12.8   *ca.* 140 B.C.

Greek culture, including athletics, spread westward as well as eastward during the Hellenistic period and Rome soon came under that influence.

Having begun [diplomatic contacts with Greece in 228 B.C.] the Romans straightway sent other ambassadors to the Corinthians and the Athenians, and it was then that the Corinthians first allowed the Romans to participate in the Isthmian Games.

195   Livy 39.22.1–2   *ca.* 18 B.C.

Even as the Romans began to enter into Greece, so they began to take Greece back with them to Rome. Athletics was a part of their loot.

Then [186 B.C., the year following his conquest of Ambrakia] for ten days and with a great show of wealth Marcus Fulvius Nobilior put on the *ludi* which he had vowed during the Aitolian War. Many actors came from Greece to pay honor to him. Then also for the first time an athletic competition was put on as a spectacle for the Romans, and a *venatio* of lions and panthers was also given, and the festival was celebrated almost as it is now with regard to number and variety of events.

196a   Plutarch, *Sulla* 12.1–6 and 19.6   *ca.* A.D. 100

With the advent of the Romans, now as conquerors rather than as ambassadors, many of the old Greek sanctuaries fell on hard times, and the athletic festival centers were not spared.

Sulla led all his forces against Athens [86 B.C.] . . . bringing to bear upon it every sort of siege-engine, and making all sorts of assaults upon it. . . . And since he needed large amounts of money for the war, he took over the sacred treasures of Greece, some from Epidauros and some from Olympia, appropriating the most beautiful and expensive of their dedications. He also wrote to the Amphiktyones at Delphi that the wealth of Apollo would rest more easily under his protection, and that either he would guard the wealth with greater safety or, if he converted the dedications to cash, he would not pay them back at a lesser rate of exchange. . . . The other treasures of Delphi were sent away to Sulla in a way so as to escape the notice of most of the other Greeks, but the silver *pithos* which was the last remaining dedication of King Kroisos of Lydia [*ca.* 546 B.C.] was too large to be carried even by wagon and the Amphiktyones were forced to cut it up. . . . [Later Sulla] expropriated half of the territory of the Thebans and dedicated it to Pythian Apollo and to Olympian Zeus, ordering that the revenues from this property be handed over to the gods as repayment for the funds which he had taken from them.

196b   Eusebius, *Chronika*   *ca.* A.D. 325

The 175th Olympiad [80 B.C.]: Epainetos of Argos won the *stadion* for boys. For the men did not compete, Sulla having moved everything to Rome.

197   Josephus, *The Jewish War* 1.426–428   A.D. 79

*With actions such as those by Sulla, and perhaps the agents of collectors like Cicero (no. **200**), it is not surprising that the old athletic festival centers needed external help.*

King Herod's beneficence to Elis was a gift not only to Greece but to the whole world, wherever the fame of the Olympic Games has reached. Seeing that these games were falling apart for lack of revenues and that this solitary relic of ancient Greece was sinking, he not only became *agonothetes* for that Olympiad when he was sailing to Rome [12 B.C.] but also produced permanent revenues so that the memory of his time as *agonothetes* would never fade.

198   Josephus, *Jewish Antiquities* 16.136–141   A.D. 93

*In the Hellenistic world which saw the spread of Greek institutions, culture, and language throughout the Mediterranean, as well as a King Herod interested in the old Greek institution of the Olympic Games (no. **197**), it is not surprising to see some elements of Greek athletics appearing in Judea.*

Kaisareia Sebaste, which Herod had been building, was finished in the twenty-eighth year of his rule [10/9 B.C.] which occurred in the 192nd Olympiad [12–8 B.C.]. Immediately there was a great festival for its dedication with the most lavish preparations. He had announced games with *mousikoi* and *gymnikoi agones,* and had prepared a large number of gladiators and wild animals, and horse races and the most lavish sorts of thing which have been manufactured for Rome and some other places. He dedicated these games to Augustus and prepared to celebrate them every four years. And Augustus sent all the supplies needed for these celebrations out of his own pocket, thus glamorizing his own *philotimia*. And Augustus' wife Julia added from her own resources no less than $6,600,000.

Those who came to the city in throngs as parts of delegations or of embassies which their native cities were sending because of the benefits with which those had been visited were welcomed by Herod with lodging and meals and continuous entertainment.

199 *IvO* 56.11–28   2 B.C.

The spread of games which were, in some sense, the equal (or the equivalent) of the old original four stephanitic *games continued throughout the Hellenistic period and into Roman times. One of the many examples is to be seen in this fragmentary inscription, discovered at Olympia, but concerning games established by the emperor Augustus at Naples. The rather imposing name of these competitions, "The Italic, Roman, Augustan, isOlympic Games and Festival," shows that their rules (so far as they are preserved on the stone) may well reflect those of the Olympic Games themselves, although it is curious that those rules would have to be inscribed at Olympia under a Roman title. Perhaps the answer lay in the last part of the inscription, which is too fragmentary to allow for full translation or comprehension, but which mentions various typical gymnic and hippic events,* mastigophoroi, *a* xystarches, agonothetai, *and sacrifices to the emperor, as well as cash prizes for musical competitions which surely were not a standard part of the Olympic Games.*

. . . no one younger than seventeen years is to be allowed to participate in the Italic *isOlympic* games. Those from seventeen to twenty years of age are to participate in the boys' category, and those older in the men's. Concerning awards: prizes are to be given to victors . . . *[about thirty letters missing on the stone]* . . . An *obsonion* is to be distributed to the athletes thirty days before the festival so that all who are competing should each be given $11 each day beginning thirty days before the festival, but beginning at the fifteenth day $27.50 is to be given to the boys, $33 to the men. In accordance with the decree of the emperor honors are to be . . . a crown of wheat. The purchase of the crown . . . *[about thirty letters missing on the stone]* . . . The crowns for any contests which either have no competitors or which end in a tie are to be dedicated by the *agonothetai* in the *gymnasion* in Naples and inscribed with the contest for which each had been the prize. Athletes who wish to be registered as competitors in the Italic Games are to appear in Naples not less than thirty days before the festival and should register with the *agonothetai* their father's name, fatherland, and the competitive event to be entered. The athletes are also to go to the *gymnasion* . . . *[about sixteen letters missing]* . . . It is necessary that each athlete be registered by his official name, whether by reference to his father or in some other way established by law. If not, he is to be fined *[amount not preserved]* by the *agonothetai*, and if he does not pay the fine, he is to be flogged. If anyone is later than the proper time, he is to give the reason for his tardiness to the *agonothetai*; legitimate excuses are illness or pirates or shipwreck. If anyone wants to lodge an accusation against him . . . *[about thirty letters missing]* . . . if he is guilty, he is to be prohibited from the games by the *agonothetai* . . .

. . . remaining part of inscription too fragmentary to translate . . .

XII
Greek Athletics in the Roman Period

200 Cicero, *Letters to Atticus* 1.10.3   67 B.C.

*This letter to Atticus follows upon two earlier letters of the same year in which Cicero had asked that his friend acquire and ship to him Greek statues which Cicero intends to use to decorate his house, and especially statues of Hermes which he wants to place in his own "gymnasium" and his own "xystos"; as seen above, no. **180**, such statues were particularly appropriate to such places. The total amount which Atticus is authorized to spend is about $112,000, and it is clear that in a Roman setting at the time of Cicero, a Greek athletic environment was part of a certain intellectual snobbery which depended ultimately upon the connections between the* palaistra *and education.*

Cicero to Atticus, Salutations,

    . . . Please do as you write about my statues and the "Herakles-herms" whenever it is most convenient for you, as well as anything else you might find that seem to you to be right for the place—you do know it—and especially for the *palaestra* and the *gymnasium*. Since I am sitting there as I write to you, the place itself is a reminder to me . . .

201   Suetonius, *Julius Caesar* 39   *ca.* A.D. 120

Suetonius, who published biographies of the first twelve emperors, here tells us of the triumphal "games" put on by Caesar in 45 B.C. From them we gain an idea of the status and importance of athletics vis-à-vis other forms of entertainment in Roman society.

Caesar's public spectacles were of various kinds. They included a gladiatorial combat, stage-plays in every quarter of Rome performed in every language, chariot races in the Circus, athletic competitions, and a mock naval battle. I shall give more detail of these spectacles.

At the gladiatorial combat in the Forum, Furius Leptinus, a man of praetorial family, fought Quintus Calpenus, a former senator and lawyer, to the death. The sons of petty kings from Asia and Bithynia performed a Pyrrhic sword dance.

One of the plays was written and performed by Decimus Laberius, a Roman knight, who thus forfeited his rank. But after the performance he was given a large sum of money and had his gold ring, the badge of knighthood, restored to him. The track in the Circus was lengthened for the races and a ditch dug around it, and young noblemen competed in driving four-horse and two-horse chariots, and rode pairs of horses jumping from one to another. The so-called Troy Game, a mock battle introduced by Aeneas, was performed by two troops of boys, one older and the other younger.

Wild beast battles took place for five consecutive days and finally there was a battle between two armies, each made up of five hundred infantry soldiers, twenty elephants, and thirty cavalry. To make room for this, the *metae* where the chariots turned in the Circus were removed and the two camps pitched in their places facing one another.

The athletic competitions were held in a temporary stadium built for the purpose in the Campus Martius and lasted for three days.

The naval battle was fought on an artificial lake dug in the lesser Codeta, between heavily manned Tyrian and Egyptian ships with two, three, and four banks of oars. Such a mob thronged to all these spectacles from all directions that many strangers had to stay in tents pitched among the roads and streets, and the press of the crowd was often such that many were crushed to death. The victims included two senators.

202   Dio Chrysostom 28.5–8   *ca.* A.D. 100

Melancomas of Caria was the most courageous and the biggest of all mankind, and the most beautiful. Had he remained a private citizen and not practiced boxing at all, I believe that he still would have become widely known simply for his beauty. Even so, all heads, even of those who did not know who he was, turned wherever he went. And yet he dressed in such a way as to escape rather than attract attention. No matter the number of boys, no matter the number of men who were exercising, when he stripped no one looked at anyone else. And although beauty customarily leads to softness, even for one who is only moderately beautiful, Melancomas was the most moderate of men despite his beauty. And though he despised his beauty, he preserved it none the less and despite his rough sport. For though he was a boxer, he was as whole as a runner. He trained so rigorously and so far exceeded others in exercising that he could remain for two whole days in succession with his hands up, and no one ever saw him drop his guard and rest as is customary with others. Thus he could force his opponents to give up, not only before he received a blow, but even before he had landed one on them. He did not consider striking or receiving a blow a sign of manliness, but as a sign of lack of stamina and of willpower. He thought it a noble achievement to last out the time without being beaten by the weight of his arms, without getting out of breath, and without being distressed by the heat.

It was for this reason that, from the time he began to compete at the Pythian Games, Melancomas was the first man in our knowledge to remain undefeated while winning the largest number and the most prestigious of crowns and defeating opponents neither feeble nor few. He surpassed his own father while still a youth, for he, the famous Melancomas of Caria who won many crowns including one at Olympia, did not remain undefeated.

Despite his splendid athletic achievements, Melancomas came to a pitiful end without having experienced any of the pleasures of life. Moreover, he was so ambitious that as he was dying [*ca.* A.D. 74] he asked his boyhood friend, Athenodoros the pankratiast, how many days were left in the competition.

203 Suetonius, *Nero* 22–25   *ca.* A.D. 120

Although athletics continued in the Greek world under the Roman Empire, they were, like anything else, subject to Roman whim as is shown most strikingly by this account of Nero's visit to Greece in A.D. 67 during which he "won" no fewer than 1,808 crowns of victory at various festivals.

Soon Nero set his heart on driving a chariot himself and in a regular race. So, after a preliminary trial in the palace garden before an audience of slaves and loafers, he made his public debut at the Circus. For this occasion one of his freedmen replaced the official who dropped the *mappa* to signal the start.

However, these incursions into the arts at Rome did not satisfy him for long, and he soon headed for Greece. His main reason stemmed from the fact that the Greek cities which sponsored regular music contests had adopted the policy of sending to him every prize for *kithara*-playing. He always accepted these prizes with great pleasure, giving the representatives of those cities the earliest audience of the day and invitations to private dinners. When the meal was over, they would beg Nero to sing and then applaud his performance resoundingly. This led him to say: "Only the Greeks are worthy of my genius, for they really listen to music." So he sailed off to Greece and, having landed, made the rounds of all the festivals.

Most contests were held only at long intervals, but he ordered them all to be held during his visit even if it meant repeating them after an irregular interval. He broke tradition at Olympia by the introduction of a music contest in the athletic games. When his freedman-secretary Halius reminded him that he was needed urgently at Rome, he would not be distracted but answered: "Yes, you have made yourself quite clear and I understand that you want me to return home. You would do better, however, by encouraging me to stay until I have proved myself worthy of my reputation."

No one was allowed to leave the theater during his performances, however urgent the reason, and the gates were kept locked. There are stories of women in the audience giving birth, and of men being so bored that they would sneak out by jumping off the wall at the back of the theater, or by playing dead and being carried away for burial. Nero's stage fright, his general nervousness, his jealousy of rivals, and his awe of the judges were more easily seen than believed. Although he was usually gracious and charming to the other competitors, whom he treated as equals, he would abuse them behind their backs and sometimes insulted them to their faces. He would bribe singers who were obviously very talented to sing off-key. He would address the judges with extreme deference and say that he had done what he could and that the outcome was now in the hands of fortune but that, since they were men of reason and experience, they would know how to remove the element of luck. When they told him not to worry he would feel a little better, but still anxious, and he mistook the silence of some for harshness, and the embarrassment of others for distaste, and admitted that he regarded every one of them with suspicion.

He observed the rules very carefully, never daring to clear his throat and even using his forearm, instead of a handkerchief to wipe the sweat from his forehead. Once, while acting in a tragedy, he dropped his scepter and quickly picked it up, but was terrified of being disqualified. The accompanist who played the flute and served as prompter for his lines swore that the slip had not been noticed because the audience was listening and enraptured; and so he took heart again. Nero insisted upon announcing his own victories and this led him to enter the competitions for *kerykes*. In order that he might destroy every trace of previous winners in his contests, he ordered that all their statues were to be pulled down, dragged away, and dumped into public latrines.

He took part in the chariot racing on several occasions, and at Olympia he drove a ten-horse team, a novelty which had been added to the festival just for him. However, he lost his balance and fell out of the chariot and had to be helped into it again. Nonetheless, even though he did not run the whole race and quit before the finish, the judges awarded him the crown of victory. On the eve of his departure for Rome, he presented the whole province where Olympia is located with its freedom, and granted Roman citizenship as well as large cash rewards upon the judges. He announced these benefactions himself from the middle of the stadium on the day of the Isthmian Games.

Returning from Greece to Naples, where he first landed, he entered with white horses through a part of the wall that had been torn down, as is the custom for victors at the sacred games. Then he entered Antium in the same way, then Albanum, and then Rome; but at Rome he entered in the same chariot that Augustus had used to celebrate his triumph long ago, and in a purple robe embroidered with golden stars and a *chlamys* and with the Olympic crown on his head and the Pythian in his right hand, and with the other crowns carried before him with legends telling where they had been won and whom he had defeated.

---

204   Suetonius, *Domitian* 4.4   *ca.* A.D. 120

Although athletics had continued in the Hellenic east under the Romans, and although they had been imported to Italian soil in the areas of the old Greek colonies toward the south (e.g., no. 199), it was not until the reign of the emperor Domitian [A.D. 82–96] that a regularly held Greek-style festival was instituted in Rome itself. These Capitoline Games were immediately included in the list of Sacred Games second only to the Olympics themselves (cf. no. 210).

Domitian also established a quadrennial contest in honor of Jupiter Capitolinus in three parts—music, equestrian, gymnic—and with quite a few more crowns of victory than is the custom now. Indeed, they competed in prose recitation in both Greek and Latin as well as in *kithara*-singing, *kithara* chorus accompaniment, and *kithara* solo playing, while in the stadium there was even a race for maidens.

XIII
Amateurism and Professionalism

205 *Hesperia* 33 (1964), 320   *ca.* 565 B.C.

*The inscription upon the base of a statue found at Nemea speaks to us as if from the statue itself. It should be contrasted with athletic inscriptions of much later times such as no. **210** below: the difference is instructive. Note also the similarly simple dedication at Olympia by Euthymos (above, no. **166b**), who was much more famous than Aristis of Kleonai.*

Aristis dedicated me to Zeus Kronios the King since he won the *pankration* at Nemea four times. Aristis is the son of Pheidon from Kleonai.

206 Aelian, *Varia Historia* 2.6   *ca.* A.D. 220

They say that Hippomachos the *gymnastes*, when an athlete who was being trained by him was wrestling and all the bystanders shouted encouragement, struck him with a *rhabdos* and said: "You have done badly and have failed to perform as you should, for if you had been technically correct, these people would not have praised you." He meant that if everything is done properly, pleasure will be given to those who have a theoretical knowledge of what ought to be done, and not to the crowd.

207   *PZenon 59060*   257 B.C.

In the early years of the twentieth century a mass of papyri was discov-
ered at some unknown site in the Fayum region of Egypt (probably near
Memphis) and then dispersed around the world into several different col-
lections. These papyri had come from the private archives of one Zenon,
the business manager of an Apollonios who, in turn, had been the
"Minister of Finance" of Ptolemy II during the last fifteen years of his
reign (285–246 B.C.). Zenon was, therefore, on the fringes of the elite and
a man of some wealth and standing. At least three letters in Zenon's
archives relate to a boy named Pyrrhos who was in some sense a ward of
Zenon. Implicit in this letter to Zenon at Memphis from Hierokles at
Alexandria, who is charged with oversight of the training and education
of the boy, is the value of a victory, and of training for a victory, in the
games. We also gain some insight into the ancient version of boarding
school.

Hierokles to Zenon, greetings! It would be nice if this finds you in good
health; we are well. You wrote to me about Pyrrhos—that I am to train him
only if I am really certain that he will win, for money is not to be thrown
away and he is not to be interrupted from his studies. Of course, only the
gods can say for certain, but it seems to Ptolemaios (the trainer) as much as
man can know, that he is already better than those currently in training who
have been at it for a longer time . . . *[gap in the papyrus]* . . . and in a very
short time there is an abundance of this. The boy approaches this level in his
training as well as in his other lessons. I speak together with the gods in saying that I have every hope that he will win a crown for you.

Please send along to Pyrrhos as soon as possible a bathing suit of
goatskin, but if that cannot be, then of light calfskin. Please also send him a
chiton and a *himation* and a mattress and a mattress-cover and a pillow and
some honey.

You wrote that you were astounded at me that I did not understand that
there was duty to be paid on all these items, but I think that you are surely
competent to send them in the "safest" way.

208   Plutarch, *Philopoimen* 3.2–4   *ca.* A.D. 100

Since Philopoemen [*ca.* 253–182 B.C.] seemed well formed for wrestling,
some of his friends and advisors urged him toward athletics. But he asked
them whether anything in athletics might damage his military training.

Then they told him the reality: that the athletic body and lifestyle are different in every way from the military, and that the diet and exercise are especially different, since athletes are always strengthening themselves with a lot of sleep and perpetual stuffing of their stomachs and fixed periods for motion and rest, and guarding their condition against every lapse or deviation from the habitual which is apt to change it for the worse. The soldier, on the contrary, has to be experienced in every sort of wandering and irregularity, and especially to be able to bear easily lack of food and sleeplessness. When Philopoemen heard this he not only avoided athletics and made fun of them, but later when he was a general he rejected all athletics with dishonor and abuse as making the most useful of bodies worthless for the contests which were truly necessary.

209 *PLond 137 (CR 7 [1893] 476)* 33/32 B.C.

*Although most of our evidence for unions or guilds of athletes comes from a later date when they were very well known (see nos. **212, 213**), this letter from Mark Antony shows that they were already well established, and demanding special treatment, before the Empire had come into being.*

Markos Antonios, Imperator, one of the triumvirs for settling the affairs of the State, to the commonwealth of the Greeks in Asia,

GREETINGS.

I willingly grant the earlier appeal to me in Ephesos by Markos Antonios Artemidoros, my friend and *aleiptes*, who was acting in concert with Charopeinos of Ephesos, the eponymous priest of the *Synodos* of Worldwide Winners of Sacred Games and Crowns . . . that I agree to write to you immediately concerning the honors and benefits which were asked of me [i.e., exemption from military service, from public duties, and from the billeting of troops, a truce during the festival of Ephesos, personal security, and the right to wear purple] and I grant this appeal because of my friendship for Artemidoros and in order to oblige their priest for the glory and advancement of the *Synodos*.

And now that Artemidoros has appealed to me again to allow them to put up a bronze plaque and to incise on it the benefits written above, I, not wishing to hinder Artemidoros in any respect, have granted that the plaque be put up as he requested.

Thus I have written to you concerning these matters.

210   *IG* XIV, 747   A.D. 107

The following inscription was discovered at Naples, and it sets forth the
career of an athlete of the first century A.D. *It tells us of the existence of*
athletic guilds or unions, of the principal games of the period, and some-
thing of their relative importance based upon the order in which they are
listed. It also indicates, especially when contrasted with no. **205** *above, a*
considerable change in athletics and athletes in the more than 650 years
between the two documents.

To Good Fortune. The Loyal and Patriotic and Reverent and Itinerant
Synodos of the Alexandrians honors Titus Flavius Archibius of Alexandria,
high priest for life of the entire *xystos*, victor incomparable, who won the
pankration in the men's category at the 220th and 221st Olympiads [A.D.
101 and 105]. In Rome at the third celebration of the Great Capitoline
Games [A.D. 94] he won the *pankration* in the *ageneios* category, and at their
fourth celebration [A.D. 98] he won the *pankration* in the men's category,
and at their fifth celebration [A.D. 102] he won the *pankration* in the men's
category, and at their sixth celebration [A.D. 106] he again won the *pankra-*
tion in the men's category, the first of mankind to do so. At the Heraklean
Victory Games held by the Emperor Nerva Trajan Caesar Augustus
Germanicus Dacicus he was crowned in the *pankration* in the men's category. At the Pythian Games he won the *pankration* in the *ageneios* category, and at the next Pythiad he won both the *pale* and the *pankration* in
the men's category, and at the next Pythiad he won the *pankration* in the
men's category, the first of mankind to do so. At the Nemean Games he won
the *pankration* in the boys' category and the *pankration* in the men's category three times in a row, the first of mankind to do so. At the Isthmian
Games he won the *pankration* in the men's category. At the Aktian Games
he won the *pale* and the *pankration* in the *ageneios* category, and at the next
festival he won the *pankration* in the men's category, the first of mankind
to do so. At Naples he won the *pankration* in the *ageneios* category and in
the next two festivals he won the *pankration* in the men's category. At the
[. . . *broken away* . . .] he won the *pale* and the *pankration* in the *ageneios*
category, and at the next two festivals he won the *pale* and the *pankration*
in the men's category, and at the next festival he won the *pankration* in the
men's category, the first of mankind to do so. At the Balbilleia Games at
Ephesos he won the *pale* and the *pyx* and the *pankration* in the men's category, the first of mankind to do so. At the sacred four-year games at Antioch
he won the *pankration* in the boys' category and at the next festival four
years later he won the *pale* and the *pyx* in the *ageneios* category, and at the

next festival he won the *pankration* in the men's category, and at the next festival again he won the *pankration* in the men's category, the first of mankind to do so. At the League of Asia Games at Smyrna he won the *pale* and the *pankration* in the *ageneios* category. At the sacred four-year games at Alexandria he won the *pankration* in the *ageneios* category and four years later he won the *pankration* in the men's category and again at the next festival he won the *pankration* in the men's category and at the next festival he won the *pale* and the *pankration* in the men's category, the first of mankind to do so. He also has victories in the *pale* and the *pankration* at the Shield of Argos Games and many other four-year games in the boys', *ageneios*, and men's categories.

211 Pliny the Younger, *Letters* 10.39, 40, 118, 119   A.D. 111

These are some of the letters between Pliny, an Imperial representative in northern Asia Minor, and the emperor Trajan. They reveal a high degree of organization within the Roman administration of the provinces, something of the conflict between the Roman dislike for athletics and the Greek world's continued interest in athletics, and something of the security felt by the athletes, probably because of their unions, in daring to negotiate with the emperor.

PLINY TO TRAJAN: The citizens of Nicaea, Sir, had their *gymnasium* burn down before my arrival. They have begun to rebuild it on a larger scale than it was before, and have voted funds for the purpose which are in danger of being wasted. The structure is poorly planned and unorganized. Furthermore, the present architect (who is, to be sure, a rival of the architect who began the work) says that the walls, even though they are twenty-two feet thick, cannot support the load placed on them, because they are rubble at the core and have no brick facing.

TRAJAN TO PLINY: Those little Greeks have a weakness for *gymnasia*. Perhaps, therefore, the citizens of Nicaea were overly ambitious in undertaking the construction of their *gymnasium*. But they will have to be content with one which is just adequate for their needs.

PLINY TO TRAJAN: Sir, the athletes are constantly complaining that they ought to receive the *obsonia* which you have established for the eiselastic games from the day when they were crowned. They maintain that it is relevant not when they may be led triumphantly into their native city, but when they actually won the contest which is the cause of the *obsonia*. Since I am to countersign the *obsonia* payments with the notation "eiselastic account," it is my strong inclination to believe that only the date when they have made their *eiselasis* is to be considered.

The athletes are also asking for the *obsonia* for victories in the games which you have designated eiselastic even though their victories at those games came before your designation. They maintain that this is only reasonable since the *obsonia* have been stopped for their victories at games which have been dropped from the eiselastic list even though their victories at those games came while those games were still on the list. I seriously question whether such retroactive rewards are to be given, and I therefore beg that you instruct me upon the intention of your benefactions.

TRAJAN TO PLINY: I do not think that anything is owed the victor in an eiselastic contest until the victor has made the *eiselasis* into his own city. No retroactive *obsonia* are owed to the athletes who won victories at the games which I have been pleased to place on the eiselastic list if the victories antedate the games' becoming eiselastic. It is no argument that they have ceased to receive the *obsonia* for their victories in games which I have removed from the eiselastic list. Although the status of those contests was changed, I did not demand that they refund what they had already received.

212 *IG XIV.1055b*   A.D. 143

*Half a century after the Capitoline Games were established in Rome (no. 204), the union of athletes had gained sufficient strength to receive their own "clubhouse" (*curia athletarum* in Latin) in Rome, as we learn from this letter from the emperor Antoninus Pius. The letter and the titles therein are still, however, in Greek, probably because the athletes were Greek.*

With Good Fortune. Emperor Caesar Titus Ailius Hadrianus Antoninus Augustus, son of the deified Hadrian, grandson of the deified Trajan Parthikos, descendant of the deified Nerva, *pontifex maximus*, with tribunician power for the sixth time, emperor for the second time, consul for the third time, and father of the fatherland to the *Xystic Synodos* of the Heraklean Athletic Winners of Sacred Games and Crowns.

GREETINGS.

I have ordered that a plot be handed over to you where you may keep your trophies and records in the area of the baths which were erected by my deified grandfather Trajan just where you congregate for the Capitoline Games. Farewell!

Negotiated by Ulpius Domesticus, head priest of the *Sympas Xystos* and of my baths. Written from Rome on May 16 in the consulship of Torquatus and Herodes.

213 *IG* XIV.1102   *ca.* A.D. 200

At the end of the second century A.D. *the tendency toward encyclopedic autobiography by athletes had continued in the same vein as the earlier example given above for Titus Flavius Archibius (no.* **210**) *but we now can see more clearly that a successful athlete, at the conclusion of his active career, could go into the administrative side of the business, both in the public area (Director of the Imperial Baths) and on behalf of his union (Xystarches). In the case of Marcus Aurelius Asklepiades this meant following closely the career of his father.*

I am the son of Markos Aurelios Demetrios, who was head priest and *Xystarches* for life of the *Sympas Xystos* and Director of the Imperial Baths, a citizen of Alexandria and of Hermopolis, a pankratiast, a *periodonikes*, and a wrestler beyond compare—I am Markos Aurelios Asklepiades, also known as Hermodoros, the eldest of the temple trustees of the great Sarapis, high priest of the *Sympas Xystos, Xystarches* for life, and Director of the Imperial Baths; a citizen of Alexandria, Hermopolis, and Puteoli; a member of the *boule* of Naples and Elis and Athens; both a citizen and member of the *boule* of many other cities; a pankratiast, an unbeaten immovable unchallenged *periodonikes* who won every contest I ever entered. I was never threatened, nor did anyone ever dare to attempt to threaten me, nor did I ever end a contest in a draw, nor debate a decision, nor withdraw, nor miss a competition, but I won my crown in the actual *skamma* of every contest I entered, and I worked my way through the preliminary qualifying events as well.

I competed in three lands: Italy, Greece, and Asia, winning the following competitions in the *pankration:* the Olympics at Pisa in the 240th Olympiad [A.D. 181], the Pythian Games at Delphi, the Isthmian Games twice, the Nemean Games twice (the second of these when my competitors withdrew), and the Shield Games of Hera also in Argos, the Capitoline Games in Rome twice (the second of these when my competitors withdrew after the first *kleros*), the Eusebeia Games at Puteoli twice (the second of these when my competitors withdrew after the second *kleros*), the Sebasta Games at Naples twice (the second of these when my competitors withdrew after the second *kleros*), the Aktian Games at Nikopolis twice (the second of these when my competitors withdrew), five games at Athens (the Panathenaic, the Olympic, the Panhellenics, and the Hadrianic twice), five games at Smyrna (the Asian Commonwealth Games twice [the second of these when my competitors withdrew], and similarly the Olympic in Smyrna and the Hadrianic Olympic), the Augusteia Games at Pergamon three times (the second of these when my competitors withdrew at the start, and the third when my competitors withdrew after the first *kleros*), three games at Ephesos (the Hadrianic, the Olympic, and the Barbilleia Games when my competitors withdrew after the first *kleros*), the Games of Asklepios at Epidauros, of Haleia at Rhodes, the Chrysanthic at Sardis, and many *chrematitic* games including the Eurykleia at Sparta and the Mantinea and others. I competed altogether for six years, but retired from competition when I was twenty-five years old because of the dangers and jealousies which were gathering around me, and after I had retired for several years, I was forced to compete in the local Olympic Games of my native Alexandria and won the *pankration* in the 6th Olympiad there [A.D. 196].

214 Philostratos, *On Gymnastics* 45   *ca.* A.D. 230

The general situation as well as the specific incident described below seem to be from Philostratos' own day, but the situation had clearly been developing over an extended period of time.

Such a luxurious lifestyle as I have just described led to illegal practices among the athletes for the sake of money. I refer to the selling and buying of victories. I suppose that some surrender their chance at fame because of great destitution, but others buy a victory which involves no effort for the luxury which it promises. There are laws against temple robbers who mutilate or destroy a silver or gold dedication to the gods, but the crown of Apollo or of Poseidon, for which even the gods once competed, they are free to buy and free to sell. Only the olive at Elis remains inviolate in accordance with its ancient glory. Let me give one of many possible examples which will illustrate what happens at the other games. A boy won the *pale* at Isthmia by promising to pay $66,000 to his opponent. When they went into the *gymnasion* on the next day, the loser demanded his money, but the winner said that he owed nothing since the other had tried after all to win. Since their differences were not resolved, they had recourse to an oath and went into the sanctuary at Isthmia. The loser then swore in public that he had sold Poseidon's contest, and that they had agreed upon a price of $66,000. Moreover, he stated this in a clear voice with no trace of embarrassment. The fact that this was told in front of witnesses may make it more truthful, but also all the more sacrilegious and infamous; he swore such an oath at Isthmia before the eyes of Greece. What disgrace might not be happening at the games in Ionia and Asia?

I do not absolve the *gymnastai* of blame for this corruption. They came to do their training with pockets full of money which they loan to the athletes at interest rates which are higher than those that businessmen who hazard sea trade have to pay. They care nothing for the reputation of the athletes, but give advice about the sale or purchase of a victory. They are constantly on the lookout for their own gain, either by making loans to those who are buying a victory, or by cutting off the training of those who are selling. I call these *gymnastai* peddlers, for they put their own interests first and peddle the *arete* of their athletes.

215 Galen, *Exhortation for Medicine* 9–14   *ca.* A.D. 180

*Galen (see no. **177**) here attacks professional athletics, but his attack may be founded in a long-standing feud between physicians and trainers. In other words, he may well be more disturbed by the training practices of his day than by professionalism, but the two were inseparable. The Hippokrates whom Galen quotes was a Greek physician who died in 399 B.C. (no. **18**).*

Come now, my boys. You who have heard what I have said to this point must push ahead with the learning of an art so that some cheat or faker will not ever teach you some useless or evil art. Thus will you recognize that those pursuits are not arts which do not have the improvement of life as their goal. Of course, you understand most of those things which are not arts such as tumbling and walking a tightrope and spinning in a circle without becoming dizzy. I am suspicious only of the pursuit of athletics which might trick some youth into thinking that it is an art because it promises strength of body and reputation among the masses and a grant of money each day from the public treasury. Therefore it is best that we give this some forethought, for a person is not so easily deceived in a matter which he has already thought out.

The race of men has in common with the gods the gift of speech and in common with dumb animals the gift of life. It is convenient in education to pay attention to the perceptible advantages of communication, for if we have this we have the greatest of goods, but lacking this we are no better than dumb animals. Now the athletic training of the body lacks this and cannot, furthermore, gain even an equal footing with the dumb animals. For who is stronger than the lions or the elephants, and who can run faster than the hare? Who does not see that we thank the gods for nothing so much as the gift of the arts, and that the best of men are honored, not because they run beautifully in the games or throw the *diskos* or wrestle, but because of their accomplishments and benefactions in the arts? Thus Asklepios and Dionysos were both men who became gods and worthy of the greatest honors, one because he gave us medicine and the other because he taught us the art of viticulture. If you do not want to believe me, then at least respect Pythian Apollo who said that Sokrates was the wisest of all men.

All natural blessings are either mental or physical, and there is no other category of blessing. Now it is abundantly clear to everyone that athletes have never even dreamed of mental blessings. To begin with, they are so deficient in reasoning powers that they do not even know if they have a brain. Always gorging themselves on flesh and blood they keep their brains soaked in so much filth that they are unable to think accurately and are as mindless as dumb animals.

Perhaps it would be claimed that athletes achieve some of the physical blessings. Will they claim the most important blessing of all—health? You will find no one in a more treacherous physical condition if we are to believe Hippokrates, who said that the extreme good health for which they strive is treacherous. And Hippokrates said something else which is liked by all: "Healthy training is moderation in diet, stamina in work." He proposed as a healthful program: "Work, food, drink, sleep, love, and all in moderation." But athletes overexert every day at their exercises, and they force-feed themselves, frequently extending their meals until midnight.

Thus too their sleep is immoderate. When normal people have ended their work and are hungry, the athletes are just getting up from their naps. In fact, their lives are just like those of pigs, except that pigs do not overexert nor force-feed themselves.

In addition to what I have already quoted, Hippokrates also said: "Excessive and sudden filling or emptying or heating or chilling or otherwise moving the body is dangerous." And he also said: "Excess is the enemy of nature." But athletes pay no attention to these or others of his wonderful sayings which they transgress, and their practices are in direct opposition to his doctrines of good health. Furthermore, the extreme conditioning of athletes is treacherous and variable, for there is no room for improvement and it cannot remain constant, and so the only way which remains is downhill. Thus their bodies are in good shape while they are competing, but as soon as they retire from competition degeneration sets in. Some soon die, some live longer but do not reach old age.

Since we have now considered the greatest physical blessing—health—

let us go on to the physical blessings which remain. With respect to beauty it is clear that natural beauty is not improved a bit for athletes, but that many athletes with well-proportioned limbs are made exceedingly fat by the *gymnastai* who take them and stuff them with blood and flesh. Indeed, the faces of some are beat up and ugly, especially of those who have practiced the *pankration* or the *pyx*. When their legs are finally broken or twisted permanently out of shape or their eyes gouged out I suppose that then especially is the beauty resulting from their way of life most clearly to be seen! While they are healthy this is the beauty which it is their good fortune to possess, but when they retire the rest of their bodies go to pot and their already twisted limbs are the cause of real deformities.

But perhaps they will claim none of the blessings which I have mentioned so far, but will say that they have strength, indeed, that they are the strongest of men. But, in the name of the gods, what kind of strength is this and good for what? Can they do agricultural work such as digging or harvesting or plowing? But perhaps their strength is good for warfare? Euripides will tell us, for he said [no. **230**]: "Do men fight battles with *diskoi* in their hands?" Are they strong in the face of cold and heat? Are they rivals of Herakles so that they too, summer and winter, go barefoot clad in a skin and camp out to sleep under the heavens? In all these respects they are weaker than newborn babies.

I think that it has become abundantly clear that the practice of athletics has no use in the real business of life. You would further learn that there is nothing worth mention in such practice if I tell you that myth which some talented man put into words. It goes like this: if Zeus had it in mind that all the animals should live in harmony and partnership so that the herald was to invite to Olympia not only men but also animals to compete in the stadium I think that no man would be crowned. In the *dolichos* the horse will be the best, the *stadion* will belong to the hare, and the gazelle will be first in the *diaulos*. Wretched men, nimble experts, none of you would be counted in the footraces. Nor would any of you descendants of Herakles be stronger than the elephant or the lion. I think that the bull will be crowned in the *pyx*, and that the donkey will, if he decides to, win the kicking crown. And so it shall be written in the *pankration*: "In the 21st Olympiad which was won by Brayer."

This myth shows quite nicely that athletic strength does not reside in human training. And yet, if athletes cannot be better than animals in strength, what other blessings do they share in?

Perhaps someone would say that they have a blessing in the pleasure of their bodies. But how can they derive any pleasure from their bodies if during their athletic years they are in constant pain and suffering, and not only because of their exercises but also because of their forced feedings? And even when they have reached the age of retirement, their bodies are essentially if not completely crippled.

Are athletes perhaps to be worshipped like kings because they have large incomes? And yet they are all in debt, not only during the time when they are competing, but also after retirement. You will not find a single athlete who is wealthier than any business agent of a rich man. Furthermore, the most important aspect of a profession is not whether you can get rich at it, but whether you can always make a living from it. I refer to a stability of income which does not exist even for the managers of rich men, nor for tax collectors, nor for merchants. Finally, athletes have big incomes while they are actively competing, but when they retire money quickly becomes a problem for them and they soon run through their funds until they have less than they started with before their careers. Does any one loan them money without property for security?

Therefore, if any of you wants to prepare to make money safely and honestly, you must train for a profession which can be continued throughout life.

216   Herodotus 3.129–133   *ca.* 430 B.C.

Demokedes, previously court physician to Polykrates the tyrant of Samos, has been captured by the Persians (519 B.C.). Darius, the Persian King, is unaware of the existence of Demokedes until there is an accident. In this story, which shows the intimate connection between athletics and the development of medicine, we realize that, even in the classical era, large sums of money were a part of athletics.

One day Darius was out hunting and twisted his ankle as he dismounted from his horse. It was a severe sprain, for the ankle had been completely dislocated. Darius had kept in attendance for some time some Egyptian doctors who had reputations for being the best of their profession, and he now summoned them. They, however, by their twisting and straining only made the foot worse. For seven days and nights Darius continued in such pain that he could not sleep. On the eighth day he was informed about the skill of Demokedes of Kroton by people who had seen him at work elsewhere. Darius ordered that he be brought forward immediately. He was brought as they found him among the slaves, dragging his chains and dressed in rags. They stood him in front of the throne and Darius asked him if he knew the art of medicine. Demokedes replied that he knew nothing of it, for he was afraid that he would never be allowed to return to Greece if he acknowledged his own skill. Darius, however, was not deceived and realized that Demokedes was concealing his skill. He therefore ordered the men who had brought Demokedes to fetch the whips and the iron spikes. With this Demokedes changed his tune and said that, although he did not understand very much, he had lived with a doctor for a time and had learned a bit about medicine. Despite this statement, Darius entrusted himself to Demokedes, and the latter, by using Greek remedies which were milder than those of his predecessors, enabled Darius to get some sleep and soon restored him to complete health. Darius, who had never expected to be able to use his foot again, presented Demokedes with two sets of gold chains which prompted Demokedes to ask if the reward for his cure was an enrichment of his slavery. Darius was amused by this and sent Demokedes off to his wives. When the eunuchs had conducted him to the wives, they introduced him as the man who had saved the King's life. Thereupon the wives each scooped a cupful of gold from a chest and gave it to Demokedes. There was so much money that a servant by the name of Skiton collected a fortune simply from what spilled over.

The history of Demokedes was that he left his native Kroton in order to escape the harsh treatment of his father. He went first to Aigina where, within the first year, he surpassed the other doctors even though he was untrained and had no medical equipment or instruments. In the second year, the people of Aigina paid him a salary of $132,000. The next year the Athenians hired him away with a salary of $220,000, and the year after that Polykrates offered him $264,000. He accepted this and so went to Samos where the Persians captured him. It was largely because of Demokedes that Krotoniate doctors came to have such a high reputation.

After his cure of Darius, Demokedes lived in a big house in Susa, took his meals with the King, and had every privilege but the one of returning to Greece. The Egyptian doctors who had first treated Darius were going to be impaled, but were released as a result of Demokedes' intervention with Darius on their behalf. In fact, Demokedes' influence with the King was such that he was also able to secure the release of a professional soothsayer from Elis who had been with Polykrates and was lying in a wretched state with the slaves.

After a short time, something else happened. An abscess developed on the breast of Atossa the daughter of Cyrus and a wife of Darius. After a time, the abscess burst and began to spread the infection. At first, while it was still small, she hid it out of shame and told no one about it; but when it grew worse, she sent for Demokedes and showed it to him. He said that he would cure her if she would promise to do for him in return whatever he might ask of her. He stipulated that he would ask for nothing which would cause her shame, and upon these terms he treated and cured her.

As her part of the bargain, Atossa convinces Darius to send Demokedes out with a Persian mission to spy upon the defenses of Greece as a preliminary to a Persian invasion. When the mission finally comes to southern Italy, Demokedes jumps ship and finds his way back to Kroton. His erstwhile Persian companions pursue him, but the Krotoniates (after some debate) refuse to give him up.

The Persians returned to Asia and made no further attempt to scout out the coasts of Greece since they had lost their guide. Just before they left Kroton Demokedes told them to inform Darius that he was engaged to be married to the daughter of Milo the wrestler whose name was held in high esteem by the King. I think that Demokedes decided to make this marriage even though it cost him a large sum of money in order to show Darius that he was important in his own homeland.

217   Pausanias 6.7.10   *ca.* A.D. 170

The role of diet in training for athletic competition was recognized in antiquity although the development of that role is not clear. We hear of a change from dried figs, wet cheese, and wheat meal to meat—a change effected by a Pythagoras who was either the famous philosopher-mathematician (ca. 582–500 B.C.) or an aleiptes of the same name (Diogenes Laertius 8.12–13; cf. Pliny, NH 23.121)—as well as the version given below.

A man from Stymphalos was Dromeus [i.e. "runner"] in name and in deed, for he won the *dolichos* twice at Olympia [484 and 480 B.C.], twice at Delphi, three times at Isthmia, and five times at Nemea. It is said that he thought up the idea of a meat diet; previously athletes had fed on wet cheese. Pythagoras made the statue.

218   Plato, *Republic* 406a–b and *Protagoras* 316d–e   390–380 B.C.

The influence of athletics on medical practices continued to develop during the late fifth century, the dramatic date of two Sokratic dialogues.

A. The followers of Asklepios did not make use of the existing "paidagogical" medicine in the treatment of illness before Herodikos. He was a *paidotribes* who became sickly and then mixed gymnastic with medical practice and thereby wore himself down first of all, and then many others; he prolonged his life too much. He paid attention constantly to his illness—which was incurable—and spent all his time on it. If he violated his strict diet by a whisker, he was in a terrible state, but thanks to his knowledge he arrived at a very old age useless for any task except staying alive.

B. I say that sophistry is an old art, but men of olden times who made use of it, since they feared its burdens, made a facade and covered it, some under the guise of poetry as did Homer and Hesiod and Simonides, while others disguised sophistry as rites and prophecies like Orpheus and Mousaios and their adherents. I sense, too, that some have used athletics to hide sophistry. These include the likes of Ikkos of Tarentum and the one still living—than whom no one is a better sophist—Herodikos of Selymbria [originally from Megara].

219 Thucydides 6.16.2   415 B.C.

During the public debate which resulted in the decision to mount an Athenian invasion of Sicily, Alkibiades presented his case for being put in command of the expedition. A part of his argument is the following, which shows something of the private wealth which was expended by competitors at the Panhellenic Games (cf. no. 67).

I think, Athenians, that I am worthy of the command. First of all, my deeds, which make me the object of public outcry, actually bring glory not only to my ancestors and myself, but also to my country, and this glory is mixed with practical advantage as well. The Greeks who had been hoping that our city was exhausted by the war came to think of our power as even greater than it is because of my magnificent *theoria* at Olympia. I entered seven *tethrippa*, a number never before entered by a private citizen, and I came in first, second, and fourth, and I provided all the trappings worthy of such a victory. For it is the custom that such accomplishments convey honor, and at the same time power is inferred from the achievement.

220 *SEG* 35.1053   *ca.* 600 B.C.

The following brief and difficult inscription was discovered on a bronze tablet at Sybaris in southern Italy. It raises fundamental questions: How could Kleombrotos dedicate a tithe of his victory prize from the Olympic Games? What is a tenth of a crown of olive leaves? Are we dealing here, at this early date, with a monetary prize awarded to Kleombrotos by his hometown in recognition of his Olympic victory?

See further below, nos. 221–223.

A gift. Kleombrotos son of Dexilaos, having won at Olympia and having promised the prize of equal length and width [?] to Athena, dedicated a tithe.

221 *IG I³ 131*   440–432 B.C.?

This decree of the Athenian people shows that, at least by the middle of the fifth century B.C. if not earlier, it was common for a city-state to reward her athletes who had been victorious at one of the Panhellenic Games with a prize worth something more than the simple crown awarded at the games themselves.

Those citizens who have won or will win at Olympia or Delphi or Isthmia or Nemea shall have a free meal every day for the rest of their lives in the *prytaneion* and other honors as well. . . . Also those citizens who have won the *tethrippon* or the *keles* at Olympia or Delphi or Isthmia or Nemea shall have a free meal every day for the rest of their lives in the *prytaneion*.

222 Diodorus Siculus 13.82.7   *ca.* 30 B.C.

In the 92nd Olympiad [412 B.C.] when Exainetos of Akragas won the *stadion*, his return home was by being led into the city in a chariot; in the parade for him there were, not to mention the other things, three hundred chariots each with a team of white horses.

223 Plutarch, *Solon* 23.3   *ca.* A.D. 100

The following passage from Plutarch's biography of the Athenian lawgiver Solon (lived ca. 650–580 B.C.; cf. nos. 35, 113) may or may not be historically accurate, but it shows that by the time of Plutarch, and perhaps much earlier, one could easily believe that money had been a part of athletics, including the stephanitic competitions, even at their inception.

[The laws of Solon stated that Athens was to] give $22,000 to a victor in the Isthmian Games, but $110,000 to a victor in the Olympic Games.

XIV
Nationalism and Internationalism

224 Pausanias 6.13.1   *ca.* A.D. 170

Pausanias fails to mention that Astylos also won the hoplitodromos *at Olympia in 476 B.C.; cf. no.* **129** *where he is listed as a Syracusan.*

The statue of Astylos of Kroton is the work of Pythagoras. Astylos won both the *stadion* and the *diaulos* in three successive Olympiads [488, 484, 480 B.C.]. Because on the two latter occasions he announced that he was a Syracusan in order to please Hieron the son of Deinomenes and king of Syracuse, the citizens of Kroton pulled down his statue and turned his house into a prison.

225 Pausanias 6.2.6   *ca.* A.D. 170

There stands a statue of Antipater son of Kleinopater of Miletus who won the *pyx* in the boys' category [388 B.C.]. Men from Syracuse, sent by the tyrant Dionysios to make a sacrifice at Olympia [no. **245**], tried to bribe Antipater's father to have the boy announced as a Syracusan. But Antipater scorned the tyrant's gift and announced that his family and he were from Miletus, and that he was the first Ionian to dedicate a statue at Olympia.

226   Pausanias 6.3.11   *ca.* A.D. 170

Dikon, son of Kallibrotos, won the Pythian Games five times in the *dromos*,
the Isthmian three times, the Nemean four times, and the Olympian once in
the *paides* [392 B.C.] and twice more in the *andres*. At Olympia the same
number of statues of him have been erected as his victories. He was recognized as being a *pais* from Kaulonia, as he was in fact. Afterward he was proclaimed as a Syracusan, for cash.

227   Pausanias 6.18.6   *ca.* A.D. 170

*Lest we think that only the Syracusans tried to "hire" a national team, the
following passage is included.*

When Sotades won the *dolichos* at the 99th Olympiad [384 B.C.] he was proclaimed as from Crete as he actually was. But at the next Olympiad he took
a bribe from the Ephesians and announced that he was from Ephesos. For
this the Cretans punished him with exile.

228   Pausanias 6.4.11   *ca.* A.D. 170

Ergoteles, son of Philanor, won the *dolichos* twice at Olympia [472 B.C.—see
no. **129**—and 464 B.C.], the same number he won at Delphi, Isthmia, and
Nemea. It is said that he was not originally from Himera, even though the
inscription on his statue says so, but a Cretan from Knossos. He was kicked
out of Knossos because of civil strife and come to Himera where he got citizenship and other honors as well. Naturally he was proclaimed at the
games as from Himera.

229   Xenophanes, fragment 2   *ca.* 525 B.C.

*The poet and philosopher Xenophanes, in his arguments for the values of
intellectual accomplishments, shows that critics and criticism of athletes
and athletics were known long before the time of Philostratos and Galen
(nos. **214** and **215**), and even before the glorification of athletes by Pindar
(nos. **248–252**).*

Even if a man should win a victory in the sanctuary of Zeus at Olympia in
the footraces or the *pentathlon* or the *pale* or the painful *pyx* or in the
dreadful struggle which men call the *pankration*, even if he should become
a most glorious symbol for his fellow citizens to observe, and win *proedria*
at the games and his meals at public expense [see above, no. **221**] and some

especially valuable gift from the state, even if he should win in the horse races, and even if he should accomplish all of these things and not just one of them, he still would not be so valuable as I am. For my wisdom is a better thing than the strength of men or horses. The current custom of honoring strength more than wisdom is neither proper nor just. For the city-state is not a bit more law-abiding for having a good boxer or a pentathlete or a wrestler or a fast runner even though the running may be the most honored event in the games of man. There is little joy for a state when an athlete wins at Olympia, for he does not fill the state's coffers.

230 Euripides, *Autolykos*, fragment 282   *ca.* 420 B.C.

The Athenian playwright Euripides, in this work of which we possess only fragments, carries on the attack against athletics a century after Xenophanes.

Of the thousands of evils which exist in Greece there is no greater evil than the race of athletes. In the first place, they are incapable of living, or of learning to live, properly. How can a man who is a slave to his jaws and a servant to his belly acquire more wealth than his father? Moreover, these athletes cannot bear poverty nor be of service to their own fortunes. Since they have not formed good habits, they face problems with difficulty. They glisten and gleam like statues of the city-state itself when they are in their prime, but when bitter old age comes upon them they are like tattered and threadbare old rugs. For this I blame the custom of the Greeks who assemble to watch athletes and thus honor useless pleasures in order to have an excuse for a feast. What man has ever defended the city of his fathers by winning a crown for wrestling well or running fast or throwing a *diskos* far or planting an uppercut on the jaw of an opponent? Do men drive the enemy out of their fatherland by waging war with *diskoi* in their hands or by throwing punches through the line of shields? No one is so silly as to do this when he is standing before the steel of the enemy.

   We ought rather to crown the good men and the wise men, and the reasonable man who leads the city-state well and the man who is just, and the man who leads us by his words to avoid evil deeds and battles and civil strife. These are the things which benefit every state and all the Greeks.

231 Plato, *Apology* 36d–e   399 B.C.

Sokrates has been found guilty of impiety and of corrupting the youth of Athens. The jury must now decide whether he should suffer the death penalty, or an alternative to be proposed by him. Such alternatives usually included exile, financial penalties, and/or disenfranchisement. Sokrates proposes as an alternative to the death penalty the following:

What is a fitting penalty for a poor man who is your benefactor and who needs leisure time for advising you? There is nothing more fitting, men of Athens, for such a man than that he be given free meals for the remainder of his life in the *prytaneion*. And that is much more fitting than such a reward for one of you who has won the *synoris* or the *tethrippon* at the Olympic Games. He makes you seem to be happy; I make you happy. And he does not need free meals; I do. If, then, I have to be penalized in accordance with my just worth, I should be penalized with free meals in the *prytaneion*.

A. RELATIONS BETWEEN THE PANHELLENIC SANCTUARIES

232 Pausanias 5.2.1–2   *ca.* A.D. 170

The following account of the "curse of Moline" is one of several attempts to explain why Elean athletes never competed at the Isthmian games. Set in mythological times and incapable of proof, it does at least show a fundamental rivalry between Olympia and Isthmia, or perhaps between Elis and Corinth.

Herakles did not distinguish himself in the war with Augeas. The sons of Actor, an ally of Augeas, were in full bloom in their valor and their age, and they were routing the allied forces of Herakles when the Corinthians announced the *spondai* for the Isthmian Games. The sons of Actor, who went off as *theoroi* to the games, were ambushed and killed by Herakles in the territory of Kleonai. While the murderer was unknown, Moline most of all the siblings tried to find him. But when she learned who he was, the Eleans demanded justice for the foul deed from the Argives, for Herakles was living in their territory at Tiryns. When the Argives refused to give them justice, the Eleans tried to get the Corinthians to exclude all Argives from the Isthmian truce. When they also failed in this, they say that Moline put curses on her countrymen if they did not boycott the Isthmian Games voluntarily. Today they still respect the curses of Moline so that Elean athletes do not participate in the Isthmian Games.

233 Pausanias 6.3.9   *ca.* A.D. 170

Hysmon of Elis, a competitor in the *pentathlon*, won a victory at Olympia [384 B.C.?] and another at Nemea, but he clearly boycotted the Isthmian games just like the other Eleans.

234 Pausanias 6.16.2   *ca.* A.D. 170

Timon [of Elis, 200 B.C.?] won victories in the *pentathlon* in all the games that Greeks hold except the Isthmian—he did not compete there and boycotted those games just like the other Eleans.

235 Plutarch, *Moralia* 675D–676F   *ca.* A.D. 100

Plutarch presents a variety of topics in the form of learned discussions where the "footnotes" are texts quoted to prove a point and to show erudition—ostensibly of the speaker who is, of course, a creation of the author.

The pine was discussed and why it became the wreath of the Isthmian Games; the occasion was a dinner in Corinth, given for us by Koukanios, the chief priest, while the Isthmian Games were in progress.

There follows a scholarly discussion of various myths about pine, interrupted by a professor of rhetoric who said:

"In the name of the gods! Didn't the pine become the wreath of the Isthmian games only yesterday or the day before that? Didn't they crown with celery longer ago? This is clear in the comedy where a miser is heard to say: 'I would be glad to sell the Isthmian Games for as much as the crown of celery is selling.'"

More citations follow, and then:

"And don't you know that they revere the pine, not as a new and imported, but as the old crown of the Isthmian games used by our forefathers?"

    Then Loukanios looked at me with a smile and said, "By Poseidon, what a lot of learned letters. It looks as if other folks have had the benefit of our lack of education and ignorance to promote the opposite point of view, that the pine was the traditional crown of the games, but the crown of celery was foreign and introduced from Nemea because of jealous rivalry with Herakles [see above, no. **232**]."

A few more citations ensue, ending with the following:

"Kallimachos makes it even clearer, for in his poem Herakles says about celery that 'The Corinthians performing much more ancient games by the shores of the Aegean will make celery the symbol of Isthmian victory out of jealous rivalry with the Nemean Games, and they will dishonor the pine which earlier crowned competitors in Corinthian land.'"

236   Pausanias 5.21.5   *ca.* A.D. 170

In his description of the Zanés (no. 103), Pausanias relates the following episode which shows that cooperation did exist, at least on occasion, between the Panhellenic sanctuaries.

They say that Kallippos the Athenian who was competing in the *pentathlon* bought off his competitors with money in the 112th Olympiad [332 B.C.]. When the Eleans had imposed fines on Kallippos and his opponents, the Athenians sent Hypereides to persuade the Eleans to forgive the penalty, but when the Eleans refused this favor, the Athenians were so filled with contempt for them that they refused to pay the money and they boycotted the Olympic Games. Finally, the god at Delphi said that he would give no oracles on any subject to the Athenians before they paid the fine to the Eleans. When the fine was thus paid, six statues were made in honor of Zeus.

B. RELATIONS BETWEEN CITY-STATES AND THE PANHELLENIC SANCTUARIES

237   Herakleides of Pontus *apud* Athenaeus 12.521F   *ca.* 340 B.C.

The Sybarites wanted to eclipse entirely the Olympic Games [*ca.* 512 B.C.] and they waited for the time of the Olympics and then by means of extraordinary prizes they tried to get the athletes to come to them instead of going to Olympia.

238a   Thucydides 5.49–50   420 B.C.

Thucydides here describes the situation when the Eleans excommunicated the Spartans from the festival at Olympia. It cannot be mere coincidence that, just before the Olympics of 420 B.C., Elis had concluded a treaty with Athens, Argos, and Mantinea against the Spartans. Xenophon, Hellenika 3.2.21–22, tells us that the Spartans were still angry about this episode when they declared war on Elis in 399/398 B.C. (see no. 239).

During this summer there were the Olympics at which Androsthenes of Arcadia won his first victory in the *pankration*. The Lakedaimonians were excluded from the Sanctuary of Zeus by the Eleans so that they could neither sacrifice nor compete in the games. The Lakedaimonians refused to pay the fine which the Eleans had imposed upon them in accordance with Olympic law for allegedly breaking the Olympic *spondai*. . . . When the

Lakedaimonians refused to pay the fine . . . the Eleans suggested that, since they were so eager to have access to the sanctuary, they should stand on the altar of Olympian Zeus and, in front of all the Greeks, swear that they would pay the fine later. Since the Lakedaimonians did not want to do this either, they were excluded from the sanctuary, the sacrifice and the contests, and sacrificed by themselves at home, while the rest of the Greeks . . . sent *theoroi* to the festival at Olympia. The Eleans were afraid that the Lakedaimonians might try to sacrifice at Olympia by force, and kept guard with the young men armed. About a thousand Argives, a like number of Mantineans, and some Athenian cavalry . . . came to help them.

A great fear came over the festival that the Lakedaimonians would march under arms, especially when a Lakedaimonian, Lichas the son of Arkesilaos, was flogged by the *rhabdouchoi* because, when his team of horses won but was announced as belonging to the people of Boeotia because he had no right to compete, he had run up and tied [a *tainia* on] the charioteer so that he could make clear that the chariot was his. Thus everyone was in a great state of fear and it seemed that something was going to happen. But the Lakedaimonians kept their peace and the celebration was completed.

238b Pausanias 6.2.2 *ca.* A.D. 170

Pausanias' version of the story of Lichas adds something of the conse-quences of the episode, including the battle described in no. 239.

Regarding Arkesilaos and his son Lichas, the father won two Olympic vic-tories, but Lichas, because the Lakedaimonians were banned from the games in his time, entered his chariot in the name of the *demos* of the Thebans, but he himself bound the *tainia* on the charioteer when he won. For this reason the *Hellanodikai* flogged him and on account of this Lichas the Lakedai-monians under King Agis invaded Elis and fought a battle inside the *Altis*. When the war was over, Lichas set up a statue here, but the Elean records of the Olympic victors do not have Lichas as the winner, but the *demos* of the Thebans.

239 Pausanias 5.20.4–5 *ca.* A.D. 170

I must not overlook the story which Aristarchos, the *exegete* [no. **133**] of everything at Olympia, told me. He said that in his own lifetime when they were repairing the roof of the Temple of Hera they found the wounded corpse of an Elean infantryman between the ceiling joist and the rafters.

This man had fought in the battle within the *Altis* between the Lakedaimonians and the Eleans [399/398 B.C.] when the Eleans were defending the place by climbing up onto the roofs of the temples and everyplace else of any similar height. It appeared to us that this man, faint from his wounds, must have crawled in here and died. Lying in a completely covered place, he suffered nothing from the heat of summer nor from the cold of winter. Aristarchos said that they gave him a burial with his weapons outside the *Altis*.

240 Xenophon, *Hellenika* 4.5.1–2 and 4.5.4   390 B.C.

Early in the fourth century, Argive imperialism resulted in the annexation of Corinth; some Corinthians welcomed their new "compatriots," others fled and allied themselves with the Lakedaimonians who invaded in the spring of 390 B.C.

Agesilaos, who was commanding the Lakedaimonians, came first to Isthmia where the Argives happened to be celebrating the Isthmian Games and sacrificing to Poseidon as if Argos were Corinth. When they learned of the approach of Agesilaos they dropped everything out of fear and ran into the city. But Agesilaos did not pursue them, even though he saw them, but pitched camp in the sanctuary, sacrificed to the god, and waited while the Corinthian exiles conducted the sacrifices to Poseidon and then the games.

As soon as Agesilaos left, the Argives returned and celebrated the Isthmian Games again from the beginning. And in that year some athletes lost twice and others were twice proclaimed victors.

. . . During the night four days later it became clear that the Temple of Poseidon was burning but no one saw who started the fire.

241 Xenophon, *Hellenika* 7.4.28   364 B.C.

During an extended war between Elis and Arkadia, the Arkadians (together with their allies the Argives, Thebans, and Messenians) captured Olympia in 365 B.C. and the next year the following infamous episode occurred (cf. above, nos. 46 and 51).

Then the Arkadians guarded Olympia most vigorously and with an Olympic year approaching [i.e. beginning at the summer solstice of 364 B.C.] they prepared to celebrate the Olympic Games together with the Pisatans who claim that they were the first to superintend the sanctuary. When the month arrived in which the Olympic Games take place, and the days on which the festival crowd gathers, then the Eleans made preparations openly and, having summoned the Achaians to help, marched on the road to Olympia. The Arkadians never thought that the Eleans would march against them, and they were organizing the festival together with the Pisatans. They had already finished the horse races, and the stadium events of the *pentathlon*. The competitors who had reached the wrestling were no longer in the stadium, but were wrestling in the region between the stadium and the altar. At this point the Eleans under arms had already reached the sacred precinct. The Arkadians did not go further out to meet them, but drew up their line on the River Kladeos which flows by the *Altis* and empties into the Alpheios. Their allies were together with them—about 2,000 Argive infantry and 400 Athenian cavalry. The Eleans drew up on the other side of the Kladeos, and as soon as they had slaughtered the sacrificial victims they advanced. Now in earlier times the Eleans had been despised by the Arkadians and the Argives in matters of war, and despised generally by the Achaians and the Athenians, but on that day they led their allies forward as men most determined and valorous. They put the Arkadians, who were the first they fell upon, to flight, and then bested the Argives who came to the rescue of the Arkadians. But when the Eleans had pursued the others into the region between the *bouleuterion* and the shrine of Hestia, their fighting did not diminish and they pushed on toward the altar. But while they were down on the ground, they were being pelted from the roofs of the stoas and of the *bouleuterion* and of the Temple of Zeus itself and some of the Eleans were killed, including Stratolas the leader of the Three Hundred. When this happened, they left off for their own camp.

The Arkadians and their company were afraid of the next day and they therefore did not pause all night long, but cut down the tents which had been so laboriously erected and built a palisade around the *Altis*. On the next day the Eleans returned and saw that the wall was sturdy and that many men were on the roofs of the temples, and therefore left for their own city. They had shown the sort of *arete* that Zeus can inspire on a given day, but which man cannot effect in many years.

242 Plutarch, *Aratos* 28.3–4   *ca.* A.D. 100

Due to his experience in speaking and in politics, and thanks to his reputation, Aratos of Sikyon was able to bring Kleonai into the Achaian League [enemy of Argos at that time, *ca.* 235 B.C.], and he brought the Nemean Games to the people of Kleonai since by tradition and propriety the games belonged to them. But the Argives also celebrated the Nemean Games at Argos, and then for the first time the right of competitors to neutrality and safety was violated, for the Achaians sold into slavery any athlete they caught traveling through their territory to compete in the games at Argos.

C. RELATIONS BETWEEN CITY-STATES AT THE PANHELLENIC SANCTUARIES

243   Pausanias 5.10.4   *ca.* A.D. 170

Pausanias begins his description of the monuments of Olympia with the Temple of Zeus and points out that on the top of the gable of the front (east) end of the Temple was a gold shield (from 457 B.C.) with the following inscription:

> The Temple has a golden shield from Tanagra,
>   The Lakedaimonians and their allies dedicated it
> A "gift" from Argives and Athenians and Ionians
>   A tithe from victory in war.

244   Pausanias 10.11.6   *ca.* A.D. 170

Delphi, like Olympia, counted among its wealth many dedications made by one city-state from its victories over another. The following example comes from a battle dating, probably, in 429 B.C.

The Athenians built a stoa from the money which they got from the Peloponnesians and their allies in war. There are dedicated the decorated prows of ships and bronze shields. The inscription on them enumerates the city-states from which the Athenians sent these first-fruits: Elis, Lakedaimonia, Sikyon, Megara, Pellene in Achaia, Ambrakia, Leukas, and Corinth.

245   Diodorus Siculus 14.109   *ca.* 30 B.C.

The Olympic Games [of 388 B.C.] were drawing near and Dionysios [tyrant of Syracuse in Sicily] sent off several *tethrippa*, much faster than the others, and tents for the festival, embroidered with gold and decorated with expensive and colorful fabrics. He also sent the best rhapsodists who were to recite his poems at the festival and ensure the fame of Dionysios—he had a mania for poetry. And he sent his brother Thearides to supervise the whole expedition.

   When Thearides arrived at Olympia, he was the center of attention because of the beauty of his tents and the number of his *tethrippa*. But when the rhapsodists began to recite the poetry of Dionysios, the crowd at first assembled because of the euphony of the reciters and all were amazed; but after they reconsidered the bad quality of the poetry, they ridiculed Dionysios and disparaged him to the extent that some dared to rip off his tents. In fact the orator Lysias who was then at Olympia urged the crowd not to allow the *theoroi* sent by that most wicked of tyrants to participate in the sacred games. . . . During the competition itself it happened by chance that some of the *tethrippa* of Dionysios spun off the track and that others smashed into one another and all were wrecked.

For other activities of Dionysios at the Olympic festival of 388 b.c., see nos. ***225*** *and* ***226***.

246   Pausanias 5.20.9–10   *ca.* A.D. 170

Within the *Altis* [at Olympia] is a round building called the Philippeion. . . . It was constructed by Philip after the fall of Greece at Chaironeia [338 B.C.], and in it are set up statues of Philip and Alexander, and of Philip's father Amyntas. These are made of gold and ivory, as are the statues of Olympias and Eurydike, Philip's wife and mother.

247   *IG* IV² 1.68.70–73   302 B.C.

The following is a clause concerning the meetings of the Greek League, originally established by Philip II of Macedon after his defeat of the Greeks at Chaironeia, as reorganized by kings Antigonos and Demetrios.

The meetings of the council will take place wherever the chairmen and the king, or the general designated by the king, announce until the war is over; when peace has come, the meetings will take place wherever the *stephanitic* games are taking place.

XV
Beauty and Reality

248 Pindar, *Olympian Ode* 7.1–16, 80–93 464 B.C.

During the first half of the fifth century B.C. the poet Pindar wrote dozens of odes in honor of victorious athletes at the Panhellenic Games. It is through his poetry more than any other single source that we form the usual picture of Classical Greek athletes and athletics, although the surviving examples of vase painting and sculpture (below, nos. 253–254) also promote an image of grace and glory. For some of the descendants of Diagoras of Rhodes, the honoree of this ode, see above, nos. 149 and 170.

As when a man takes up in his wealthy hand
a drinking cup brimming with the dew of the vine,
and gives it to his new son-in-law,
toasting his move from one home to another
to the joy of his drinking companions
and in honor of his new alliance and thus makes him,
in the presence of his friends, an object of envy
for the true love of his marriage bed;
Just so do I send my liquid nectar, gift of the Muses,
sweet fruit of my talent to the prize winners,

and please the winners at Olympia and Pytho.
Truly blessed is he who is surrounded by constant good repute,
for the Grace who gives the bloom to life now favors one, then
  another
with both the sweet-singing lyre and the variegated notes of the flute.
To the accompaniment of both have I now come
with Diagoras to his land while singing of
Rhodes, daughter of Aphrodite, bride of Apollo.
I have come to honor his fighting form and his skill in boxing
and the great man himself who was crowned by the Alpheios
and by the Kastalian spring and to honor his father Damagetos.
Twice crowned with the laurel has been Diagoras,
and with his good fortune four times at famed Isthmia,
and again and again at Nemea and at rocky Athens.
Nor is he a stranger to the bronze shield at Argos,
nor to the prizes in Arcadia and at Thebes.
And he has won six times at Pellana and Aigina
while at Megara the stone tablet tells the same story.
O father Zeus, give honor to this hymn for a victor at Olympia,
and to his now famous *arete* in boxing.
Grant him grace and reverence among his townsfolk and among
  foreigners.
He travels the straight path which despises *hubris*,
and he has learned well the righteous precepts of good forefathers.

249 Pindar, *Pythian Ode* 8.70–98   450 B.C.

In Megara you have a prize already, Aristomenes,
and in the plain of Marathon, and three victories
in Hera's games in your home of Aigina.
But now you fell heavily and from high and with malice
  aforethought
upon the bodies of three opponents.
For them there was at Delphi no decision
for a happy homecoming like yours,
nor did happy laughter awaken pleasure in them
as they ran home to their mothers.
They slunk through the back alleys, separately and furtively,
painfully stung by their loss.

But he who has won has a fresh beauty and
is all the more graceful for his high hopes
as he flies on the wings of his manly deeds
with his mind far above the pursuit of money.
The happiness of man grows only for a short time
and then falls again to the ground,
cut down by the grim reaper.
Creatures of a day, what is a man? what is he not?
Man is but a dream of a shadow.
But when a ray of sunshine comes as a gift from the gods,
a brilliant light settles on men,
and a gentle life.

250   Bacchylides 8.1–9, 21–36, 97–104   451 B.C.?

This victory ode for Automedes of Phlious was written by Bacchylides, a
slightly younger contemporary of Pindar, and it is one of many that reveal
that Pindar was not the only poet whose business was based on the glorifi-
cation of athletes, or at least of victorious ones.

O golden-distaffed Graces grant
Man-persuading fame
For a divine prophet of violet-eyed Muses
Stands prepared to hymn Phlious
And Nemean Zeus' prosperous plain
Where white-armed Hera reared
Sheep-slaughtering roar-reverberating
Lion, first of Herakles' lauded labors . . .
. . . from famous games at Nemea
Are men renowned whose golden hair
with biennial wreath is crowned.
And now Automedes has been given
Such victory by the god.
For among the pentathletes he stood out
Even as the full brilliant moon
Dims the stars at midnight
Thus did his wondrous body shine
Among the boundless circle of Hellenes
As he hurled the wheel-like *diskos*
And into lofty heavens launched the

Branch of dark-leaved elder wood
To the gasp of the crowd now in his grasp
Or polishing off his wrestling opponents.

Zeus has given to you, Phlious,
City god-honored and unravaged,
As your home and as a boon to
Demeter and Dionysos.
Let all men praise whomever wins
A boon of gold-sceptered Zeus,
But with revel-songs may you recount
The *pentathlon* victory of the son of Timoxenos.

---

251   Pindar, *Isthmian Ode* 2.1–21   472 B.C.?

At the beginning of this victory ode Pindar reveals something of the under-lying business of glorifying athletic success.

Men of old, Thrasyboulos, who mounted the
Stage of the golden-wreathed Muses
With splendid lyre in hand
Swiftly shot out sweetened songs for a boy
Who was *kalos* and had the most pleasant
Ripeness reminding one of Aphrodite on her beautiful throne
For the muse was then not yet a profiteer nor yet a hired hand
Nor were sugared soft-voiced songs silver-plated for sale by
    Terpsichore.
But now she demands our attention for that saying of Argive
    Aristodemos
Which so nearly approaches today's truth: "Money, Money, makes
    the Man,"
Said he who lost together wealth and friends.

But you are wise and I do not ignore that I must sing of the horsy
    Isthmian
Victory of Xenokrates, your father . . .

252a   Pindar, *Nemean Ode* 5.1–11   485 B.C.

I am no sculptor who carves
statues doomed to stand on their bases.

I send forth on every merchant ship, on every mail boat,
my sweet song to speed from Aigina and announce that
stalwart Pytheas son of Lampon has won the crown
for the *pankration* at the Nemean Games.
And he still a lad showing on his cheeks a summer tan,
a delicate sign of youthful bloom.

252b Scholion to Pindar, *Nemean Ode* 5.1

They say that the family of Pytheas came to Pindar and asked him to write
a victory ode for him. When Pindar demanded $66,000, they said it would
be better to make a statue in his honor than a poem. Later they gave up and
returned to pay his price. Thus he begins [the poem] by reproaching them
and says that he doesn't make works that sit in one place, but that his poems
reach everywhere so that the *arete* of those who are praised is known to
many.

253 Lucian, *Philopseudes* 18   ca. A.D. 170

*Stories of the supernatural include one of a statue that roams the house at
night; here the speaker wants the auditor to understand of which statue he
speaks.*

"As you enter," he asked, "have you not seen that most beautiful statue set
up in the courtyard, a work of Demetrios the portrait-maker?" "Do you
mean the *diskos*-thrower," I said, "the one bent over as if at the start, looking back at the *diskos*-holding hand, crouching down slightly, looking like
he is cocked to spring up with the throw?" "Not that one," he said, "the
diskobolos of which you speak is one of the works of Myron. Neither do I
speak of the one next to it, the beautiful statue which is binding a ribbon on
his head, for that is the work of Polykleitos."

254 *Anthologia Graeca* 16.54–54A   [460 B.C.]

As you were in life, Ladas, flying before
          wind-foot Thymos
Barely touching the ground with
          the tips of your toes,
Just so did Myron cast you in bronze

engraving all over your body
    Expectation of the crown of Pisa.

He is full of hope, with the breath on
    the tips of his lips
Blowing from within his hollow ribs
    bronze ready to jump
Out for the crown—the base cannot
    hold it back
Art swifter than the wind.

255   Aristophanes, *Birds* 904–957   414 B.C.

In this comedy, Peisthetairos and others begin a new kingdom of the birds as a replacement for and an improvement upon the real world ruled by men, but problems continue to appear. One of these is in the form of an itinerant poet, and it is quite clear that Aristophanes was thinking of Pindar and of others like him, and we are thereby warned not to accept at face value the poetic glorifications of ancient athletes.

PEISTHETAIROS: Let us pray as we sacrifice to the feathered gods.

POET [enters singing]: O my Muse, praise the blessed Cloud-cuckoo-land, and hymn her fame in song.

PEISTHETAIROS: What in the world is this? Tell me, who are you?

POET: I am a sweet-tongued warbler, a song-bird and poor servant of the Muses.

PEISTHETAIROS: How can you be a slave and wear your hair so long?

POET: I am no slave, but all we teachers are poor servants of the Muses.

PEISTHETAIROS: Is that why your cloak is so shabby and poor? But tell me, poet, what ill wind has blown you here?

POET: I have been composing sweet songs and lovely poems to celebrate your Cloud-cuckoo-land.

PEISTHETAIROS: You cannot have been composing such anthems. When did you begin?

POET: Long, long ago did I begin to sing the praises of this state.

PEISTHETAIROS: I have not yet celebrated the tenth day since the founding of this state.

POET: Ah, but the Rumor of the Muses is as swift as the flashing feet of horses; but give to me whatever you choose willingly.

PEISTHETAIROS: He'll make trouble for us now unless we give him something to get rid of him. Hey, you there, you have a leather jacket and a *chiton.* Take off your jacket and give it to this wise poet.

POET: This gift my Muse accepts
    and not at all unwilling,
    but turn your mind to learn
    of Pindar's word fulfilling.

PEISTHETAIROS: Can't we get rid of this fellow?

POET: Through the nomadic Skythia wanders Straton
    with no undershirt to display,
    Disgraced by jacket with no *chiton.*
    Please perceive my point, I pray.

PEISTHETAIROS: Sure. I perceive that you want the *chiton* too. Hey, you, take if off. We have to help the poet. Here, poet, take it and go away.

POET [exiting]: I am leaving, for I have made pretty songs for the city.

PEISTHETAIROS: Thank God! This is an evil I never hoped for, that he would find our city so soon.

256   Isokrates, *Antidosis* 166   353 B.C.

At the age of eighty-two, the orator and political scientist Isokrates lost a court case by the negative vote of an Athenian jury. Feeling that he was generally misunderstood and unappreciated by his fellow citizens, Isokrates wrote a self-justifying pamphlet in which he included the following argument.

It would be the height of absurdity if Pindar the poet was so honored by our ancestors for the single line in which he called Athens the bulwark of Greece that they made him a *proxenos* and gave him a gift of $220,000, but I who have paid our city and our forefathers much greater praise and written such beautiful eulogies am not to be accorded the simple honor of living out my days in peace.

Isokrates and Aristophanes (above, no. **255***) are both referring to the same fact: Pindar and Myron (as well as other poets, artists and sculptors) were paid for their works. Thus if we today are to view ancient athletics objectively, we must understand two principles. First, Pindar and others glorified athletes not merely because they thought that athletes were worthy of glorification, but also because they were paid to do so. Secondly, the athletes who commissioned these words or statues had sufficient wealth to be able to pay for depictions, whether verbal or visual, of their arete. Some athletes may have inherited their wealth, but others, such as Theagenes of Thasos,* *clearly owed their financial status to their* arete. *This does not diminish their accomplishments, but it does remind us that many of the same glories and many of the same problems—potential or realized—that we confront today in athletics were first confronted by the ancient Greeks more than two millennia ago. Their true experience can be more edifying for us than the fiction of their perfection.*

Nobility and valor, greed and avarice, glory and glorification, unions and contract negotiations, heroics and heroization, corruption and vilification, the evolution of physical competitions (including women's competitions) into an entertainment industry, and the development of noncompetitive physical exercise for the non-athlete were all present in the athletic world of two millennia ago. In short, nearly every aspect of athletics we know today existed already in that distant but kindred world.

From across the centuries the echoes of arete *call us to examine its successes, and its failures, to discard and avoid those venal practices which were rightfully condemned in antiquity, and to emulate those noble experiences that have been recounted for us. But first we must learn to examine critically both the praises of a Pindar and the reproaches of a Euripides.*

Appendix

I. THE EVENTS OF THE OLYMPIC GAMES AND THE DATE WHEN
EACH WAS ADDED TO THE OLYMPIC PROGRAM

stadion	776 B.C.	*pyx* for *paides*	616 B.C.
diaulos	724 B.C.	*hoplitodromos*	520 B.C.
dolichos	720 B.C.	*apene*	500 B.C.
pentathlon	708 B.C.	(dropped in 444 B.C.)	
pale	708 B.C.	*kalpe*	496 B.C.
pyx	688 B.C.	(dropped in 444 B.C.)	
tethrippon	680 B.C.	*synoris*	408 B.C.
pankration	648 B.C.	*salpinktes*	396 B.C.
keles	648 B.C.	*keryx*	396 B.C.
stadion for *paides*	632 B.C.	*tethrippon* for *poloi*	384 B.C.
pale for *paides*	632 B.C.	*synoris* for *poloi*	264 B.C.
pentathlon for *paides*	628 B.C.	*keles* for *poloi*	256 B.C.
(dropped immediately)		*pankration* for *paides*	200 B.C.

II. THE EVENTS OF THE PYTHIAN GAMES AND THE DATE WHEN EACH WAS ADDED TO THE PYTHIAN PROGRAM

kithara-singing	586 B.C.	*pentathlon* for *paides*	586 B.C.
aulos	586 B.C.	*pyx* for *paides*	586 B.C.
aulos-singing (dropped immediately)	586 B.C.	*dolichos* for *paides*	586 B.C.
		diaulos for *paides*	586 B.C.
stadion	586 B.C.	*tethrippon*	582 B.C.
diaulos	586 B.C.	*kithara*	558 B.C.
dolichos	586 B.C.	*hoplitodromos*	498 B.C.
pentathlon	586 B.C.	*synoris*	398 B.C.
pale	586 B.C.	*tethrippon* for *poloi*	378 B.C.
pyx	586 B.C.	*pankration* for *paides*	346 B.C.
pankration	586 B.C.	*synoris* for *poloi*	338 B.C.
keles	586 B.C.	*keles* for *poloi*	314 B.C.
stadion for *paides*	586 B.C.		

Select Bibliography

The student of ancient athletics has been assisted immeasurably by the appearance in 1984 of two good and thorough bibliographic reference works which render a full listing of scholarship before that date superfluous and unnecessary.

Thomas F. Scanlon, *Greek and Roman Athletics: A Bibliography* (Chicago 1984).
Nigel B. Crowther, "Studies in Greek Athletics," *Classical World* 78 (1984) 497–558 and 79 (1985) 73–135.

Since the appearance of those two reference works, a large number of books and articles on athletics have appeared. The following list of works is not complete, and is limited to English-language publications, but it will provide starting points for further study of various subjects:

Alcock, Susan E., "Nero at Play? The Emperor's Grecian Odyssey," in J. Elsner and J. Masters (eds.), *Reflections of Nero: Culture, History and Representation* (London 1994) 98–111.
Alexandri, Olga (ed.), *Mind and Body: Athletic Contests in Ancient Greece* (Athens 1989).
Bandy, Susan J. (ed.), *Coroebus Triumphs* (San Diego, 1988).
Bell, David, "The Horse Race (κέλης) in Ancient Greece from the Pre-Classical Period to the First Century B.C.," *Stadion* 15 (1989) 167–190.
Boe, Alfred F., "Sports in the Bible," in Bandy 218–229.
Bonfante, L., "Nudity as a Costume in Classical Art," *American Journal of Archaeology* 93 (1989) 543–570.
Brophy, Robert, and Mary Brophy, "Deaths in the Pan-Hellenic Games II: All Combative Sports," *American Journal of Philology* 106 (1985) 171–198.
Brulotte, Eric L., "The 'Pillar of Oinomaos' and the Location of Stadium I at Olympia," *American Journal of Archaeology* 98 (1994) 53–64.

Christesen, Paul, "The Emergence of Civic Nudity in Archaic Greece," manuscript.

Coulson, William, and Helmut Kyrieleis (eds.), *Proceedings of an International Symposium on the Olympic Games* (Athens 1992).

Crowther, Nigel B., "The Age Category of Boys at Olympia," *Phoenix* 42 (1988) 304–308.

———, "Euexia, Eutaxia, Philoponia: The Contests of the Greek Gymnasium," *Zeitschrift für Papyrologie und Epigraphik* 85 (1991) 301–304.

———, "The Olympic Training Period," *Nikephoros* 4 (1991) 161–166.

———, "Rounds and Byes in Greek Athletics," *Stadion* 18 (1992) 68–74.

———, "More on 'drómos' as a Technical Term in Greek Sport," *Nikephoros* 6 (1993) 33–37.

———, "Numbers of Contestants in Greek Athletic Contests," *Nikephoros* 6 (1993) 39–52.

———, "Reflections on Greek Equestrian Events: Violence and Spectator Attitudes," *Nikephoros* 7 (1994) 121–134.

———, "The Role of Heralds and Trumpeters at Greek Athletic Festivals," *Nikephoros* 7 (1994) 135–156.

———, "Greek Equestrian Events in the Late Republic and Early Empire: Africanus and the Olympic Victory Lists," *Nikephoros* 8 (1995) 111–124.

———, "Athlete and State: Qualifying for the Olympic Games in Ancient Greece," *Journal of Sport History* 23 (1996) 34–43.

———, " 'Sed quis custodiet ipsos custodes?' The Impartiality of the Olympic Judges and the Case of Leon of Ambracia," *Nikephoros* 10 (1997) 149–160.

———, "Athlete as Warrior in the Ancient Greek Games: Some Reflections," *Nikephoros* 12 (1999) 121–130.

———, "The Finish in the Greek Foot-Race," *Nikephoros* 12 (1999) 131–142.

Crowther, Nigel B., and Monika Frass, "Flogging as a Punishment in the Ancient Games," *Nikephoros* 11 (1998) 51–82.

Edmondson, Jonathan C., "The Cultural Politics of Public Spectacle in Rome and the Greek East," in Bettina Bergmann and Christine Kondoleon (eds.), *The Art of Ancient Spectacle* (Washington 1999) 77–95.

Evjen, Harold D., "Competitive Athletics in Ancient Greece: The Search for Origins and Influences," *Opuscula Atheniensia* 16 (1986) 51–56.

———, "The Origins and Functions of Formal Athletic Competition in the Ancient World," in Coulson and Kyrieleis, 95–104.

Gallis, Kostas J., "The Games in Ancient Larisa: An Example of Provincial Olympic Games," in Raschke (1988) 217–235.

Gebhard, Elizabeth R., "The Evolution of a Pan-Hellenic Sanctuary: From Archaeology Towards History at Isthmia," in Nanno Marinatos and Robin Hägg (eds.), *Greek Sanctuaries, New Approaches* (London and New York 1993) 154–177.

Glass, Stephen L., "The Greek Gymnasium: Some Problems," in Raschke (1988) 155–173.

Golden, Mark, *Children and Childhood in Classical Athens* (Baltimore and London 1990).

————, "Equestrian Competition in Ancient Greece: Difference, Dissent, Democracy," *Phoenix* 51 (1997) 327–344.

————, *Sport and Society in Ancient Greece* (Cambridge 1998).

————, *Sport in the Ancient World from A to Z* (London and New York, 2004).

Herrmann, Fritz Gregor, "Wrestling Metaphors in Plato's 'Theaetetus'," *Nikephoros* 8 (1995) 77–110.

Jackson, Donald F., "Philostratos and the Pentathlon," *Journal of Hellenic Studies* 111 (1991) 178–181.

Johnston, Alan W., "*IG* II^2 2311 and the Number of Panathenaic Amphorae," *BSA* 82 (1987) 125–129.

Kefalidou, Eurydice, "Ceremonies of Athletic Victory in Ancient Greece," *Nikephoros* 12 (1999) 95–109.

Kennell, Nigel M., *The Gymnasium of Virtue* (Chapel Hill and London 1995).

Kokolakis, Minos, "Intellectual Activity on the Fringes of the Games," in Coulson and Kyrieleis, 153–158.

Kyle, Donald G., *Athletics in Ancient Athens* (Leiden 1987).

————, "Philostratus, 'Repêchage,' Running and Wrestling: The Greek Pentathlon Again," *Journal of Sport History* 22 (1995) 60–65.

————, "The First Hundred Olympiads: A Process of Decline or Democratization?" *Nikephoros* 10 (1997) 53–76.

Langdon, Merle, "Scoring the Ancient Pentathlon: Final Solution?" *Zeitschrift für Papyrologie und Epigraphik* 78 (1989) 117–118.

————, "Throwing the Discus in Antiquity: The Literary Evidence," *Nikephoros* 3 (1990) 177–184.

Larmour, David H. J., *Stage and Stadium* (*Nikephoros* Beihefte 4, Hildesheim 1999).

Lattimore, Steven, "The Nature of Early Greek Victor Statues," in Bandy 245–256.

Lee, Hugh M., "Modern Ultra-long Distance Running and Philippides' Run from Athens to Sparta," *The Ancient World* 11 (1984) 107–113.

————, "The 'First' Olympic Games of 776 B.C.," in Raschke (1998) 110–118.

————, "*SIG*^{3} 802: Did Women Compete Against Men in Greek Athletic Festivals?" *Nikephoros* 1 (1988) 103–118.

————, "Yet Another Scoring System for the Ancient Pentathlon," *Nikephoros* 8 (1995) 41–55.

————, "The Later Greek Boxing Glove and the 'Roman' Caestus: A Centennial Reevaluation of Jüthner's 'Über Antike Turngeräthe,'" *Nikephoros* 10 (1997) 161–178.

————, "The Ancient Olympic Games: Origin, Evolution, Revolution," *Classical Bulletin* 74 (1998) 129–141.

————, "Venues for Greek Athletics in Rome," in S. K. Dickison and Judith P. Hallett (eds.), *Rome and Her Monuments: Essays on the City and Literature of Rome in Honor of Katherine Geffcken* (Wauconda 2000) 215–239.

Mallwitz, Alfred, "Cult and Competitions Locations at Olympia," in Raschke (1998) 79–109.

Matthews, Victor, "The Greek Pentathlon Again," *Zeitschrift für Papyrologie und Epigraphik* 100 (1994) 129–138.

Matz, David, *Greek and Roman Sport: A Dictionary of Athletes and Events from the Eighth Century B.C. to the Third Century A.D.* (Jefferson, N.C. 1991).

McDonnell, Myles, "The Introduction of Athletic Nudity: Thucydides, Plato, and the Vases," *Journal of Hellenic Studies* 111 (1991) 182–193.

———, "Athletic Nudity among the Greeks and Etruscans: The Evidence of the 'Perizoma Vases,'" in École française de Rome (ed.), *Spectacles sportifs et scéniques dans le monde étrusco-italique* (Rome 1993) 395–407.

Measham, Terence, Elisabeth Spathari, and Paul Donnelly, *1000 Years of the Olympic Games: Treasures of Ancient Greece* (Sydney 2000).

Millender, Ellen, "Athenian Ideology and the Empowered Spartan Woman," in Stephen Hodkinson and Anton Powell (eds.), *Sparta: New Perspectives* (Swansea 1999) 355–391.

Miller, Stella G., "Macedonians at Delphi," in Anne Jacquemin (ed.), *Delphes cent ans après la grande fouille* (Paris 2000) 263–281.

Miller, Stephen G., "Stadiums," *The Oxford Encyclopedia of Archaeology in the Near East,* Vol. 5 (Oxford 1997) 74–75.

———, "Naked Democracy," in P. Flensted-Jensen, T. H. Nielsen, L. Rubinstein (eds.), *Polis & Politics* (Festschrift M. H. Hansen, Copenhagen 2000) 277–296.

———, *Nemea II: The Early Hellenistic Stadium* (Berkeley and Los Angeles 2001).

———, "The Organization and Functioning of the Olympic Games," in Phillips and Pritchard 1–40.

———, *Ancient Greek Athletics* (New Haven 2004).

Morgan, Catherine, *Athletes and Oracles: The Transformation of Delphi and Olympia in the Eighth Century B.C.* (Cambridge 1990).

Morison, William W., "Attic Gymnasia and Palaistrai: Public or Private?" *Ancient World* 31 (2000) 140–144.

Mouratidis, John, "Anachronism in the Homeric Games and Sports," *Nikephoros* 3 (1990) 11–22.

Nagy, Gregory, "Pindar's *Olympian* 1 and the Aetiology of the Olympic Games," *Transactions of the American Philological Association* 116 (1986) 71–88.

Neils, Jenifer (ed.), *Goddess and Polis: The Panathenaic Festival in Ancient Athens* (Princeton 1992).

———, (ed.), *Worshipping Athena: Panathenaia and Parthenon* (Madison 1996).

Neils, Jenifer, and S. V. Tracy, *The Panathenaic Games* (Princeton 2003).

O'Sullivan, Patrick, "Victory Song, Victory Statue: Pindar's Agonistic Imagery and Its Legacy," in Phillips and Pritchard 75–100.

Papalas, Anthony J., "Boy Athletes in Ancient Greece," *Stadion* 17 (1991) 165–172.

Patrich, Joseph, "Herod's Hippodrome/Stadium at Caesarea and the Games Conducted Therein," in L. Rutgers (ed.), *What Athens Has to Do with Jerusalem* (*Essays in Honor of Gideon Foerster,* Louvain 2002) 29–68.

Percey, William Armstrong, III, *Pederasty and Pedagogy in Archaic Greece* (Urbana and Chicago 1996).

Pfeiffer, Ilja Leonard, "Athletic Age Categories in Victory Odes," *Nikephoros* 11 (1998) 21–38.

Phillips, David, and David Pritchard (eds.), *Sport and Festival in the Ancient Greek World* (Swansea 2003).

Poliakoff, Michael B., "Deaths in the Pan-Hellenic Games: Addenda et Corrigenda," *American Journal of Philology* 107 (1986) 400–402.

———, *Combat Sports in the Ancient World: Competition, Violence, and Culture* (New Haven 1987).

———, "Melankomas, ἐκ κλίμακος, and Greek Boxing," *American Journal of Philology* 108 (1987) 511–518.

Raschke, Wendy, "Aulos and Athlete: The Function of the Flute Player in Greek Athletics," *Arete* 2 (1985) 177–200.

——— (ed.), *The Archaeology of the Olympics* (Madison 1988).

———, "Images of Victory: Some New Considerations of Athletic Monuments," in Raschke (1988) 38–54.

Reed, Nancy B., "A Chariot Race for Athens' Finest: The *Apobates* Contest Re-Examined," *Journal of Sport History* 17 (1990) 306–319.

Reeder, Ellen D., *Pandora: Women in Classical Greece* (Princeton 1995) 363–373, *et passim.*

Sansome, David, *Greek Athletics and the Genesis of Sport* (Berkeley and Los Angeles 1988).

Scanlon, Thomas F., "Combat and Context: Athletic Metaphors for Warfare in Greek Literature," in Bandy 230–244.

———, "*Virgineum Gymnasium:* Spartan Females and Early Greek Athletics," in Raschke (1988) 185–216.

———, "Race or Chase at the Arkteia of Attica?" *Nikephoros* 3 (1990) 73–120.

———, *Eros and Greek Athletics* (Oxford 2002).

Serwint, Nancy, "Female Athletic Costume at the Heraia and Prenuptial Initiation Rites," *American Journal of Archaeology* 97 (1993) 403–422.

Siewert, Peter, "The Olympic Rules," in Coulson and Kyrieleis 111–117.

Sinn, Ulrich, *Olympia: Cult, Sport, and Ancient Festival* (Princeton, Markus Weiner 2000).

Spathari, Elsi, *The Olympic Spirit* (Athens 1992).

Steiner, Deborah, "Moving Images: Fifth-Century Victory Monuments and the Athlete's Allure, " *Classical Antiquity* 17 (1998) 123–149.

Swaddling, Judith, *The Ancient Olympic Games*[2] (Austin 1999).

Sweet, Waldo, "Protection of the Genitals in Greek Athletics," *Ancient World* 11 (1985) 43–52.

Tzifopoulos, Yannis Z., " 'Hermerodromoi' and Cretan 'Dromeis,' " *Nikephoros* 1 (1998) 137–170.

Valavanis, Panos, *Hysplex: The Starting Mechanism in Ancient Stadia* (Berkeley and Los Angeles 1999).

Vanhove, Doris (curator), *Olympism in Antiquity* I (Lausanne, International Olympic Committee editions, 1993).

——, *Olympism in Antiquity* II (Lausanne, International Olympic Committee editions, 1996).

——, *Olympism in Antiquity* III (Lausanne, International Olympic Committee editions, 1998).

van Nijf, Onno, "Athletics, Festivals, and Greek Identity in the Roman East," *Proceedings of the Cambridge Philological Society* 45 (1999) 176–200.

Vos, M. F., "Aulodic and Auletic Contests," in H. A. G. Brijder, et al. (eds.), *Enthousiasmos: Essays on Greek and Related Pottery Presented to J. M. Hemelrijk* (Amsterdam 1986) 121–130.

Wacker, Christian, "The Record of the Olympic Victory List," *Nikephoros* 11 (1998) 39–50.

Waddell, Gene, "The Greek Pentathlon," *Greek Vases in the J. Paul Getty Museum* 5 (1991) 99–106.

Welch, Katherine, "Negotiating Roman Spectacle Architecture in the Greek World: Athens and Corinth," in Bettina Bergmann and Christine Kondoleon (eds.), *The Art of Ancient Spectacle* (Washington 1999) 125–148.

Young, David C., *The Olympic Myth of Greek Amateur Athletics* (Chicago 1984).

——, "How the Amateurs Won the Olympics," in Raschke (1988) 55–78.

——, "First with the Most: Greek Athletic Records and 'Specialization,'" *Nikephoros* 9 (1996) 175–198.

Index and Glossary

Numbers in **bold face** refer to the entry number in the text above; those in regular type to page references, usually so noted.

The *agonothetes* had general responsibility for the conduct and the smooth functioning of the games, and at times also for underwriting their finances: **65, 77, 82, 104, 109, 118, 162, 191, 197, 199**

AGORA. The marketplace of every city, usually an open square surrounded by buildings, which served as the commercial and civic/political center of the city: **15, 44, 83, 157, 167a, 189**

AIGINA AND AIGINITANS: **94, 216, 249, 252**

AISCHINES

Against Ktesiphon 179–180: **118**

Against Timarchos 9–12: **183**

AITOLIAN LEAGUE: **191**

AJAX, son of Oileus: **1**

AJAX, son of Telamon: **1, 187**

AKADEMY, a *GYMNASION* of Athens: **123, 144, 182**; p. ix

AKANTHOS OF LAKEDAIMONIA: **4**

AKON (or *akontion*). A light spear or javelin, to be distinguished from the heavier military or hunting spear: **47, 53, 54, 62, 63, 64, 65, 153**

AKONITI. Literally, "dustless," a term used to designate a victor who had won without a contest. This was usually the result of his opponents' physical or psychological incapacity to compete with him, and initially was used exclusively of the heavy events of wrestling, boxing, and the *pankration*: **167a, 170**

AKRAGAS: **17, 129, 135, 143, 222**

ALEIMMA (pl. *aleimmata*). Literally, anything used for anointing such as an unguent or oil, but technically a fund which provided oil for young athletes: **185**

ALEIPTES (pl. *aleiptai*). Literally, one who anoints, an "oiling man," which came to be the name used of a trainer who specialized in massages: **209, 218**

ALEXANDER I OF MACEDON: **92**

ALEXANDER IV OF MACEDON, THE GREAT: **31, 84, 139, 143, 171a, 172a, 190, 246**

ALEXANDER SEVERUS: **84**

ALEXANDRIA: **74, 78, 79, 84, 110, 180, 207, 210, 213**

ALKIBIADES OF ATHENS: **67, 116, 219**

ALPHEIOS RIVER: **45, 98, 149, 161, 241, 248**

ALTIS. The sacred grove at Olympia, an area surrounding the Temple of Zeus, defined in the fourth century B.C. by a wall. In theory, everything within the *Altis* was sacred and all secular activities and buildings were kept outside this open square: **51, 73, 103, 163a, 170, 239, 241, 246**

AMBRAKIA: **109, 195, 244**

AMMONIOS, *On Similar and Different Words* 23: **62**

AMPHIKTYONIC COUNCIL AT DELPHI: **75, 76, 192, 196a**

AMPHOTIS (pl. *amphotidai*). Literally, something around or over the ears; used of ear-protectors for boxers: **42**

AMYKOS OF BEBRYKIA: **39**

ANABATES (pl. *anabatai*). Literally, one who mounts, a rider, but used sometimes as a synonym for *apobates*: **72**

ANACHARSIS OF SKYTHIA: **7, 35, 113, 127**

ANAXIMENES OF CHIOS: **143**

[ANDOKIDES], *Against Alkibiades* 29: **116**

ATHENAEUS, *The Gastronomers*
    1.14F–15A: **176**
    9.509B: **171b**
    10.412F: **163b**
    10.414F–415A: **74**
    12.521F: **237**
    12.539C: **190**
    13.561C–D: **181**
    13.565F: **122**
    13.609E–610A: **161**
ATHENS AND ATHENIANS: **13, 15, 28, 30, 31, 68, 69, 79, 88, 89, 116, 118, 119, 120, 121, 129, 130, 131, 136, 143, 144, 145, 155, 162, 167a, 170, 172a–b, 180, 182, 186, 187, 194, 196a, 213, 216, 219, 221, 223, 231, 236, 238, 241, 243, 244, 248, 256;** pp. ix, xii, 17, 18, 29, 49, 50, 53, 81–86, 94, 107, 124, 135, 180, 183, 210, 213, 214, 215, 222, 223, 225, 229, 230
ATHLOTHETES (pl. *athlothetai*). Literally, one who sets out a prize; used as the title of one who organized games with prizes, an ancient "promoter." Essentially synonymous with *agonothetes* and, sometimes, *Hellanodikes:* **33, 109, 119**
ATTICUS: **200**
AUGUSTUS: **198, 199**
AULETES. One who plays the *aulos:* **76**
AULOS (pl. *auloi*). Generally any woodwind instrument, but usually and specifically a flute. Competitions in playing the *aulos* were a part of some festivals including those at Delphi, Isthmia, and Athens, but not at Olympia and Nemea. There were also competitions in singing to the accompaniment of the flute, *aulos*-singing, although this contest at Delphi was dropped immediately after its initial performance: **75, 76, 77, 120;** p. 202
AUTOMEDES, son of Timoxenos of Phlious: **250**
AURELIUS HELIX: **96**
AUTOMEDON: **1**

BACCHYLIDES 8.1–9, 21–36, 97–104: **250**
BALBIS. An area in the stadium track marked off for the *diskos* throwers. Sometimes used generally of the starting line for the runners: **55, 99**
BATER. Generally, that which is tred upon, like a threshold. Used of the taking-off place for the *halma* and, more generally, for the starting line in the stadium.
BCH
    64–65 (1940–41) 175: **167b**
    77 (1953) 389: **136**
BEAUTY CONTESTS: **161**
BEBRYKIA: **39**
BELISTICHE OF MACEDONIA: **160**
BIBASIS: **156**
BOMONIKES (pl. *bomonikai*). Literally, an altar-winner. Used in a technical sense at Sparta of the young men who endured the greatest flogging: **127**
BOULE. The council or senate in a city-state. The Olympic *boule* consisted of 50 Eleans who had general control over the Olympic festival. The meeting place of

any *boule* was generally called the *bouleuterion:* 82, 83, 90, 108, 119, 167, 184, 186, 187, 213, 241

BOXING. See *Pyx*

BOYS. The youngest category of competitors at the games, and of members of the *palaistra;* see also *pais:* 64, 75, 77, 93, 98, 120, 124, 129, 162, 163a, 170, 189, 191, 196, 199, 210, 214, 225

BRASIDAS OF LAKEDAIMONIA: 111

CAESTUS. The boxing glove of Roman times. A leather strap wrapped around the hands and usually loaded or studded with pellets of lead or iron.

CAPITOLINE GAMES: 96, 204, 210, 212, 213

CASTOR: 39

CATAPULT: 187

CHAIRON OF PELLENE: 171a–b

CHARMOS: 174

CHIONIS OF SPARTA: 60, 61

CHIOS AND CHIANS: 88, 129, 130, 143, 191

CHITON. Thin unisex undergarment like a long tunic or T-shirt: 158, 207, 255

CHLAMYS. A heavy cloak or mantle worn especially, but not exclusively, by cavalrymen, and the "uniform" of the *epheboi:* 186, 203

CHOREGOS. A private citizen who undertook the economic sponsorship of a festival or a team in a competition: 183. See also 67 and 121.

CHREMATITIC. The adjective applied to games where the prizes were either of money or of monetary value as, for example, in the Panathenaic Games at Athens; derived from *chrema* or money: 213

CHRISTOS: 10

CHRONOS: 11

CICERO: 197

    Tusculan Disputations 5.3.9: 128

    Letters to Atticus 1.10.3: 200

CID

    1.3: 100

    2.139: 81

CIRCUS. Generally, the Latin word for circle, but usually the name for the oval horse race track in Roman times. The most famous of these was the Circus Maximus at Rome: 31, 201, 203

CORINTH AND CORINTHIANS: 66, 71, 80, 82, 84, 88, 129, 143, 145, 194, 232, 235, 240, 244; p. 74

DAIDALOS OF SIKYON: 108

DAMAGETOS, son of Diagoras of Rhodes: 170

DAMARETOS OF HERAIA: 26

DAMEAS OF KROTON: 163a

DAMOXENOS OF SYRACUSE: 38

DANCING. To the extent that dancing was a part of athletics, it was military in nature and formed a part of the ephebic training: 2, 120, 121, 155, 188, 201

DARIUS OF PERSIA: 216

ISTHMIA OR ISTHMIAN GAMES: **46, 69, 77, 84, 88, 113, 137, 145, 162, 167a, 170, 171a, 182, 194, 203, 210, 213, 214, 218, 221, 223, 226, 228, 232, 233, 234, 235, 240, 248, 251**; pp. 58, 61, 209, 213, 231

ITHAKA: **2**

IvO

    56: **199**
    64: **133**
    144: **166b**
    160: **151b**
    225: **98**

JAMES 5.14: **10**

JASON: **39**

JASON, high priest at Jerusalem: **193**

JAVELIN. See *akon.*

JOSPHEUS

    Jewish Antiquities 16.136–141: **198**

    Jewish War 1.426–428: **197**

JUDEA: **193, 198**

JULIUS CAESAR: **201**

JUMPING. See *halma.*

KAIKINOS RIVER: **166a**

KAISAREIA: **198**

KALLIPATEIRa OF RHODES (or Pherenike): **149, 170**

KALLIPPOS OF ATHENS: **236**

KALOKAGATHIA. A composite word from the Greek *kalos kai agathos,* "beautiful and good," signifying physical and moral excellence: **182, 187**

KALPE. Name of an equestrian event at Olympia for a brief period. The evidence indicates that it was either a race for mares, or a race which involved the rider jumping off and running along the horses for a part of the race. These two possibilities are not, of course, mutually exclusive: **72, 77**; p. 201

KAMPE. Literally, a bending or turning. Used of the general area where the turn was made in the footraces and horse races, or of the turn itself: **69**

KAMPTER (pl. *kampteres*). The name of the post where the turn was made in the footraces and the horse races: **81**

KANON (pl. *kanones*). Generally, any straight rod or stick, but sometimes a measuring stick or ruler of variable length: **52**

KAPROS OF ELIS: **95**

KASTALIA. The name of a spring near Delphi: **81, 248**

KELES. A riding horse and the name of the horseback race. The length seems to have been six laps, or twelve lengths, of the hippodrome: **69, 71, 120, 129, 182, 221**; pp. 94, 201, 202

KERYX (pl. *kerykes*). Any herald, but including those who won the competition at Olympia and were rewarded with the honor of calling events and announcing victors: **73, 124, 143**; p. 201

KITHARA. The harp or lyre. *Kithara* playing, as well as singing to the accompani-

4.73.6–10: **85**
27.9.3–13: **140**
POLYDAMAS, son of Nikias of Skotussa: **143, 165, 168**
POLYDEUKES OF LAKEDAIMONIA: **37 ,39**
POLYKLEITOS OF ARGOS: **253**
POLYKRATES OF SAMOS: **216**
POSEIDON: **1, 66, 69, 145, 215, 235, 240**
POxy
  II.222: **129**
  III.466 ii: **36**
PRODOKOS OF KEOS: **143**
PROEDRIA. The right of sitting in reserved front-row seats in the theater, at the games, and elsewhere, given to distinguished guests and accomplished citizens: **229**
PROSKENION. The forepart of a tent or a stage-curtain. Perhaps here an awning: **81**
PROTAGORAS OF ABDERA: **65**
PROXENOS. A citizen and inhabitant of one state who is a friend to and representative of another state; a consul: **136, 256**
PRYTANEIS. Rulers, lords, chiefs. In Athens a standing committee of citizens selected by lot who had direct and daily responsibility for governing: **29**
PRYTANEION. A building in every ancient city-state where the eternal flame of the city was housed on a hearth, where new citizens were enrolled, and where guests of the state were invited for free meals: **115, 187, 221, 231**
PRYTANIS OF KYZIKOS: **103**
PSALTES (pl. *psaltai*). A singer with *kithara* accompaniment; a music teacher: **184**
PSAMMIS OF EGYPT: **105**
PTOLEMY II PHILADELPHOS: **207**
PTOLEMY III EUERGETES: **78, 140**
PUBLIUS CORNELIUS ARISTON: **98**
PYGME, PYGMACHIA. Synonyms for *pyx*.
PYRRHIC (dance): **120, 121, 201**
PYTHAGORAS OF SAMOS (and Kroton): **128**
PYTHEAS, son of Lampon of Aigina: **252**
PYTHIA AND PYTHIAN GAMES (see also Delphi): **60a, 63, 68, 75, 76, 77, 80, 81, 84, 87, 108, 137, 162, 164, 167a, 170, 191, 192, 196a, 202, 203, 210, 213, 215, 226, 249**; pp. 61, 202, 209
PYTHOKRITOS, son of Kallinikos of Sikyon: **76**
PYX. The boxing in which the victor was decided as the *pankration*. The boxers wore *himantes* and there were no round or time limits, although the boxers might take short breaks by mutual consent: **1, 2, 5, 35, 37–41, 48, 59, 79, 95, 103, 120, 124, 129, 140, 164, 166a, 167a, 170, 173, 188, 202, 210, 215, 225, 229, 248**; pp. 201, 202
PZenon 59060: **207**

RHODES: **20, 52, 94, 104, 149, 213, 248**
RIVISTA DI FILOLOGIA (1956) 55–57: **52**

ROME: **4, 6, 60c, 96, 147, 194, 195, 196, 197, 198, 201, 203, 204, 210, 212, 213**

SAKADAS OF ARGOS: **76**

SALAMIS: **102, 142, 187**

SALPINKTES (pl. *salpinktai*). A trumpeter. The victor in the competitions at
   Olympia won an olive wreath and the honor of signaling the athletic and equestrian events to the crowd: **73**; p. 201

SEG

   15.501: **52**
   27.261: **185**
   35.1053: **220**

SIG[3]

   402: **191**
   630: **192**
   802: **162**
   1080: **79**

SIKYON AND SIKYONIANS: **31, 34, 46, 56, 76, 77, 108, 141, 162, 242, 244**

SIXTEEN WOMEN: **86, 157, 158**

SKAMMA (pl. *skammata*). Literally, that which has been dug, a pit or a trench.
   This was the name of the pit where the jumpers in the *halma* landed, and of
   the wrestling "ring" where the soft earth would break falls: **52, 60e, 213**

SOKRATES: **15, 49, 60, 66, 131, 132, 144, 147, 182, 215, 231**

SOLON OF ATHENS: **35, 113, 223**

SOPHIST: **15, 45, 60c, 66, 132, 139, 143, 145, 147, 182, 218**

SOPHOKLES, *Elektra* 681–756: **68**

SOPHRONISTES (pl. *sophronistai*). Literally, one who makes something moderate,
   a chastiser. As a technical term, *sophronistai* were annually elected officials at
   Athens, one from each of the ten Athenian tribes, each official charged with
   supervising the training and welfare of the *epheboi* from his tribe: **186**

SOSTRATOS OF SIKYON: **34, 46**

SOSTRATOS OF PELLENE: **169**

SOTADES OF CRETE (or Ephesos): **227**

SOTERIA GAMES at Delphi: **191**

SPARTA AND SPARTANS (see also Lakedaimonia): **5, 28, 31, 37, 39, 68, 127, 129,
   143, 151a–c, 152, 153, 154, 159, 189, 213, 238**; pp. 21, 25, 46, 213, 216

SPHAIRA (pl. *sphairai*). Any ball, glove, sphere, etc. The word occurs in athletic
   contexts as a playing ball (as in **177**), and as a sort of padded practice boxing
   glove (**40–41**). It is sometimes said by modern scholars that the *sphairai* gloves
   were used in actual boxing competitions, but the evidence for this is slight.

SPHAIRISTERION (pl. *sphairisteria*). A room in the *palaistra* for playing ball: **81,
   180**

SPONDAI (the pl. of *sponde*). The sacred rites which began a treaty or truce, conse-
   quently used of the truce itself: **88, 232, 238**

SPONDOPHOROS. Literally, a truce bearer; an official at Olympia and elsewhere
   who traveled throughout Greece (like the *theoros*) to announce the truce for the
   celebration of the festival: **133**

the hippodrome in a general way for the finishing line and the turning post, and in an even more general way as the "mark" or "goal": **1, 2, 23, 52, 68**

TETHRIPPON (pl. *tethrippa*). A team of four horses, a four-horse chariot, and the race for the four-horse chariot which was twelve laps or 24 lengths of the hippodrome: **4, 75, 107, 116, 129, 141, 182, 219, 221, 231, 245**; pp. 79, 201, 202

TEUKROS: **1**

THEAGENES, son of Timosthenes of Thasos: **95, 165, 166a, 167a–b**; p. 198

THEAGENES OF THESSALY: **126**

THEARODOKOS (sometimes spelled *theorodokos*). A "*theoros*-receiver," akin to a *proxenos*, who served as a kind of representative of a given festival in his hometown. When the *theoroi* of that festival arrived at his town, the *thearodokos* was responsible for greeting them, providing them with hospitality, and expediting their work: **136**

THEBES AND THEBANS: **95, 129, 140, 196a, 238b, 248**; p. 188

THEMISTOKLES: **102, 142**

THEOKRITOS, *Idylls* 22.27–135: **39**

THEOPHRASTOS: **161**

    Characters 16: **9**

THEORIA. Literally, a looking at or a viewing of something. Technically, a delegation, embassy, or mission (the members of which were called *theoroi*) sent on behalf of a city-state to oracles or other city-states or the Panhellenic festivals: **67, 116, 155, 219**; cf. **88, 134, 135, 191, 193, 232, 238, 245**

THERSIPPOS OF ERCHIA: **29**

THESSALY AND THESSALIANS: **103, 124–126, 167a, 168**

THUCYDIDES

    1.6.5–6: **4**

    3.104: **155**

    4.121.1: **111**

    5.49–50: **238**

    6.16.2: **219**

    8.9.1–10.1: **88**

TIMAGORAS OF CHALKIS: **80**

TIMON OF ELIS: **234**

TISAMENOS OF ELIS: **50**

TITUS FLAVIUS ARCHIBIUS OF ALEXANDRIA: **210**

TORCH-RACE. See *lampadedromia*

TRAJAN: **210, 211**

TRIREME. The warship of ancient Greece, powered by three superimposed banks of oars on each side; the careful coordination of 198 rowers was tested in local races: **67, 121, 170**; cf. **120**

TROILOS OF ELIS: **107**

TROY: **1, 2, 201**

TRYPHOSA, daughter of Hermesianax: **162**

VENATIO. Hunting, used of shows in the Roman amphitheater involving the hunting and slaughtering of wild animals: **195**

VERUS: **117**

Sources for the Chapter-Opening Sketches

Ch. I: Geometric kantharos, eighth century B.C. Dresden, State Art Collection

Ch. II: Red-figure krater, 510 B.C. Berlin, State Museum

Ch. III: Red-figure krater, 480 B.C. Copenhagen, National Museum

Ch. IV: Red-figure kylix, 500 B.C. Munich, Ancient Collection

Ch. V: Red-figure choe, late fifth century B.C. Paris, Louvre

Ch. VI: Marble statuette of Diogenes the Cynic, original 330 B.C. Rome, Villa Albani

Ch. VII: Bronze statuette of female runner, late sixth century B.C. London, British Museum

Ch. VIII: Red-figure stamnos, early fifth century B.C. Philadelphia, University Museum

Ch. IX: Relief on marble lekythos, mid-fourth century B.C. Athens, National Museum

Ch. X: Red-figure kylix, early fifth century B.C. Berlin, State Museum

Ch. XI: Silver tetradrachma of Alexander, 325 B.C. Berkeley, Hearst Museum

Ch. XII: Mosaic from the Baths of Caracalla, third century A.D. Rome, Lateran Collection, Vatican

Ch. XIII: Panathenaic amphora, late sixth century B.C. Naples, National Museum

Ch. XIV: Panathenaic amphora, 530 B.C. Madrid, National Archaeological Museum

Ch. XV: Marble copy of statue by Myron, original mid-fifth century B.C. Rome, National Museum

Compositor: BookMatters, Berkeley
Text: 10/13 Aldus
Display: Aldus